D0375126

THE PREACHERS OF CULTURE
A Study of English and Its Teachers

The Preachers of Culture

A Study of English and Its Teachers

MARGARET MATHIESON

ROWMAN AND LITTLEFIELD

Totowa, New Jersey

First published in the United States 1975
by ROWMAN AND LITTLEFIELD, Totowa, N.J.

Library of Congress Cataloging in Publication Data

Mathieson, Margaret.
    The preachers of culture.

    Includes bibliographical references.
    1. English language – Study and teaching. I. Title.
LB1631.M39   1975   420'.7   75-17992
ISBN 0-87471-752-3

Printed in Great Britain
by Redwood Press, Trowbridge, Wiltshire.

Acknowledgements

I should like to thank my father, P. Powis, for the care and patience with which he typed and checked the manuscript of this book.

I am also grateful to Lawrence Pollinger and the estate of the late Mrs Frieda Lawrence for permission to use 'What Have They Done to You' by D. H. Lawrence from *The Complete Poems of D. H. Lawrence*.

Contents

Introduction

In *Culture and Anarchy* Matthew Arnold expressed his misgivings about the difficult task ahead for the 'preachers' of culture. They were, he forecast, likely long to have ' a hard time of it' in this country. This book, which shows how teachers of English in schools came, fairly early in the subject's history, to be identified as these preachers, asks why they have had such a hard time, and tries to give some answers. It sets out to examine the ideology of English in schools, to find explanations for its growth, and to discuss the implications of educationists' persistent demands for teachers with outstanding personal qualities.

During the last century, English as a school subject has risen in status, widened in interpretation and taken on a powerful sense of moral purpose. From its beginnings as two rudimentary skills (reading and writing) within the useful knowledge of the nineteenth-century's elementary school curriculum, English has come to be regarded as 'coexistent with life itself'.[1] It is seen as the school subject which concerns itself with 'the personal development and social competence of the pupil'.[2] Teachers appear to agree, in a general fashion, that the experience of literature, creative activity, critical discrimination and classroom talk constitute the character-building elements in today's curriculum. The titles of three influential books—*English for Maturity* (1961), *Growth through English* (1966) and *Sense and Sensitivity* (1967) —suggest that English has come to be seen as central to children's moral and emotional development.

This book consists of three parts. Two of these consider the changing role of English in the curriculum, discussing the relationship between its redefinitions and developments in educational theory and wider society. They show how the emergence of English as an important school subject has coincided with educational expansion, urban development and technological change. They also examine its growth in relation to the decline of the classical curriculum in universities, public schools and grammar schools, and the decline of religion as a character-building force.

Part I outlines the history of English as a school subject until the publication in 1921 of the government Report, *The Teaching of English in England*, by which time progressive ideas had begun to affect official views about English in education. It begins with the central issues of the nineteenth-century curriculum debate between supporters of classical and scientific studies and suggests that this debate's underlying assumptions and the tones in which it was conducted affected the initial claims made for English studies. Then comes a discussion of the influences upon English of the Victorian liberals, the contributors to Farrar's 1868 collection, *Essays on a Liberal Education*, and even more importantly the poet, Matthew Arnold. The next two chapters in this first section discuss the early effects upon definitions of English in schools of two elements which were to become more significant during this century: fear about the corrupting influence of cheap press and film; and developmental theories of education which stressed the value of personal activity and artistic experience in a child's total growth. This Part ends with a description of the ideology of English studies in schools as it existed after the First World War, drawing not only upon the 1921 Report but also upon contemporary textbooks and suggestions to teachers made by school inspectors.

Part II describes the subject's development until the present day, identifying four major influences upon the increasingly powerful ideology within English for pupils' personal and social improvement. These influences are: the growing official acceptance of progressive theories of education; the persistent anti-industrialism shared by most educators concerned with English studies; F. R. Leavis and the Cambridge School of English; and the coming together of concern about working-class children's failure to achieve at school and the growth of socio-linguistics. This part ends with a review of descriptions of the 'good' English teacher, from 'preachers' to 'psycho-analysts'. This historical discussion shows that English today has come to be viewed less as a 'subject' and more as a 'way of life'.[3] During the past hundred years it has been held increasingly responsible for humanising all the nation's children, through literature, through creative use of their native language and through critical discrimination between art and the products of commercial entertainment. Viewed as a network of activities inside which children can achieve emotional, social and moral development, English has come to be seen as the school subject which, more than any other, requires teachers to have outstanding personal qualities. At every stage of the subject's growth, during which new hopes have been invested in it as a liberalising force, fresh demands have been made for inspirational teachers. In response to what they have seen as a worsening cultural crisis, educationists have recurrently called for exceptional teachers to face unsympathetic conditions in the schools and the 'forces' of modern urban society. After discussing some of the discrepancies between official descriptions of good English teachers and the academic and social backgrounds of recruits to the profession at the beginning of this century,

Part III explores some of the likely tensions in English teaching today, particularly those which can affect classroom relationships.

Notes

1. W. R. Mullins, *A Study of Significant Changes in the Theory of the Teaching of English to Older Pupils in Elementary and Secondary Modern Schools, 1860–1960*, unpublished MEd thesis, University of Leicester (January, 1968), p. 281.
2. *Half Our Future* (HMSO, 1963), p. 173.
3. J. R. Squire and R. K. Applebee, *Teaching English in the United Kingdom* (Illinois, USA, NCTE, 1969), p. 235.

Part I

FROM THE CLASSICS TO ENGLISH LITERATURE

The First Hopes

Chapter 1

The Curriculum Debate

'Not only, however, for intellectual discipline is science
the best; but also for moral discipline.'

Herbert Spencer, *Science and Religion*

As a school subject, English first existed simply as instruction in the
basic skills of reading and writing. In the early elementary schools
children from humble backgrounds were taught English so that they
they would be able to read the Bible for themselves and have access
to useful knowledge. In the Mechanics' Institutes some literature was
included in the instruction, on the grounds that its study would protect
young workers against the corrupting effects of seditious political
material and the sensational products of the cheap press. The ancient
universities, public schools and grammar schools ignored English
throughout the nineteenth century. This neglect was partly because of
confidence in the superior humanism of the classics, and partly because
of the vernacular's despised association with working-class education,
the utilitarianism of elementary school, Mechanics' Institute and
London University. Nevertheless, despite the universities' and public
schools' persistent contempt for English studies, these institutions'
ideals inspired the earliest insistence upon the subject's morally
educative value. Although the elementary schools and the Mechanics'
Institutes were engaged in the actual teaching of English, it was from
the high-status establishments with their ideal of a liberal education
that the notion of English as a character-building subject drew much
of its strength.

This Part begins with a consideration of the assumptions underlying
the nineteenth-century debate about the relative worth of classical and
scientific subjects. Although this debate involved several important
issues, such as middle-class resentment of entrenched traditional
attitudes and anxiety about our technological inferiority to Germany,
France and America, its importance for English rests in the contestants' shared assumption about the need for a liberalising core to
the curriculum. All the participants—Darwin, Spencer and Huxley,
with their commitment to scientific studies, and Arnold, Ruskin and

Thring, with their faith in literature—shared the notion that, at its centre, the curriculum should embody morally educative subjects; they all expressed their respective claims by reference to the subject's character-building potential. They seemed to share the Victorian desire for certainty (what G. M. Young calls 'a childlike craving for certitude, as if the natural end of every refuted dogma was to be replaced by another dogma').[1] Thus, when this debate was finally resolved in favour of English, we find that this subject has inherited the high ideals and impassioned tones of voice of the participants.

Criticism of the ancient universities and the public schools came from the radical educational reformers, from leading scientists and from the late nineteenth-century progressives. Perhaps the most severe—and the most significant for the way in which English was to develop—was that which insisted that classics' teaching was failing, at every level, to achieve its main aim, which was to provide a liberal education. Between 1808 and 1811, a series of attacks was published in the *Edinburgh Review* criticising the stultifying clerical control of the universities and the limits this imposed on what should be a liberal education. In 1830 a contributor to the *Edinburgh Review* expressed dissatisfaction not only with the narrowness of the public school curriculum in its refusal to provide anything outside classical studies, but also with its failure to liberalise pupils through their acquaintance with classical literature. He claimed, of a typical pupil:

'He has not read a single book of Herodotus, or Thucydides, or Xenophon, or Livy, or Polybus or Tacitus; he has not read a single Greek tragedy or comedy; he is utterly ignorant of mathematical or physical science, or even of arithmetic; the very names of logical, moral, or political science, are unknown to him. Modern history and modern languages are, of course, out of the question. Is this creditable to the most celebrated public school of England?'[2]

Essays on a Liberal Education (1868) bitterly accused the ancient universities of failing to reconsider the meaning of a liberal education in the light of changing knowledge. Since Oxford and Cambridge determined what was taught in schools, they were failing to recognise their responsibility within the country's system of education. John Seeley asserted: 'Education, in fact, in England, is what the universities choose to make it'.[3] In 'A Liberal Education and Where to Find It' (1868), T. H. Huxley described Oxford and Cambridge as 'half clerical seminaries, half race-courses, where men are trained to win a senior wranglership, or a double first, as horses are trained to win a cup, with as little reference to the needs of after life in the case of the man as in that of the racer'.[4] One of the chief anxieties expressed in Farrar's collection, *Essays on a Liberal Education*, is about the deadlock in relationships between universities and public schools.

'It simply amounts to a reciprocal abnegation of responsibility since the University professes to reward because the Schools teach, and the Schools to teach because the University rewards . . . . How long are we to suffer nine-tenths of our boys to be addled because it is thought necessary to put them all through a process that shall hatch out of their entire numbers a few Senior Classics or Craven Scholars?'[5]

The accusation that dominated the criticism directed at universities and schools was that a liberal education had degenerated into the sterile routine of grammar drill and exercise of mere memory. Few pupils, critics argued, reached those heights where their characters would be trained through encounters with the great minds of the past. Thomas Huxley maintained that the difficulties involved in mastering the classical language hindered the progress of most pupils towards any real appreciation of classical literature. In reality, a classical education

'. . . means getting up endless forms and rules by heart. It means turning Latin and Greek into English for the mere sake of being able to do it, and without the smallest regard to the worth or worthlessness of the author read.'[6]

Critics of the exclusively classical curriculum claimed that many boys left public schools, after years spent on composition and grammar, detesting their studies and ignorant of the literature towards which these studies were designed to lead. Darwin, commenting upon his studies at Shrewsbury, refers to them as 'a blank',[7] and the Clarendon Commission reported, after its investigation, that it found 'far too many boys emerged from the public schools with little knowledge even of the classics, with less of modern subjects, and with no mental cultivation or interest in study'.[8] Dull, mechanical teaching, far from achieving the stated objectives of developing characters and training minds, was failing to help boys achieve fluency and elegance in their own language.

The most persistent and acrimonious criticism, however, stemmed from middle-class dissatisfaction with the classical and clerical exclusiveness of the universities and public schools. In the *Edinburgh Review* (1810), the Edgeworths expressed their impatience with the limitations and inflexibility of the classical curriculum.

'The advantages which are derived from classical learning by the English manner of teaching involve another and very different question; and we will venture to say that there was never a more complete instance in any country of such extravagant and overacted attachment to any branch of knowledge, as that which obtains in this country with regard to classical knowledge. A young Englishman goes to school at 6 or 7 years old, and he remains in a course of education till 23 or 24 years of age. In all that time, his sole and exclusive occupation is learning Latin and Greek . . . . If you have neglected to put other things in him, they will never get in afterwards, if you have fed him only with words he will remain a narrow and limited being to the end of his existence.'[9]

Throughout the 1830s, 'all publications in any way expressive of middle-class standpoint are in full cry against the state of university learning, at Oxford in particular'.[10] Throughout the first part of the century articles appeared in the *Westminster Review* and the *Edinburgh Review* continually pointing to the narrowness and inappropriateness of the classical curriculum and agitating for inclusion of the sciences. In 1825, the *Westminster Review* stated bitterly that 'Westminster, Harrow, Winchester and Eton are seminaries for monks.'[11] In 1832, the *Quarterly Journal*, expressing dissatisfaction with the teaching in public schools, asked: 'Is it reasonable that they [boys of 15] should not even know arithmetic or be able to write their own language with reasonable accuracy?'[12] Mack draws attention to the part played by the eighteenth-century radicals (the Edgeworths, Adam Smith, Godwin and Cobbett), all of whom had attacked the classical curriculum's irrelevance to society and had recommended the inclusion of scientific studies. Even modern languages would not 'conduce towards cotton spinning or abolishing the Poor Laws'.[13] In 1825 the *Westminster Review* insisted that there must 'be science, on which the wealth and power of Britain depends'.[14] Throughout the nineteenth century and until many years after the First World War, the failure of the ancient universities and public schools to take scientific education seriously was held responsible for Britain's worsening technological inferiority to France, Germany and America. Comparing Britain with Germany where in 1825, the Giessen laboratory had been founded and, by 1865, the aniline dye industry, Cardwell writes:

'The universities were concerned with the liberal education of men of a privileged class who would later adopt suitable professions or else follow a life of leisure. The educational ideal was the Christian gentleman; if he was a scholar, then so much the better; if not, then he would benefit from the corporate life in the university.'[15]

He argues that, although some progress had been made to promote scientific education in this country—for example the Mechanics' Institutes and the Society for the Diffusion of Useful Knowledge were in existence; by the mid-century some science was included in the syllabuses of the older universities; the Government School of Science and Owen's College had been founded; and science degrees had been introduced at London—the Paris Exhibition of 1867 revealed how far behind other countries Britain had fallen. Cardwell points to the irony of this country's spread of industrialisation and its failure to organise national education. He suggests that the universities' self-image as establishments for training gentlemen was responsible for this. Science in this country was conducted by 'a brilliant group of semi-amateurs',[16] and the universities were largely 'closed to research and advancement of learning'.[17] Their lack of interest meant that there was nothing here to match the German structure of primary schools, state secondary schools, *Gymnasia, Progymnasia* and *Realgymnasia*. These encouraged the development of applied and theoretical science to the highest levels, and produced science teachers for the schools. Placing responsibility on the ancient universities, Cardwell's criticism echoes the charges expressed in *Essays on a Liberal Education* about the schools' dependence upon university curricula. He says:

'Even if we assume that industrial requirements on their own can break down an iron curtain of Latin and Greek, buttressed by class privilege and underpinned by the Established Church, we can hardly suppose that they could create a syllabus of studies and researches which is not understood by the educational authorities of the time. In whatever way industrial requirements express themselves . . . they cannot be wiser to see further than the received notions and ideas of those concerned with education.'[18]

Before considering the universities' and public schools' resistance to all this criticism, it is useful to note the ways in which this dissatisfaction was likely to have affected the growth of English studies. Of most significance was the criticism which suggested that upper-class educational establishments were failing to provide a liberal education, either because of the dull routine teaching or because of the failure to include modern knowledge. This is the important criticism as far as English is concerned, because of its assumption that provision of a liberal education mattered most of all. It is this assumption which impelled scientists to support their subject as being 'of the greatest worth' and, in time, the supporters of English to make similar claims. On the other hand, the very criticism which concentrated upon the failure of the upper-middle-class educational establishments to meet the needs of a modern industrial nation, to keep pace with foreign competition, is likely to have been partly responsible for the persistent neglect of English. Upper-class revulsion from the unpleasant urban realities of Victorian England, their dislike of commerce, strengthened their commitment to classical and Christian ideals. University tutors and many public school headmasters thus resisted those studies which, with scientific subjects, they identified with the working- and middle-class institutions such as the Mechanics' Institutes and the Dissenting Academies. When it was proposed that English literature should be included in the public schools' curricula since it was more likely to inspire enthusiasm for art than the classical texts, the proposal was rejected, in part, because most headmasters associated the native literature with working-class education, industrialism and manual labour.

It is helpful to look briefly at some expressions of resistance to proposals for the study of science. In response to attacks upon its limited interpretation of a liberal education and the suggestion that this should begin to include science, Oxford replied that 'physical knowledge neither is nor ought to be an essential part of a liberal education'.[19] Thomas Arnold, in a lecture to the Rugby Mechanics' Institute, stated emphatically:

'Physical science alone can never make a man educated; even the formal sciences, valuable as they are with respect to the discipline of the reasoning powers, cannot instruct the judgement; it is only moral and religious knowledge which can accomplish this.'[20]

Moberley, explaining Winchester's refusal to accept the Clarendon Commission's recommendation to include science in the curriculum, stated his convictions in similarly confident tones:

'Classical learning is the inheritance of all former ages. Combined with its allied subjects of philology and history, it puts a person into the possession of all the inherited wisdom of the ages.'[21]

For these headmasters, the classics, in their embodiment of tradition and authority, held with Christianity the unique power to educate. They represented the heritage of Greece and Rome, and by giving

opportunities for an initiation into the aesthetic, political and philosophical realms of European civilisation, they offered that wisdom
through which character could best be developed. In classical studies,
headmasters were convinced that they possessed the 'monopoly of the
roads to true liberal goals'.[22] They provided, moreover, an intellectually tough discipline, the experience of which, the faculty theory suggested, could be transferred to other activities in the outside world.
All this, in addition to their obvious power of conferring superior
social status upon their students, gave classical studies, in many headmasters' eyes, unassailable advantages over other subjects. Therefore,
inspired as they were, under Thomas Arnold's influence, by notions
of moral revival which stemmed from German idealism, convinced
by faculty theories of mental training, and bitterly opposed to utilitarian conceptions of vocational education, headmasters resisted the
introduction of science subjects into their schools. As they saw it, the
classical curriculum, allied with Christian teaching—an important
element in public school life—ennobled the character, and its methods
disciplined the mind. Hence the study of physical sciences appeared
inappropriate, superfluous and unnecessarily expensive. Science, which
they identified with utilitarianism and trade, was an unlikely require-
ment for the sons of landed gentry or the traditional professions of
Church and law. Moreover, unlike the classics with its long, respectable tradition in schools, science appeared to be in a state of confusion.
As G. M. Young points out:

'To all complaints of the classical curriculum there was one convincing answer: there were hundreds of people who could teach it,
there was hardly anyone who could teach anything else ."If you want
science", Faraday told a Royal Commission, "you must begin by
creating science teachers".'[23]

In addition, the teaching of science subjects threatened increased
spending upon space and teaching facilities—expense which public
schools, continually under pressure from financial problems, were
unwilling to bear. The classics, therefore, dominated public schools'
timetables throughout the century, classics masters being accorded
considerably higher status than those of other subjects. When, late in
the century, modern languages and science were introduced into
public schools' curricula, they were limited to the timetables of the
less-able pupil. At Lancing, in 1885, the modern side 'consisted at
first of one despised form, the members of which were debarred from
entering the sixth. It existed. No one had the least wish for it to exist
and it was a sort of parasite.'[24]

P. W. Musgrave, discussing the classics in upper-class education
this century, refers to the public school masters' conviction that
classical studies equip pupils to withstand our 'mechanised, com-
mercialised, industrialised existence'.[25] He suggests that anti-
industrialism strengthens support today for continued study of classical
subjects, much as it hardened the nineteenth-century headmasters'
resistance to utilitarianism. As will be discussed in detail in Part II,
hostility to modern urban society has also had an important bearing
upon the growth of English in schools. When English replaced
classical subjects in those schools for whose pupils the classics
were inappropriate, it drew much power from its supporters' distaste
for contemporary conditions. Commenting upon this element in
nineteenth-century upper-class education, Musgrave writes:

'But those who knew Greece naturally turned from Cobbett and the
Manchester school to Pericles and Plato, from Leeds and Wigan to
Athens, from self-satisfied mercantilism to a civilisation without
machines or vast towns or great resources or a soul.'[26]

For a century and a half then, from the dissatisfied middle class
who wished to enter public schools and universities and transform
them to accommodate their needs, from the radicals who insisted
upon the inclusion of useful knowledge, from the progressives who
followed Rousseau in their emphasis upon learning through things
rather than words, critics attacked a curriculum limited to the study
of classical texts. The universities and public schools, however, stub-
bornly resisted successive series of critical articles and the recommendations of commissions and scientists. They maintained their
unshaken confidence in what they believed to be the superior
humanism of the classics and the truth of the faculty theory. Public
school headmasters, distrusting the notion of progress through scientific discovery and application, were unimpressed by references to
foreign competition, suspicious of the anti-religious associations with
the scientific cause, and untroubled by any need to provide their pupils
with the means of earning their living. They continued therefore in
those ways by which they had succeeded in the past in producing
Christian gentlemen. As T. W. Bamford points out:

'Fundamentally, the schools and the rest of the country were different
worlds . . . . All this had no effect on the schools whatsoever, and they
were still pursuing the same line that had suited an out-of-date agricultural society dominated by landowners.'[27]

Because the public schools despised and distrusted science, identifying it with grubby industrialism and godlessness, because they refused to take seriously the scientists' criticism of their classical education, nothing less than impassioned insistence upon the value of science was likely to be effective in championship of its cause. Something which emerges clearly from this curriculum debate is the strong notion of a central, totally educative subject. Since defenders of the classics claimed that these studies provided the complete education, supporters of scientific studies opposed them by making similar claims in equally elevated tones. Thomas Arnold's affirmation, 'it is only moral and religious knowledge which can accomplish this [a man's education]',[28] helps to explain Thomas Huxley's emotional plea for the study of science:

'Leave out the Physiological sciences from your curriculum and you launch the student into the world, undisciplined in that science whose subject matter would best develop his powers of observation; ignorant of facts of the deepest importance for his own and others' welfare; blind to the richest sources in God's creation; and unprovided with that belief in a living law and an order manifesting itself in and through endless change and variety, which might serve to check and moderate that phase of despair through which, if he take an earnest interest in social problems, he will assuredly sooner or later pass.'[29]

In 'Science and Culture' (1887), Huxley maintained that 'for the purpose of attaining real culture, an exclusively scientific education is at least as effectual as an exclusively literary education'.[30] In 1882 'On Science and Art in Relation to Education', Huxley quoted approvingly a statement made by a master at Clifton College to the effect that certain branches of science (exercised) 'an influence as much moral as intellectual'.[31] The serious claims by Huxley in *Essays on a Liberal Education* for the value of scientific studies, like those voiced by Michael Faraday to the Clarendon Commission, testify to the strength of the notion of the morally edifying and mentally improving subject. In 'Science and Religion' Herbert Spencer insisted upon the moral value of engaging in scientific activity. Answering the question which he puts about the subject 'of most worth', he said: 'Not only, however, for intellectual discipline is science the best; but also for moral discipline.'[32]

Those engaged in the curriculum debate felt that they were living in a time of crisis and, therefore, stated their views in tones of considerable urgency. Christians who felt that religious certainty was threatened by publications such as Darwin's *Origin of Species,*

Spencer's *Essays* and Bishop Colenso's *Statistical Inquiry into the Arithmetic of the Pentateuch*, supported subjects embodying spiritual and aesthetic values against Spencer's and Huxley's advocation of science in education. Literary men like Ruskin and Matthew Arnold, who disliked the 'mechanical' aspects of nineteenth-century England and feared the threat to cultural standards represented by the cheap press, supported the study of literature in desperate tones. Scientists who believed that the traditional classical studies were failing to humanise scholars because of their narrowness and incomprehensibility, and their irrelevance to society as a whole, argued their case with equal passion.

Ann Low Beer speaks of the 'desperate need for certainty'[33] in her comments on the intellectuals of Spencer's generation, who had discarded orthodox religion and yet sought some other system of thought which could answer their doubts and give them clear-cut principles. This desperate need seems partly to account for the nature of support given to new subjects. It also appears that nothing less than exaggerated championship of those subjects could hope to dislodge the confident superiority of the classics, even when they were achieving so little in many pupil's education.

The argument underlying this account of the curriculum debate is that it was to have far-reaching effects on English studies. All those who took part assumed that, in any sound education, there must be a liberal, truly humanising, morally improving subject at its centre. The classicists and scientists established, in their dispute, a mode of argument and created a combative mood in which recommendations were made in tones of desperate urgency. When English was recommended for inclusion in the expanded system of national school education, and later in universities, its supporters naturally shared the classicists' and scientists' assumptions. Their uneasy defensiveness about its status frequently sharpened their insistence upon its central value. The teachers of English, however, have been given a far heavier burden than the classics' tutors. The numbers of pupils to be 'protected' and 'improved' have increased massively and have been drawn from humbler social backgrounds. Much of the support given to English in the school curriculum has come from educators holding gloomy views of modern urban society and repeatedly reminding the teachers of its state of cultural crisis. And unlike the nineteenth century's unified view of the kind of character-building demanded of the classical curriculum, today's highly diversified society provides its English teachers with no single sense of purpose.

Notes

1. G. M. Young, *Victorian England: Portrait of an Age* (London, Oxford University Press, 1953), p. 75.
2. *Edinburgh Review* (April 1830); quoted by E. C. Mack, *Public Schools and British Opinion*, an examination of the relationship between contemporary ideas and the evolution of an English institution (London, Methuen; and New York, Columbia University Press, 1938–41), 2 vols; Vol. 1, p. 73.
3. J. Seeley, 'Liberal Education in Universities', in *Essays on a Liberal Education* (London, Macmillan, 1868), p. 146.
4. T. H. Huxley, 'A Liberal Education and Where to Find It' (1868), in *Science and Education* (London, Macmillan, 1895), p. 79.
5. Rev. F. W. Farrar, 'Of Greek and Latin Verse Composition', in *Essays on a Liberal Education*, op. cit., pp. 219 f.
6. T. H. Huxley, op. cit., p. 100.
7. N. Barlow (ed.), *The Autobiography of Charles Darwin* (London, Collins, 1958), p. 27.
8. Quoted by Mack, op. cit., p. 34 .
9. *Edinburgh Review*, Vol 15 (1809–10), p. 456.
10. B. Simon, *Studies in the History of Education, 1780–1870* (London, Lawrence & Wishart, 1960), p. 91.
11. *Westminster Review*, Vol. 4, No. 7 (July 1825), pp. 147 ff.
12. *Quarterly Journal*, Vol. 3, No. 6 (April 1832), pp. 268 f.
13. *Westminster Review*, Vol. 4, No. 7 (July 1825), p. 150.
14. Ibid., p. 155.
15. D. S. L. Cardwell, *The Organisation of Science in England* (London, Heinemann, 1957), p. 58.
16. Ibid., p. 242.
17. Ibid., loc. cit.
18. Ibid., p. 245.
19. *Quarterly Journal*, Vol. 3, No. 14 (April 1834).
20. T. Arnold: quoted by T. W. Bamford, *The Rise of the Public Schools* (London, Nelson, 1967), p. 92.
21. Quoted by W. F. Connell, *The Educational Thought and Influence of Matthew Arnold* (London, Routledge, 1950), p. 188.
22. Mack, op. cit., p. 390.
23. Young, op. cit., p. 97.
24. Bamford, op. cit., p. 63.
25. Sir Richard Livingstone, *A Defence of Classical Education* (1916); quoted by P. W. Musgrave, *Sociology, History and Education* (London, Methuen, 1970), p. 31.
26. Musgrave, op. cit., p. 31.
27. Bamford, op. cit., p. 89.
28. Arnold, op. cit., p. 66.
29. T. Huxley, 'On the Educational Value of the Natural History Sciences', in *Science and Education* (London, Macmillan, 1895), p. 65.
30. T. Huxley, 'Science and Culture', in ibid., p. 141.

31. T. Huxley, 'On Science and Art in Relation to Education', in ibid., p. 167.
32. Sir Herbert Spencer, 'Science and Religion', in A. Low Beer (ed.), *Spencer* (London, Collier-Macmillan, 1969), p. 55.
33. Low Beer (ed.), op. cit., Introduction, p. 7.

Chapter 2

Essays on a Liberal Education

'I feel sure that if the schoolmaster is ever to be, as I
think he ought to be, a missionary of culture . . . he
must make the study of modern literature a substantive
and important part of his training.'

Henry Sidgwick, *Essays on a Liberal Education*

The content and tone of the recommendations made for the study of
English by contributors to Dean Farrar's volume, *Essays on a Liberal
Education*, seem very likely to have significantly influenced the subject's growing ideology. Like Matthew Arnold, these writers responded
to the issues raised in the classics-science debate by making very high
claims for the benefits which the study of English literature could give
to their pupils. As was noted in Chapter 1, the commitment of educators to the notion of a centrally educative subject compelled the
supporters of new studies to express their justifications in tones of
considerable moral seriousness. Thus, Farrar's contributors, in common with later figures in the field of English from Matthew Arnold
to F. R. Leavis, make, in their discussion of teachers, references to
'missionaries of culture' to convey their lofty conception of the new
subject's responsibility. Like Arnold, the writers in Farrar's volume,
in spite of their high valuation of English literature, still assume the
superiority of the classics. Although much more flexible than most
public school headmasters, who insisted upon the study of the classics
for all their pupils, Sidgwick and Hales wish to confine their study to
the most able pupils only. Thus, these writers' convictions about the
supremely liberalising influence of classical studies were something in
the nature of a mixed blessing. Their recommendations for English
literature drew obvious strength from their belief in the power of
great literature to humanise, and led them to support its introduction
into the schools in morally exalted tones, but their assumption of the
inferiority of English to the classics helped to perpetuate the social
divisiveness against which, in 1921, the Newbolt Committee was to
protest so vigorously. Much of this protest was to take the form of
even more extravagant claims for the benefits of English studies in
schools.

Before looking at the recommendations for English made in *Essays on a Liberal Education*, it is useful to recall that their lofty tones derive not only from the assumptions underlying the nineteenth-century curriculum debate, but also from the writers' anxieties about the low status of English, from elementary school to university. Although the memorising of literature was gradually introduced into the elementary schools in the second half of the century, the theory of English teaching in these schools 'centred on providing primary literacy in terms of functional skills. Facility in these skills, because they tended to be drills taught in isolation, became an end in itself rather than a means, reflecting thereby some of the chief educational theories of the times.'[1] Like the utilitarians, whose theories hardened university and public school resistance to the inclusion of science and English into their curricula, identifying both with soulless vocational training, Robert Lowe performed a dubious service for the subject when he recommended its study in terms of its practical value. In his address, 'Primary and Classical Education' (1867), he stressed the importance of what he called 'practical things' rather than 'speculative things', insisting that 'the present is more important than the past'.[2] Condemning classical studies as the 'worship of inutility' he recommended the study of English, arguing that education should be 'preparation for actual life'. Although differing profoundly from Matthew Arnold in his approach to the problem of educating a growing population in an industrial society, he came to what seemed to be, on the surface, a similar conclusion as the poet. 'I believe it will be absolutely necessary', Lowe told the House of Commons in 1867, 'that you should prevail upon our future masters to learn their letters.'[3] Lowe appeared to share the views expressed by contributors to *Essays on a Liberal Education* when, in a letter, he wrote:

'First, I recommend to your notice a subject generally overlooked in our public schools, and that is—what do you think?—the English language, the language of Bacon and of Shakespeare . . . is it not time that we who speak that language, read that language . . . should know something about it?'[4]

But as far as elementary education was concerned, Lowe's motives for introducing requirements in English were governed by economic expediency. Lowe wrote to R. R. W. Linger, Secretary of the Committee of the Council on Education, about these requirements in reference to the Revised Code of 1862:

'It was more a financial than literary preference. Had there been any other branch of useful knowledge the possession of which could have been ascertained with equal precision, there was nothing to stop its admission. But there was not.'[5]

The following advertisement, which appeared in 1832 for Billesdon Academy, suggests that English, like science, was taught there in reaction against what was considered the uselessness of the classics and their irrelevance to middle-class pupils' needs: 'Many young gentlemen have left the seminary highly accomplished in English grammar, a qualification of peculiar importance in every respectable station in life.'[6] The impression given of English being the poor man's Latin is reinforced by the remarks made by George Combe, founder of Williams' Secular School, 1840, about his curriculum's lack of humanist element in its omission of classical studies. On Combe's decision to add poetry, painting and sculpture to his curriculum, Campbell Stewart comments that these were offered as a substitute; 'in adding the study of literature . . . he was pioneering liberal studies, possibly to fill the gap formerly supplied by the study of classical cultures'.[7] Proposals that English be studied in schools often made explicit their writer's acceptance of its low social status. When the Taunton Commission revealed that nearly half the endowed schools in England were no longer teaching Latin and Greek, and that whatever was taking place in these schools was of a deplorably low standard, the Commissioners endorsed a suggestion made by Rev G. C. Bradley of Marlborough that modern subjects should be encouraged in schools of inferior social status. In a letter to the Commission in 1868, Bradley says:

'. . . above all, I would give unusual weight to the teaching of English language, literature and history, to the attempt to humanise and refine a boy's mind by trying early to familiarise him with English poetry and to inspire him with a taste for the best authors I could place before him.'[8]

Earlier, in 1861, the Newcastle Commission had recommended that 'student teachers should study English language and literature, just as the Greek and Latin classics are read in superior public schools'.[9]

The contributors to *Essays on a Liberal Education*, several of whom were scientists critical of the public school's narrow view of human knowledge and their failure to teach classical literature meaningfully, wrote about English studies in schools in a way that had important effects on its emerging ideology. They were, clearly, looking to English to make good the deficiencies of the classics; they were 'feeling their way towards the position which regarded English studies as replacing the classics'.[10] Several developments in schools in the mid-nineteenth century help to account for the elevated tones in which these writers refer to English literature. They disliked Bentham's and Spencer's deliberate exclusion of literature from their recommended subjects for study, an exclusion explained by their hostility to the public schools' literary curriculum. Moreover, most endowed grammar schools were neglecting English literature entirely, and teaching classical studies ineffectually. Finally, the elementary schools' concentration upon useful knowledge taught through mechanical drills added to a profound concern about what many Victorians saw as a cultural crisis in education.

Of the contributors to Farrar's volume, T. H. Huxley and H. Sidgwick gave the strongest emphasis to the value of English studies. Elsewhere, Huxley had expressed his anxiety about the shortcomings of the schools. In 'A Liberal Education and Where to Find It' (1868), he expressed both his dissatisfaction with working-class and middle-class education and his interest in the possibilities of the native language. About elementary education, he wrote that a child learns: 'To read, write and cypher, more or less well; but in a very large number of cases not so well as to take pleasure in reading, or to be able to write the commonest letter properly.'[11] And about middle-class education in the inferior endowed schools and academies he stated:

'There is a little more reading and writing of English. But for all that, everyone knows that it is a rare thing to find a boy in the middle and upper classes who can read aloud decently, and who can put his thoughts on paper in clear and grammatical (to say nothing of good and elegant) language . . . . He might never have heard that there once lived certain notable men called Chaucer, Shakespeare, Milton, Voltaire, Goethe, Schiller.'[12]

After condemning the uselessness of his own classical education, Huxley advocates the study of English in all schools. It is interesting, however, that although Huxley expresses concern about the importance of literary culture and its part in pupils' enrichment, he assumes the effectiveness of classical teaching methods, and suggests that these be transferred to English.

'I would assuredly devote a very large portion of the time of every English child to the careful study of the models of English writing of such varied and wonderful kind as we possess, and, what is still more important, and still more neglected, the habit of using that language with precision, with force, and with art. I fancy we are almost the only nation in the world who seem to think that composition comes by nature.'[13]

Henry Sidgwick's essay in Farrar's volume is probably of even greater significance for the growth of English in schools. The content and tone of his convictions about the humanising power of literature and about the responsibility of teachers, anticipate many later claims. While it is true, and closely related to the type of statement which he makes about English, that Sidgwick feels that a genuine preference for Greek and Latin writing shows 'the purest, severest and most elevated literary taste',[14] he is very concerned about the inaccessibility of the classics to all but a very few. When he condemns English philistinism and athleticism, he places responsibility for these failings firmly upon the insufficiently literary education in the schools. He thus shares the view held by other contributors that most pupils never experience what he believes to be the humanising effects of literature because their minds are exhausted by linguistic struggles. He said that the young boy's mind, during a typical public school education, 'instead of being penetrated with the subtle and simple graces of form, is filled to the brim with thoughts of gender, quantity, tertiary predicates, uses of the subjunctive mood'.[15] Attacking the public school view that, since the complete study of Greek and Latin provided a perfect education, its half study would provide a satisfactory half perfection, Sidgwick insists instead upon the need for more literature. Attacking the classical curriculum's critics who wished to remove any sort of study of literature from the schools on the grounds that it was frivolous and useless, he again insists upon the benefits of shifting attention to English. Thus, he supports the inclusion of more literature because he believes in its character-building element. If it had to be faced that the classics were inaccessible to the great majority, and at that time were very badly taught, Sidgwick believed that the solution lay with the introduction of English. He was firmly convinced that English literature could provide those vital formative experiences which most pupils missed in their linguistic battles with Latin and Greek.

'Let us demand instead that all boys, whatever their special bent and destination, be really taught literature; so that as far as possible, they may learn to enjoy intelligently poetry and eloquence; that their views and sympathies may be enlarged and expanded by apprehending noble, subtle and profound thoughts, refined and lofty feelings; that some comprehension of the varied development of human nature may ever abide with them, the source and essence of a truly humanising culture.'[16]

What remains important for future anxieties about English, however, is that both Sidgwick and Hales assume the superiority of the classics to English literature. Hales advocated the study of English for those who would not proceed to university, arguing that, since classical education for most boys meant its neglect and an escape from it as soon as possible, it would be more reasonable to replace what it was intended to achieve by the study of English. Speaking of the boy unlikely to go to university, Hales said:

'In fact, he is not at all at his ease in the society of the classics, he cannot converse naturally with them, justly estimate and admire their calm and placid beauty, their noble dignified grace. He must find society more accordant with his tastes and abilities.'[17]

Clearly, in spite of the supporting rhetoric, or perhaps explaining it, English, for all its richness, remained, even for its defenders, the lower-status subject, fit only for those pupils unable or unwilling to aim beyond it. Little wonder, therefore, that Oxford and Cambridge, and those schools which either wanted their pupils to gain entry there or wanted to satisfy parents in their provision of a gentleman's education, continued to ignore English. London University, having introduced it as a student's subject, made every attempt to confer respectability upon it by adding philological requirements, as Oxford and Cambridge were to do later in the century.

Today, a roughly similar relationship exists between subject specialists and supporters of interdisciplinary work. The supremacy of the classics has finally disappeared—qualifications in Latin are no longer demanded by the ancient universities—and English is widely accepted as their replacement as the humanising centre of the school curriculum. Many teachers are worried, though, about the difficulties faced, by working-class children in particular, when reading major texts in English literature, and are adopting thematic approaches involving easier and shorter extracts. When English teachers resist these developments, their reluctance for their subject to be dismantled for interdisciplinary projects and themes reflects something of the Victorian headmasters' suspicion of vernacular literature as it previously threatened the classics. There are differences, of course, which illustrate major changes in the climate of educational discussion. Today, the supporters of English studies, like G. H. Bantock and David Holbrook, want children from all social backgrounds to be able to experience great literature and creative activity, at their own levels, whereas the nineteenth-century headmasters wished to preserve the classics as a liberal education for their upper-class pupils only. They were unconcerned, sometimes enthusiastic, about the introduction of English literature into elementary schools, as long· as this did not interfere with their own curriculum. And today, unlike the Victorian pioneers for English studies, the supporters of interdisciplinary work tend to believe in the value of their innovative curriculum for all pupils, not only the average and less able, and even for university students.

Unlike the contributors to *Essays on a Liberal Education* who implied, or readily acknowledged, the superiority of the classics, contemporary innovators in the interdisciplinary field rarely acknowledge the superiority of English. Today, supporters of English in schools believe that its benefits should be enjoyed by all pupils, unlike those classicists who advocated their curriculum for an élite; similarly, today, supporters of interdisciplinary work commend it for all pupils, unlike Arnold, Sidgwick and Hales who proposed that their new subject, English literature, be mainly for those in middle- and working-class schools.

Chapter 3, which considers the importance of Matthew Arnold's contribution to the growth of English studies in schools, also discusses the effects, in this century, of his acknowledgement, like Sidgwick's and Hales's, of the superiority of the classics. Unlike the great scientists such as Huxley, who utterly condemned the exclusiveness and aridity of the classical curriculum in public schools and universities, proposing a thoroughgoing reorganisation of upper-class education, Arnold and other literary men were happy to leave the classics in supremacy. Unwittingly, therefore, although they made major contributions to the growth of English in elementary and, later, secondary education, their assumptions about its inferiority intensified the bitterness of debate about its worth during the first half of this century. If these literary figures' acceptance of the superiority of the classics over English studies was, in some measure, responsible for the traditional curriculum's persistence at public schools and ancient universities this century, then they can be said to have played a part in creating some of the Newbolt Committee's anxieties about the social divisiveness in England, and its passionate recommendations of English studies as a 'bond' between the classes. Similarly, it can be argued that their assumptions contributed, indirectly, to the indifference which F. R. Leavis had to contend with when struggling to dislodge the classics at Oxford and Cambridge and to replace them by English as the central humanising study. Victorian liberals accepted the class divisions in their society and were, in general, unquestioning in recommending different liberal educations for different kinds of schools. Therefore, when English came to be viewed, in part, as a solution to social inequalities, support for it had to be expressed in tones of almost religious insistence in order that it should be given attention in those institutions where classical studies had remained unchallenged for so long.

Notes

1. W. R. Mullins, *A Study of Significant Changes in the Theory of the Teaching of English to Older Pupils in Elementary and Secondary Schools, 1860–1960*, unpublished MEd thesis, University of Leicester (January 1968), p. 256.
2. Sir Robert Lowe, 'Primary and Classical Education', an Address delivered before the Philosophical Institution of Edinburgh, Friday, 1 November, 1867; revised by the author in 1867 (Edinburgh, Edmonston & Douglas, 1867), pp. 15 ff.
3. Sir Robert Lowe, Debate on the 1867 Reform Act, Parliamentary Debates CLXXXVIII, 1549.
4. Sir Robert Lowe to R. R. W. Linger; quoted by Martin Patchett, *Life and Letters of Viscount Sherbrook* (London, Longman Green, 1893), Vol. 2, p. 335.
5. Ibid., p. 335.
6. *Leicester Chronicle* (7 January 1832), quoted by B. Simon, *Studies in the History of Education 1780–1870* (London, Lawrence & Wishart, 1960), p. 113.
7. W. A. C. Stewart and W. P. McCann, *The Educational Innovators* (New York, Macmillan, 1967), Vol. 1, p. 284.
8. Rev. G. C. Bradley, Letter to Taunton Commission, *Report of Schools Inquiry*, Vol. 4 (1868), p. 420.
9. The Newcastle Commission, Report of the Royal Commission appointed to Inquire into the State of Popular Education in England, 1861, Vol. 1, p. 120.
10. J. W. Adamson, *English Education, 1789–1902* (Cambridge, Cambridge University Press, 1930), p. 428.
11. J. Huxley, 'A Liberal Education and Where to Find It', in *Science and Education* (London, Macmillan, 1895), p. 87.
12. Ibid., pp. 92 f.
13. T. Huxley, 'On Science and Art in Relation to Education', in *Science and Education*, op. cit., p. 185.
14. H. Sidgwick, 'The Theory of Classical Education,' in *Essays on a Liberal Education* (London, Macmillan, 1868), p. 106.
15. Ibid., p. 116.
16. Ibid., pp. 129 f.
17. J. W. Hales, 'The Teaching of English', in *Essays on a Liberal Education*, op. cit., p. 331.

Matthew Arnold

'Good poetry does undoubtedly tend to form the soul
and character; it tends to beget a love of beauty and
of truth in alliance together; it suggests, however
indirectly, high and noble principles of action, and it
inspires the emotion so helpful in making principles
operative. Hence its extreme importance to all of us;
but in our elementary schools its importance seems
to me at present quite extraordinary.'

Matthew Arnold, *Report* (1880)

Like other contestants in the curriculum debate, Matthew Arnold was
committed to the notion of a central educative subject which would
'form the soul and character'. He, too, believed in the ideal of a liberal
education, expressing his convictions about its importance in all the
nation's schools in tones of religious intensity. For the growth of
English, his passionate insistence upon the value of literary culture
has been of outstanding significance. Fearing the likely persuasiveness of scientists' claims to moralise pupils through their discipline,
Arnold felt compelled to argue for the superiority of literature in the
strongest terms. His passion drew additional force from his anxieties
about developments in his society which had, in his view, brought
about a severe cultural crisis. During the political unrest of the 1860s
and 1870s—the Second Reform Bill, trade union disturbances, Fenian
outrages, the Murphy riots in Birmingham and Manchester—Arnold
feared the price to be paid for the lack of central planning in our
schools. During such times he felt that there was a desperate need for
literary culture in the elementary schools.

Although his attitude towards the masses' likely receptivity to
culture was, at times, ambivalent, Arnold stated in most of his writing
that culture should not remain the exclusive privilege of the few, but
by 'apostles of equality'[1] should be diffused among the many, in the
middle and working classes; it was the task of education to achieve
this. He proposed that the unsuccessful classics' teaching in the great
public schools should not be abolished but reformed, and that English
literature should be introduced at every other level in the nation's

schools. Sharing the Romantic poets' belief in the moral superiority of the artist, Arnold argued that England's cultural crisis could be met only by the dissemination of great literature and the creation of conditions under which standards of critical refinement could be maintained. Resisting nothing less than the increasing confidence and influence of science in a commercially minded age, as well as all those elements in Victorian England which he feared as disruptive, Arnold's recommendations for the study of literature were, predictably, made in tones of passionate conviction. His faith in what it might achieve and, implicitly, his expectations of successful teachers, have played a very important part in the growth of this century's ideology of English in schools. Arnold was profoundly troubled by what he called the 'external' nature of Victorian society, competitive, materialistic, practical and complacent. Worship of material progress threatened to displace religion; 'scientific' criticism of the Bible encouraged scepticism; utilitarianism excluded literature from middle-class education in the Academies and emphasised the value of the merely useful in the elementary schools. For Arnold who, in 1848, said, 'I see a wave of more than American vulgarity, moral, intellectual and social, preparing to wash over us',[2] imparting culture to all classes meant making 'reason and the will of God prevail'[3] and helping to stem the 'common tide of men's thoughts in a wealthy and industrial community', to save 'the future as one may hope from being vulgarised, even if it cannot save the present'.[4]

Persistent attacks on the classical curriculum increased Arnold's anxieties about the precarious position of a liberal education. They strengthened his belief in the need for reform in the public schools and in the need for the study of literature in the elementary schools. He feared, particularly, that the curriculum in schools for the working classes merely reflected the 'mechanism' of the outside world.

'The great fault of the instruction in our elementary schools is that it at most gives to a child the mechanical possession of the instruments of knowledge, but does nothing to form him, to put him in the way of making the best possible use of them.'[5]

Herbert Spencer's insistence upon science as 'the knowledge of greatest worth' and Thomas Huxley's claims that science promoted breadth and elevation of mind, even more than those accusations that the literary curriculum hindered our competitive progress against foreign powers, drove Arnold into a position of antagonism to science and impassioned defence of literature. In *Friendship's Garland*, Lycurgus Academy, Peckham, is satirised thus:

'None of your antiquated rubbish—all practical work—latest discoveries in science—mind constantly kept excited—lots of interesting
experiments—lights of all colours—fizz! fizz! bang! bang! That's
what I call forming a man.'[6]

Supporters of science who claimed that its study developed valuable
abilities forced Arnold, in 'Literature and Science', to write in
defensive and assertive tones about the humanities. Separating them
from instrumental knowledge which, he insisted, cannot be directly
related to the 'sense which we have in us for beauty' or the 'sense
which we have in us for conduct',[7] he stated his personal preference
thus: 'If one is driven to choose, I think I would rather have a young
person ignorant about the moon's diameter. . . . Letters will call out
[the great majority's] being at more points, will make them live more.'[8]
Expressing even more emphatically his reluctance to admit science
into the school curriculum as the 'more useful alternative' for
literature and history, Arnold said in his General Report for 1876:

'To have the power of using, which is the thing wished, the data of
natural science, a man must, in general, have first been in some sense
"moralised"; and for moralising him it will be found not easy, I think,
to dispense with those old agents, letters, poetry, religion. So let not
our teachers be led to imagine, whatever they may hear and see of the
call for natural science, that this literary cultivation is unimportant.
The fruitful use of natural science itself depends, in a very great
degree, on having effected in the whole man, by means of letters, a
rise in what the political economists call the standards of life.'[9]

Thomas Arnold, influenced like other great public school headmasters by the moral idealism of German education, had passed on
to his son his deep distrust of what he saw as the godless, restless,
'mechanical' society produced by Benthamite rationalism. As Connell points out: 'Above all there ran through the lives of both father
and son a missionary zeal for the transformation and elevation of
society.'[10] In Matthew Arnold's view, a society which appeared to
lack central control, whose religion had become the worship of
machinery and wealth, needed, not scientific education, but the
'beneficent function' of literature which had 'immense work to do
in the middle region between religion and science'. 'I do hope', he
wrote, 'that what influence I have may be of use in the troubled times
which I see before us as a healing and reconciling influence.'[11]

Above all, it was to poetry that Arnold looked for the redemption of
the middle and lower classes in a society which was not only politically

disturbed but appeared to be losing religion at the same time as it was threatened by science. The religious role which he desired for poetry is clear here, when he says:

'We should conceive of poetry worthily, and more highly than it has been the custom to conceive of it. . . . More and more mankind will discover that we have to turn to poetry to interpret life for us to console us, to sustain us. Without poetry, our science will appear incomplete; and most of what now passes with us for religion and philosophy, will be replaced by poetry.'[12]

Moral zeal, therefore, which was a characteristic both of the Victorian headmasters concerned about the development of their pupils into leaders of society, and of the evangelicals anxious to protect the newly literate masses against corrupting reading matter, is clearly an important part of Arnold's support for literature. Reinforcing it is the notion which Raymond Williams refers to as belief in the moral superiority of the artist, a belief which, he argues, had developed largely from the Romantic poet's alienation from his society. Williams, who discusses this in detail in the first chapter of *Culture and Society*, and continues to refer to it throughout the rest of his book, suggests that the Romantic tendency, in reaction to society's neglect of the artist after the disappearance of patronage, was to find compensation in equating art with what was superior in experience. Romantic critical theories redefined relations between literature and life by promoting literature to the level of life, poetry to experience itself. In *The Prelude*, Wordsworth refers to poetry as 'a power like one of Nature's',[13] while Shelley insisted that 'Poetry strengthens the faculty which is the organ of the moral nature of man, in the same manner as exercise strengthens a limb.'[14] Williams argues that the dissatisfaction of the artists not only with their exclusion from society (as publishers replaced patronage), but with the kind of industrial society which was developing, led to an insistence upon the superiority of art in that it is 'natural' rather than 'mechanical'. He says that 'under pressure, art became a symbolic abstraction for a whole range of general human experience . . . a general social activity was forced into a status of a department or province, and actual works of art were in part converted into a self-pleading ideology'.[15] At a time when society was obviously becoming 'external' in its values, art offered a different and superior set of values against the widespread acceptance of utility and acquisitiveness; it became indeed the 'Court of Appeal',[16] by which a society constructing its relationships in terms of the cash nexus might be condemned. From Coleridge, through Arnold, to F. R.

Leavis, the need has been expressed for a class of cultivated men whose concern is with the quality of their society's life. Since 'quality' had come to be identified with or even equated with the ability to respond to and discriminate between great works of art, this élite has been distinguished above all by its degree of literary culture.

The intensity of Arnold's critical response to his 'external' society has had far-reaching effects upon the study of English in schools. Convinced of the morally educative power of literature, he proposed its study so that society's imperfections could be counteracted at a time when science appeared to be gaining support in middle-class education and, as he stated it, 'the masses are losing the Bible and religion'.[17] In his view, there was a desperate need for culture, that is literary culture, among the British middle and working classes, the Philistines and Populace. Arnold believed culture to be 'a study of perfection. It moves by the force, not merely or primarily of the scientific passion for pure knowledge, but also of the moral and social passion for doing good',[18] and that it was 'the great help out of our present difficulties'. He therefore made repeated recommendations that ways be found to bring culture into the schools. Since the classics were obviously inaccessible and inappropriate to the expanding elementary school population, Arnold, like the contributors to *Essays on a Liberal Education* who were concerned about middle- and upper-class pupils, wished to see the teaching of English improved. Concurring, paradoxically, with Robert Lowe and the utilitarians who had been asserting the claims of English over Greek and Latin, and with Thomas Huxley who detected 'no pleasure in reading', Arnold suggested that elementary school children should study the best models of English poetry. Indeed, the introduction of learning poetry by heart by children and pupil teachers was Arnold's contribution to the advancement of English in schools.

Throughout Arnold's work are frequent expressions of his distress about the existence of class divisions in English society. His recommendations, in particular about the need for literature in elementary education, derive partly from his desire to see a broadening of the basis of that 'sweetness and light' which culture represented to him. The following extract anticipates not only the emotional tones of proposals for better English teaching to be made in the 1921 Report, but also the hope that its success would bind together England's divided social classes.

'If I have not shrunk from saying that we must work for sweetness and light, so neither have I shrunk from saying that we must have a broad basis, must have sweetness and light for as many as possible.

[Culture] seeks to do away with classes; to make the best that has been thought and known in the world current everywhere; to make all men live in an atmosphere of sweetness and light, where they may use ideas, as it uses them itself, freely—nourished, and not bound by them. . . .[19] This is the social idea; and the men of culture are the true apostles of equality. The great men of culture are those who have had a passion for diffusing, for making prevail, for carrying from one end of society to the other, the best knowledge, the best ideas of their time . . . .'[20]

As several critics have pointed out, there is considerable ambivalence in Arnold's work between this egalitarianism and his occasionally contemptuous attitude towards the masses. Sometimes his remoteness from working-class life and, thus, lack of sympathy with its conditions, takes the form of unpleasant arrogance: 'And so they are thrown back upon themselves, upon their beer, their gin and their fun.'[21] Sometimes he expresses doubts about the capacity of the masses to receive the 'best ideas of their time'. The emphatic nature of the following assertion certainly seems inconsistent with his wish to broaden the basis of culture's 'sweetness and light'.

'The mass of mankind will never have any ardent zeal for seeing things as they really are; very inadequate ideas will always satisfy them. On these inadequate ideas reposes, and must repose, the general practice of the world.'[22]

And, with statements such as these, there comes a further element in Arnold's contribution to the growth of English in schools which has persisted throughout this century. Despair with what is seen as the threats represented by the mass media, and frustration with education's apparent failure to equip the masses to resist, have frequently provoked serious and compassionate people in the field of English to express similar superiority and contempt. F. R. Leavis, who has been even more influential than Arnold in achieving an important place for English in schools, has, like Arnold, in spite of his professed concern with quality of life, exhibited both arrogance and remoteness in his contemptuous references to 'telly and bingo'.

Arnold, unlike Leavis, G. H. Bantock and David Holbrook, who are very close to him in their concern about the quality of children's lives unrefined by engagement with great literature, often expressed his anxieties about inequality in his society. He failed, however, in common with several contributors to *Essays on a Liberal Education*, to realise that, to some extent, by his support for the retention of the traditional classical curriculum for the public schools, Latin for older secondary pupils, and English for the lower-middle-class and elementary-school pupils, he was responsible for the perpetuation of class differences. He seemed to think that by advocating the study of English poetry in the elementary schools, he was broadening the basis of that 'sweetness and light' which culture represented to him. But as long as English was studied only by working-class children, girls, Mechanics' Institute apprentices and audiences for WEA lectures, it remained a low-status subject, despised by the great public schools and universities. It is interesting to note both the reluctance of head-masters to include English literature in their curricula and the crusading tones of the subject's supporters. The curriculum con-troversy, arising to a considerable extent out of opposing claims made by rival social classes, took place in a climate of bitterness and sus-picion. Claimants stated their cases with passionate eloquence, the tones of which have had, in the case of English in particular, lasting effects upon the ideology of the subject. Robert Lowe, who let it be known that, for reasons of expediency, he favoured the study of English rather than Greek or Latin, was criticised by H. H. Almond, a public school headmaster. Almond did concede that he would admit English into schools: 'sometimes when boys are tired with a hard run and a football match . . . sometimes a spare quarter hour when a regular lesson has been quickly got over, may be utilised in this way.'[23]

Although Arnold's persuasive rhetoric implies his realisation that English needed defence against neglect and contempt as a low-status subject, it appears inconsistent with his endorsement of continued study of the classical curriculum in public schools. His hopes for the promotion of a common culture seem to be contradicted by this, and to be unrealistically optimistic when, in attempts to confer respecta-bility upon English, he introduced that same drudgery of memorising poetry which was alienating upper-class pupils from their classical studies. A common culture was unlikely to be achieved by retention of traditional teaching methods transferred, for working-class pupils, to models of the English classics. His recommendations, however, caused English to be given greater time and attention in the schools. In 1861, he commended 'learning by heart extracts from good authors' as 'an excellent discipline for pupil teachers'.[24] Recitation, he said 'afforded a useful discipline . . . out of the mass of treasures thus gained . . .' would grow 'a more precious fruit' for 'all but the rudest natures would be insensibly nourished by that which [was] stored in them, and their taste [would be] formed by it'.[25] As a result of Arnold's efforts, in 1871 English literature and grammar was made a 'specific subject' to be taught to individual pupils in Standards IV, V and VI.

This did much to raise the status of recitation and to extend English beyond its early study as a useful subject. Although pleased by this change, Arnold felt that the passages chosen were frequently unsuitable for children, who recited without understanding. He recommended that 'the recitation should be turned into a literature lesson',[26] one of many suggestions made to teachers by the Inspectorate who tended to underestimate the difficulties this raised for those elementary school teachers whose cultural background was very insecure. By 1882, English moved from being an optional to a compulsory 'class' subject. Arnold expressed his approval of extending recitation to more pupils in a way which interestingly anticipates present-day ideas; if a child, he said, was brought 'to throw himself into a piece of poetry', he was being involved in 'an exercise of creative activity'.[27]

Throughout his career, Arnold, with a moral zeal as strong as Wesley's and a sense of the artist's superiority as fervent as the Romantic poets', advocated the study of poetry for the complacent, Philistine middle class and the brutalised lower class, both threatened by the 'tide of American vulgarity'. Moral zeal which he inherited from his father, defensiveness into which the opposition drove him, with their claims about the power of science to form the mind and character, and concern about his society's political unrest, all led Arnold to state the case for literature in tones whose passion and vagueness have characterised much of the argument about the subject. In the 1871 Report, Arnold refers to literature as 'the greatest power available in education';[28] in the 1880 Report, he says that poetry

'undoubtedly tends to form the soul and character; it tends to beget a love of beauty, of truth, in alliance together; it suggests, however indirectly, high and noble principles in action . . . hence its extreme importance to all of us, but in our elementary schools, its importance seems to me at present, quite extraordinary.'[29]

Expressions of warm agreement with his diagnosis of what he saw as Victorian England's cultural crisis testify to Arnold's affinity with many educators in English throughout this century. His hostility to the practical, 'external', 'do-as-you-like' elements in modern industrial society, his suspicions of science, and his commitment to what he believed to be the refining power of literature for people without religion have all commended him to later educators dissatisfied with the way the world has been going. It is interesting to notice the striking similarities between the content and tone of Arnold's recommendations for the study of poetry and those expressed in the 1921 government Report on the *Teaching of English in England*. Like Arnold, the contributors to this Report insisted upon the desirability of uniting society's divided classes by means of a literature in a common language. They expressed their faith in its 'unifying tendency', in the national literature's power to serve as a 'bond'. Like Arnold, they referred to teachers as the 'missionaries of culture' who would carry their enthusiasm and personal commitment to the value of literature into an unresponsive, even hostile society. Sharing Arnold's anti-industrialism, philanthropy, faith in the spiritually educative power of literature, they envisaged something like a crusade of English teachers working in the schools to promote society's unity and salvation. Many educators, responding to the problems involved in what they saw as the schools' responsibility to disseminate liberal culture throughout all levels of society, demanded outstanding personal qualities from the teachers. And as the 'problem' grew more complex and difficult, these demands for good teachers became more insistent and extravagant.

Throughout this century, educators concerned with English in schools have expressed their admiration for Arnold, acknowledging his influence upon their views. F. R. Leavis, about whom Denys Thompson says (as could have been said about Arnold) 'he has contended ceaselessly and vigorously for literature as something that matters to us and our civilisation,'[30] writes about his debt to Arnold in facing 'a crisis more severe' in contemporary conditions. G. H. Bantock, a pupil of Leavis's who has been influential in promoting the study of English in schools, develops Leavis's acknowledgement in an article in *Scrutiny*:

'The importance of Matthew Arnold as an educationalist—the reason why, today, we need so much to turn to him for light—seems to me to be in two directions. There is his diagnosis of a particular cultural situation, a situation which since Arnold's day has not only grown worse, but has grown worse along the lines that Arnold indicated; and there is his appreciation of the necessity of tackling the current degeneration of standards by a clear-sighted understanding of essential distinctions to be made between means and ends.'[31]

Several major figures in literature and education this century have been strongly attracted to Arnold's way of thinking about his society. Many of those who have been responsible for the growth of English in schools have sympathised with his criticism of commerce, science, 'mechanical' curricula and teaching methods. Fearing the effects of our loss of religion, convinced about men's need for deeper satisfactions beyond material gain and—a development since Arnold—

anxious about the disappearance of small agricultural communities, they, too, have placed immense faith in the personally enriching, improving power of literature. Basil Willey summarises the key reasons for Arnold's special role in his introduction to the poet's achievement in *Nineteenth-Century Studies*:

'Instead, in Arnold, we encounter a new phenomenon, the "literary" intelligence playing freely upon the great concerns of human life. He was the first to see and to proclaim the importance, for the modern world, of the qualities of mind and spirit which literary culture can give . . . . He knew, and had "felt along the heart", the deep malady of his time, and for that very reason could diagnose it and spend the greater part of his life in trying to cure it.'[32]

Notes

1. Matthew Arnold, *Culture and Anarchy* (Ann Arbor, University of Michigan Press, 1965), p. 113.
2. Matthew Arnold, *Letters of Matthew Arnold, 1848–1888*, Vol. 1, ed. G. W. E. Russell (London, Macmillan, 1895), p. 4.
3. Arnold, *Culture and Anarchy*, op. cit., p. 112.
4. Ibid., p. 98.
5. Matthew Arnold, General Report for the Year 1872, in *Reports on Elementary Schools, 1852–1882* (London, HMSO, 1908), p. 147.
6. Matthew Arnold, *Friendship's Garland* (London, Smith, Elder, 1903), pp. 50 f.
7. Matthew Arnold, 'Literature and Science' (1882), in *Discourses in America* (New York, Macmillan, 1906), p. 105.
8. Ibid., pp. 127 ff.
9. Matthew Arnold, General Report for the Year 1876, in *Reports on Elementary Schools, 1852–1882*, op. cit., p. 178.
10. W. F. Connell, *The Educational Thought and Influence of Matthew Arnold* (London, Routledge, 1950), p. 278.
11. Matthew Arnold, *Letters of Matthew Arnold, 1848–1888*, Vol 1., op. cit., p. 41.
12. Matthew Arnold, *Essays in Criticism* (London, Macmillan, 1908), Second Series, p. 2.
13. William Wordsworth, *The Prelude*, Book XIII C313 (London, Edward Mixon, 1850), p. 465.
14. Percy Shelley, 'A Defence of Poetry', in *Shelley's Literary and Philosophical Criticism* (London, Henry Froude, 1909), p. 131.
15. Raymond Williams, *Culture and Society, 1780–1950* (New York, Anchor Books, 1960), p. 51.

16. Ibid., p. 52.
17. Matthew Arnold, *Literature and Dogma* (London, Nelson [1910]), p. 290.
18. Matthew Arnold, *Culture and Anarchy*, op. cit., p. 91.
19. Ibid., pp. 112 f.
20. Ibid., p. 112.
21. Matthew Arnold, 'Equality', in *Mixed Essays, The Works of Matthew Arnold* (London, Edition de Luxe, 1903–4), pp. 91 f.
22. Ibid., loc cit.
23. H. H. Almond, 'Mr Lowe's Educational Theories Examined from a Practical Point of View' (Edinburgh, Edmonston & Douglas, 1868), p. 21.
24. Matthew Arnold, General Report for the Year 1861, in *Reports on Elementary Schools, 1852–1882*, op. cit., p. 88.
25. Ibid., loc. cit.
26. Matthew Arnold, General Report for the Year 1874, in ibid., p. 163.
27. Matthew Arnold, General Report for the Year 1882, in ibid., pp. 228 f.
28. Matthew Arnold, General Report for the Year 1871, in ibid., p. 142.
29. Matthew Arnold, General Report for the Year 1880, in ibid., pp. 200 f.
30. Denys Thompson, *Directions in the Teaching of English* (Cambridge, Cambridge University Press, 1969), Introduction, p. 9.
31. G. H. Bantock, 'Matthew Arnold, HMI', in *Scrutiny*, Vol. 18, No. 1 (June 1951), p. 32.
32. Basil Willey, *Nineteenth-Century Studies* (London, Chatto & Windus, 1949), pp. 252 f.

Chapter 4

Literature and the Threats from Commerce

'... one of the richest fields of our spiritual being is
left uncultivated—not indeed barren, for the weeds
of literature have never been so prolific as in our day.'

The Newbolt Report (1921)

Thus far, Matthew Arnold stands out for the severity with which he criticised his society. He makes it very clear that he recommended the inclusion of English literature in the elementary school curriculum because he feared the power of commercial, 'mechanical' forces in a rapidly industrialising nation. Artists, critics and teachers this century who have shared his fear have, as we shall see later, made a special contribution to English studies by developing critical discrimination as a crucial exercise at school and university level. Because F. R. Leavis was committed to the notion of English as the central humanising subject, wishing to raise its status as a discipline in the face of the classicists' and scientists' contempt for a 'soft option', he devoted his teaching and writing to demonstrations of fine critical responses to writers' use of language. Moreover, since, like I. A. Richards, Leavis feared what he viewed as the coarsening effects upon our emotions of the language of bad art—advertising, cinema, cheap fiction—he pointed out the need for our schools to encourage critical discrimination in order that children should be able to resist their appeal. Because he played such a significant part in establishing Cambridge English, it is his work which, later, will be given the closest attention in the discussion of critical discrimination in school English.

At this stage, however, it is interesting to note that much support was given to the study of English literature—long before its acceptance at Oxford and Cambridge—because it was believed that this subject could protect readers against the corrupting effects of cheap fiction and the newspapers. Right from its beginnings as a recommended subject for study in schools, it was hoped that English literature would provide experiences which would lift pupils above the commercial world's crude sensationalism. In this chapter, a selection of supporters' views have been chosen to illustrate this optimism accompanying the growing recognition of English as an important part of the curriculum.

D. J. Palmer, who analyses in detail this aspect of the development of English as a university subject, shows that the recommendation of good books as a defence against corruption has a long history. As early as 1660, Charles Hoole was concerning himself with the problem of educating pupils whose future lives did not require a classical background. Anxious about the possible ill effects of neglecting the character-building elements in their education, Hoole wrote:

'Non-improvement of children's time after they can read English any whit well, throweth open a gap to all loose kinds of behaviour. . . . And their acquaintance with good books will (by God's blessing) be a means so to sweeten their (otherwise sour) natures, that they may live comfortably towards themselves, and amiably converse with other persons.'[1]

Palmer also quotes from the Reverend Vicesimus Knox's *Elegant Extracts* of 1824. Knox was concerned with a problem, the anxiety about which, as Palmer points out, will lead to greater insistence upon the moral power of literature during the nineteenth century. As Knox wrote in his Preface:

'There is no good reason to be given why the mercantile classes, at least of the higher order, should not amuse their leisure with any pleasures of polite literature. Nothing perhaps contributes more to liberalise their minds, and prevent that narrowness which is too often the consequence of a life attached, from the earliest age, to the pursuits of lucre.'[2]

In 1826, in a sermon called 'The Tendency of Prevalent Opinions about Knowledge', the Reverend H. J. Rose pleaded a case for the study of literature, supporting his proposal by reference to Wordsworth's belief in poetry as a humanising power. This sermon, 'in which the writer fully accepts Wordsworth's definition of the poetic imagination as endowed with profounder moral insight, a deeper truth than that comprehended by a scientific mind',[3] usefully illustrates how the Romantic view of the artist's superiority had fused with nineteenth-century moral earnestness to advance recommendations for English studies. As literacy spread, and the cheap press flourished, the study of literature was recommended less generally against 'loose behaviour' and the 'pursuit of lucre', but more specifically against the power of sensational fiction to deprave and corrupt.

From this century's perspective, the threats embodied in Victorian cheap fiction appear fairly harmless. Today, when radio and television are in almost every home, when cinema-going is a regular entertainment, and when advertisements reach inside and outside the home, many English teachers see themselves engaged in a daily struggle against the debasement of language. Convictions about the cheapening, trivialising effects of cinema, radio and pop music lead many of them to increase their efforts to stimulate creativity, enthusiasm for literature, and to encourage critical discrimination. English teachers, since the 1930s, have been urged by Leavis and his pupils to join a crusade against those forces in commercial entertainment which they hold responsible for the severity of the cultural crisis they fear in contemporary society. Nevertheless, even though radio, television, cinema and pop music were a hundred years away, many Victorian educators were deeply worried about the likely power of the 'penny dreadfuls' to demoralise their youth of all classes.

Before 1852, when repeal of the Stamp Duty produced an explosion of daily newspapers, most disapproval was concentrated upon the popular, low-priced magazines, imitations of the Gothic novels of Walpole, Ann Radcliffe and Gregory 'Monk' Lewis. Although these publications, which grew enormously in popularity in the 1830s and 1840s, were not aimed at the juvenile market, their appeal for the young of every class drew bitter criticism from everyone concerned about the level of culture in public and elementary schools. Indeed, one of the charges which was expressed by the critics of the classical curriculum as taught in nineteenth-century schools was that it failed to defend pupils against the attractions of the popular press. It was maintained that the poor teaching of classical languages, which rarely let pupils appreciate their literature, had produced only boredom and distaste, thus leaving them vulnerable to the appeal of the vulgar and sensational. Fearful of what they were convinced was the power of the cheap press to corrupt its readers, unconvinced that the classics were successfully stimulating pupils' pleasure in literature, and anxious about the exclusion of art from the Benthamite curriculum in the Academies, several Victorians supported the study of English literature as a defence against commercial forces. In *Essays on a Liberal Education*, Sidgwick quoted from a contribution to the *Quarterly Review* in support of his argument about the unsatisfactory state of classics teaching in schools. The contributor wrote:

'Much more is it a thing to wonder at and be ashamed of, that, with such a literature as ours, the English lesson is still a desideratum in nearly all our great places of education, and that the future gentry of the country are left to pick up their mother tongue from the periodical works of fiction which are the bane of our youth and the dread of every conscientious schoolmaster.'[4]

A selection of titles suggests this fiction's affinities with the Gothic novels: *The Calendar of Horrors, The Maniac Father, Vice and Its Victims, The Castle Fiend, Varney and the Vampire.* The genre was characterised by cruelty, suffering and the grotesque; blood, entrails, instruments of torture and skeletons trailed and rattled through the novels' inevitable caves, dungeons, prisons and vaults.

In 1856 Bagehot expressed his condemnation of the persistent exploitation by publishers of the public's appetite for sensationalism in its fiction.

'Exaggerated emotions, violent incidents, monstrous characters, crowd our canvas. They are the resource of a weakness which would obtain the fame of strength. Reading is about to become a series of collisions against aggravated breakers, of beatings with imaginary surf.'[5]

Although by the 1850s, ill-printed tales of crime, torture, vampires and ghosts had lost some of their most horrifying elements, the situation had become even worse for young readers. Publishers, ambitious to make a fortune out of the recently literate working classes, realised that it was worth while aiming specifically at the juvenile market. Thus, in addition to the hundreds of tales about Dick Turpin, Jack Sheppard and Charlie Peace published in mid-century, there appeared those written with deliberate appeal for the young. In these, nuns, monks, highwaymen and criminals gave way to heroes drawn from groups such as boy apprentices. It seems very likely, from the frequently expressed anxiety about the pernicious effects of their content and style, that both sorts of tales were popular with young readers. The most commonly expressed fear was that these stories about romanticised villains would encourage the young to wrongdoing by imitation, particularly since publishers too seldom included sufficiently severe retribution to act as a likely deterrent. That same faculty theory which supported continued inclusion of the classics in the curricula of public and grammar schools lent force to condemnation of the penny dreadfuls, their immorality and their style. The *Edinburgh Review* complained that: 'Bombastic rant, high-flown rhodomontade and the flattest fustian flow from the lips of all speakers alike.'[6]

Convinced that fine literature brought about improvement of character, the nineteenth-century supporters of English studies for the masses were equally certain about the ill effects of reading books and papers of poor quality. The leading article in the *Edinburgh Evening Despatch* (1889) demonstrates its writer's certainty about this in its criticism of the nation's schools; he takes it for granted that blame for the success of popular fiction rests with the schools and that this success has had disastrous implications for the pupils' characters.

'From the mere observation of the methods and partial results it is difficult to avoid coming to the conclusion that our primary schools have for their chief aim the dissemination of penny-dreadful reading, and the use of chalks upon the walls of public buildings. . . .'[7]

As anxieties increased during the century about the failure to defend elementary school pupils against the corrupting attractions of newspapers, magazines and novelettes, recommendations were made to include more poetry in the schools' curriculum. Matthew Arnold, as we have seen, was particularly influential in this area, having repeatedly urged in his reports the value of memorisation by children of great poetry. As deeply anxious as he had been, the contributors to the Report of the Committee on Education, 1895–6, advocated the inclusion of a wide range of authors in school libraries because, they said, this would help to diminish the attractions of 'pernicious matter'. Edmund Holmes, whose contribution to the changing approaches to creative work is discussed elsewhere, made his attitude towards popular fiction very plain in *What Is and What Might Be*. He said that one of the prices being paid for the failure of elementary education was children's surrender to 'vicious and demoralising literature';[8] they were, he insisted, 'taking so readily to this garbage because they have lost their appetite for wholesome food'.[9]

Gradually, as a result of the continued efforts made by Arnold to draw attention to the inadequacies of the elementary school curriculum, and of increasing alarm about the kind of threat which popular fiction represented, theory and practice in England 'were designed to encourage the training of taste, the taking of pleasure in superior prose works'.[10] There is little doubt that the advance of English as a school subject can partly be explained by the coincidence of spreading literacy with the commercial success of cheap fiction; literature, it was clearly hoped, would act as a defence against the penny-dreadful. The Preface to Macmillan's *The Progress to Literature* (1914) illustrates this expectation at the same time as it reveals what was beginning to be seen as the teacher's responsibility. The editor, introducing his literary extracts, referred to them as 'one of the most effective intellectual and moral weapons in the teacher's armoury'.[11] As educators' hostility to cheap fiction intensified, the teacher's obligation to defend his pupils against it was described in correspondingly strong terms. W. S. Tomkinson, for example, insisted that the teacher 'must set his face against printed rubbish'.[12] By 1921 it seemed very obvious to the subject's supporters that if the teacher succeeded in creating enthusiasm for good books in his pupils, he was achieving far more than the stimulation of new interests—he was improving characters. Part of the civilising experience of imaginative engagement with great literature was thought to be the resistance it created to the damaging effects of the second-rate. Edmund Holmes's and W. S. Tomkinson's disease imagery conveys their shared conviction about the power of popular entertainment to put children's whole development at risk. Both writers accept the progressive theory of growth. Equally, both see this growth as nurtured by high art and threatened by newspapers, cheap fiction and, by this time, films. In the section where he considers the influence of the cinema, Tomkinson's advice to teachers of English contains several interesting assumptions: 'Children who are reared on the strong meat of the picture palaces will come to the more delicate viands of literature with dulled palates and jaded appetites.'[13]

Not surprisingly, he fears the appeal of the visual, and generally sensational, as likely to be more attractive to children than the efforts required for appreciation of the printed page. Moreover, in common with many educators, he assumes that an enthusiasm for the cinema will preclude the possibility of enjoyment of literature. However, what is striking, retrospectively, is his version of high art, his assumption that the life-style associated with appreciation of its delicacy is desirable for the total population. As if unaware of the energy and complexity of great art, Tomkinson, in his opposition to the cinema, is recommending high art's fragility, almost effeteness, for the improvement of the newly literate population. The imagery which he chooses to convey his hope for pupils' refinement has the unsatisfactory effect of emasculating literature and conferring its vigour upon the new medium whose influence he fears.

Abundant evidence, both of the concern which was being felt about the poor quality of popular reading matter and of the hope which was coming to be invested in English, can be seen in the 1921 Report on *The Teaching of English in England*. The contributors to this

Report—university dons, inspectors, headmasters, headmistresses, selected teachers of English—deplored the mechanical way in which reading had been taught in Victorian elementary schools. They claimed that this method, ignoring literature, had left pupils 'the helpless prey of anything which appears in print. In this fact we see the root cause of the enormous increase in the proportion of worthless printed matter during the last fifty years'.[14] The Report's criticism of nineteenth-century teaching methods is illuminating. It reveals the writers' immense faith in the power of education and, importantly for the strengthening ideology of English teaching, contains their conviction that English, well taught, would provide successful defence against cheap fiction. Sharing Matthew Arnold's belief in the moral power of literature, the Newbolt Report pleads a passionate case for the serious inclusion of English in every child's timetable. Hostility to commercial forces and the religious fervour of their hopes for literature are both evident in the following extract.

'We claim that no personality can be complete, can see life steadily and see it whole, without that unifying influence, that purifying of the emotions which art and literature can alone bestow. It follows then from what we have said above that the bulk of our people, of whatever class, are unconsciously living starved existences, that one of the richest fields of our spiritual being is left uncultivated—not indeed barren, for the weeds of literature have never been so prolific as in our day.'[15]

Accepting the Romantic notion of the superiority of art to the rest of life, a notion which strengthened as anti-industrialism deepened, as well as the theory of transfer from knowledge to behaviour, the contributors assert the inseparability of fine literature from quality of life. Dissemination of liberal culture, traditionally the monopoly of the leisured classes, throughout the whole of society, was becoming defined as the special mission of the English teacher. The great majority's preference for cheap fiction and films to great literature indicated, to many educators, a worsening cultural crisis. In many cases their response was to demand exceptionally gifted men and women to teach in the schools. Since literature was held to be essential to the good life, and its widespread appreciation seemed to be threatened by the conditions of modern industrial society, the solution could only be envisaged in terms of some sort of miracle workers. Statements of faith about what good English teaching might achieve appear in every chapter of the Newbolt Report. It was from such assumptions about the redemptive power of literature and the 'threat' of commercial forces that later insistence upon the need for exceptional teachers drew much of its force.

Notes

1. C. Hoole, *A New Discovery* (1660), edited by E. T. Campagnac (1913), Part 1, pp. 24 ff.; quoted by D. J. Palmer in *The Rise of English Studies* (London, Oxford University Press for the University of Hull, 1965), p. 10.
2. Rev. Vicesimus Knox, *Elegant Extracts*, edited by V. Knox, Preface, 1824 edn; quoted by Palmer, op. cit., p. 13.
3. Palmer, op. cit., p. 18.
4. *Quarterly Review*, Vol. 117, p. 418; quoted by H. Sidgwick in *Essays on a Liberal Education* (London, Macmillan, 1868), pp. 109 f.
5. W. Bagehot, 'Essays on Mr Macaulay' (1856); quoted in *From Dickens to Hardy: Pelican Guide to English Literature*, edited by Boris Ford (1958), Part 1, p. 47.
6. *Edinburgh Review* (1887); quoted by E. S. Turner, *Boys Will Be Boys* (London, Michael Joseph, 1948), p. 56.
7. *Edinburgh Evening Despatch* (July 1889), leading article, p. 42.
8. Edmond Holmes, *What Is and What Might Be* (London, Constable, 1911), p. 232.
9. Ibid., loc. cit.
10. W. R. Mullins, *A Study of Significant Changes in the Theory of the Teaching of English to Older Pupils in Elementary and Secondary Modern Schools, 1860–1960*, unpublished MEd thesis, University of Leicester (January 1968), pp. 136 f.
11. R. Wilson (ed.), 'Preface' to *The Progress to Literature*, Stages 4–6 (London, Macmillan, 1914).
12. W. S. Tomkinson, *The Teaching of English. A New Approach* (Oxford, Clarendon Press, 1921), p. 219.
13. Ibid., p. 220.
14. *The Teaching of English in England* (London, HMSO, 1921), p. 147.
15. Ibid., p. 257.

Chapter 5

Progressive Theories and Creativity

'The child strives after the expression of himself
and does it in the same way as the poet—by
creative work.'

The Teaching of English, A New Approach (1921)

Part I has been looking carefully at expressions of the early hopes for
English as a school subject. It has described the circumstances which
gave rise to claims about its value, and at the same time has been
sensitive to the writers' moods and tones. Thus far, it has shown how
the argument about a subject 'of most worth', conducted as it was at
a time of widespread concern about the curriculum in an expanding
system of education, has moved English literature forward for serious
consideration. Towards the end of the nineteenth century, however,
proposals for English in schools were broadening to include pupils'
own composition. As a result of growing official interest in progressive
educational theories, the emphasis gradually changed from copying
and memorising to creativity. Convictions about the importance of
the individual's emotional life, notions of growth through activity,
and, later, romantic views about children as artists, were bringing discussion of the creative element into proposals for English teaching.

Part II, which concentrates upon developments in English during
this century, will show the extent to which artists', critics' and
teachers' anti-industrialism explains their enthusiasm for creativity
in schools. Leading critics of commercial culture, like G. H. Bantock
and David Holbrook, urge the revival of 'genuine' popular culture,
through the schools' encouragement of children's art, drama and
personal writing. At this stage, however, we shall look at the role of
progressive theories of education in broadening the educators' view
of English studies. Early in the subject's history they appear to have
strengthened the case for literature and stimulated recommendations
for children's creative work. European and American theories, fusing
with the native experimental tradition and coinciding with anxieties
about suitable curricula for the great majority, had the effect of
opening up the narrow view of English as two useful skills and

memorising great literature. This chapter discusses the way in which 'composition' came to be differently defined, and shows how this was the special contribution of progressive theories. After the First World War, particularly, English took on new possibilities, because it was then that more widespread interest was aroused in the relationship between individual growth and self-expression. Many educators who were affected by the mood of disillusionment, and suspected that the classical curriculum and traditional teaching methods were personally destructive, gave strong support to what they believed to be the emotionally liberating experiences of literature and creativity.

Since Rousseau, European theorists had likened the educational process to the cultivation of plants. Not until the 1870s, however, after the foundation of the Froebel Society, did their ideas about growth, the school environment and experiences which fostered the developing child, become influential in the country. In the first half of the nineteenth century, critics of the public schools' curricula and teaching methods had been mainly concerned with the introduction of useful subjects in addition to, or as replacement for, classical studies. Although it had been frequently suggested that children failed to work enthusiastically because classical studies lacked interest, no one had advocated the deliberate encouragement of self-expression, Froebel's *Darstellung*. The work of the Edgeworths, radical late-eighteenth-century educators, usefully illustrates the difference between the English educators who recommended change and the European educators who were interested in the role of play and self-expression. *On Practical Education* shows the preoccupation of the Edgeworths with the techniques for transmitting knowledge and the competing claims of science and the classics for primacy in the curriculum. Towards the end of the nineteenth century, however, Darwin's evolutionary theory provided what seemed to be an acceptable basis for Rousseau's and Froebel's view of the child as a developing organism whose growth demands careful nurture. Gradual acceptance of the European educational ideas about the vital role of free expression in this growth brought a change of emphasis in thinking about the purpose of composition writing in school. Whereas the Codes of 1862 and 1871 make it clear that a child's experience of writing in school was limited to dictation, and linked with skills of copying, transcribing and spelling, the Cross Commission of 1886–8 pointed out that English ought to consist of more than exercises in grammar,[1] advising teachers to devise schemes of work related to pupils' interests. Its members realised that by inviting his pupils to write a teacher could involve them in both work and play, thus meeting Froebel's requirements that individual development should be stimulated by interest. They appear to have recommended a new approach to writing, out of their sympathy with Froebel's view of creative expression as a process which satisfies the 'innate urge of the organism to push out to greater life, and to make its adjustments and contributions to the greater unity of which it is a part'.[2] Circular 322, issued in 1893, accepts Froebel's notion of development. This document, issued by the Education Department, illustrates how the theories of faculty psychology were being replaced by Froebel's conception of physical and mental growth, a conception which recognised the importance of children's spontaneous activity, and the need to involve children themselves in the learning process. The *Instructions to Inspectors*, issued in 1895 and 1896, draw unmistakeably, in the sections on composition, on the 'interest' theories of European and American educationalists. Professor Armytage, noting the importance of American ideas in this area, argues that the problems of educating immense numbers from mixed racial backgrounds produced the need in America for an optimistic belief in the possibilities of the educational environment. These problems stimulated the intensive study of child development undertaken at the end of the nineteenth century. In 1891, at the Pedagogical Seminary, G. Stanley Hall published his studies on children's ideas and aptitudes, work which was later developed in his volumes on *Adolescence*. In 1895, the British Association of Child Study was formed, through which J. J. Findlay introduced John Dewey's ideas into this country. The Bryce Commission on Secondary Education, 1895, drew upon Findlay's services. This meant that recognition of Dewey's theories was taking place at a level where they were likely to affect the attitudes of the Inspectorate. It is usful to notice the difference between the statement made by the Committee of the Council on Education in 1875 on 'the value of learning by heart generally as a means of storing children's memories with noble and elevating thoughts'[3] and the view expressed in the *Handbook of Suggestions*, issued by the Board in 1905, which criticises excessive burdening of children's memories. By 1915, the published *Suggestions* condemn memorising as being the 'merest mechanical drill'.[4] Clearly, 'interest' theories were influencing the Board's thinking since, by 1905, it was being proposed that composition was to have its origin in children's experiences and that it should form a part of every lesson because it could function as 'a common bond ... unifying the whole curriculum'.[5] Philip Hartog in *The Writing of English*, published in 1908, criticised the employment by teachers of methods used in classics teaching, arguing that spelling and grammar were best taught incidentally and that any continuous writing by pupils should be about subjects related to their experience and interests. Composition, the Report of a Conference on the Teaching in Elementary Schools, 1909, stated, should be 'considered as a systematic practice in self- expression'.[6] Progressive theories were, it appears, beginning to make an impact.

The coinciding of new theories in science and education with widespread dissatisfaction and uncertainty about traditional teaching methods brought about increasing commitment to the notion of children's involvement in the learning process. This had special relevance to the question of children expressing themselves, in composition, about what interested them. Darwin's theories accelerated the acceptance of developmental ideas about physical and mental differences between pupils. Froebel's notions about the value of sensory experiences and spontaneity in the learning process undermined support for memorising and copying. Dewey's theories of motivation, and his stress on the importance of direct experience and interest turned teachers' attention to children's lives as the material for their compositions. As the idea of the child as a developing personality displaced the view of him as a passive receptacle for useful information, greater emphasis was placed upon the role of English in schools. Through composition particularly, it offered opportunities for self-expression, inviting the child to participate in the learning process as an active, responsible being. By 1921, contributors to the *Report on the Teaching of English in England* were pointing out that composition was not 'merely a subject' and were arguing that the correction which took place in schools should be through methods which 'fostered the creative impulse'.[7] What must be emphasised, however, is that these developments were mainly confined to policies for the elementary schools. With the exception of the occasional outstanding teacher, such as Caldwell Cook, progressive thinking about the desirability of play and, more particularly, the value of self-expression in the development of the whole child, made little impression upon the public and grammar schools. Notions about the benefits of creativity entered educational thinking in this country through the kindergarten. In time, composition in English was proposed by the Inspectorate for those elementary school children who were unlikely to experience the civilising effects of composition within classical studies. Later we shall see how theories about education through art and artistic activity played an important part in bringing composition into a central position as an activity offering opportunities to everyone for personal development.

Although they were few in number, and their views unacceptable to the public schools, several headmasters and teachers in progressive schools made lasting contributions to the growth of English. Deeply critical of what they thought was the arid, rigid nature of the public schools' classical curriculum, these educators, valuing individuality and the emotional life, offered curricula which embodied a life-style very different from that of the traditionally educated, upper-class Englishman. In his introduction to *Abbotsholme* (1900), sub-titled 'for English boys of the . . . directing classes',[8] Cecil Reddie argued that stories in a foreign language failed to touch the boys' emotions, and in his first chapter he developed one of his central beliefs.

'In the conviction that the imaginative faculty is best developed by the education of the innate creative instinct, it is proposed to train boys as far as possible through the creation of objects of their daily lives, especially where these can be made beautiful.'[9]

One of the strongest influences upon official thinking about the curriculum and teaching methods was probably G. S. Hall's work on *Adolescence* which was published in 1905. Attacking the traditional drill methods which were designed to produce uniform accuracy in pupils, Hall asserted that 'Individuality must have a longer tether. There is nothing in the environment to which the adolescent nature does not keenly respond'.[10] Claiming that the study of English had failed, in that pupils' use of their own language and capacity to appreciate literature were deteriorating, Hall cited as the cause of this 'the excessive time given to other languages just at the psychological period of greatest linguistic plasticity and capacity for growth'.[11] Like Reddie, Hall attacked Latin grammar as being inadequate to 'legislate for the free spirit of our magnificent tongue,'[12] going on to say that 'to enforce a curriculum without interest suggests the dream'.[13] Edward Holmes, in *What is and What Might Be* (1911), insisting that the 'business of the teacher is to foster the growth of the child's soul'[14] referred to the child as the 'victim' of traditional teaching methods.

'For a third of a century, from 1862–95, self-expression on the part of the child may be said to have been formally prohibited by all who were responsible for the elementary education of the children of England, and also to have been prohibited *de facto* by all the unformulated conditions under which the elementary school was conducted.'[15]

Holmes was interested in the separateness and uniqueness of each child. He gave his support to the encouragement of composition, believing that self-expression aided the growth of this individuality. In the section which considers the role of composition, he said:

'I mean by composition the sincere expression in language of the child's genuine thoughts and feelings. The effort to express himself [in language] tends, in proportion as it is sincere and strong, to give breadth, depth and complexity to the child's thoughts and feelings and through the development of these to weave his experiences into the tissue of his life.'[16]

Work in English and the quality of children's lives were becoming more and more closely identified in the writings of the progressive educators. Holmes says, in his discussion of the value of self-realisation, 'I am entering a region in which the idea of education begins to merge itself into the larger idea of salvation'.[17] Others, as well as the most committed progressives, were now paying serious attention to the way in which children's growth could be affected by teaching methods. Although Norwood and Hope do not mention 'self-expression' specifically in *Higher Education of Boys in England* (1909), they defend their suggestion that schools should move away from the historical approach to literature in the following terms.

'This disregard [of the historical approach] is deliberate, and is based on the belief that is is wiser to consider the boys' development, rather than the formal growth of the subject matter.'[18]

When they discuss the education of working-class children who, they felt, were leaving school at too early an age to work, Norwood and Hope plead for the school experience of such boys to be one which provided for 'mental and moral growth'.[19]

The educator who had the most influence upon the broadening perception of the role of English studies in pupil's growth was Caldwell Cook, 'a pioneer, for he dared to be unconventional in a period of conventionality in the teaching of English'.[20] Like Rousseau, Cook affirmed the special qualities of childhood. Recommending approaches to learning through the pupils' interest in their play, he derided the traditional teacher's 'beautiful system, a course of work schemed, graded and ordered in admirable shape. . . .'[21] Insisting that it was more realistic and much more productive to begin with the child and his interests in the classroom, he said:

'Let us have outline schemes by all means, but leave the details to the hour in which it will be told us what we shall do. Let us remember that without interest there is no learning, and since the child's interest is all in play it is necessary whatever the method in hand, that the method be a play method.'[22]

Attacking what he called the traditional schools' 'everlasting slavery to books', he asked teachers to rid themselves of the 'tyranny of print' for a little while so they could discover how much more could be achieved if their starting-points were the interest and activity of 'life itself'.[23]

Cook was deeply critical of the classical curriculum's supremacy in public school education and of the teaching methods associated with it. He deplored teachers' treatment of English as a foreign tongue and their subordination of it to other languages so that it featured mainly in the introduction of formal studies to be developed in Latin and Greek. Instead, Cook wished to bring English to the centre of classroom experience, to encourage poetry reading and writing, and the use of the native language in talks and debates. The affinity of his book, *The Play Way*, with progressive theories about childhood, the romantic, optimistic assumptions, is illustrated by its recurrent references to 'delight', 'joy' and 'pleasure', and its references to the 'natural free activity of children'.[24] In his summary of Cook's work at the Perse School, Beacock notes the similarity between his convictions about 'interest' and 'activity' and statements made later in the Spens Report. The following extract is very like several passages in 'General Principles of *The Play Way*'.

'We have learnt that just as men work best when their hearts are in their job, so boys and girls work best when they are interested in their work and see its purpose . . . .'[25]

Coldwell Cook's importance in the history of English studies in schools is evident from the enthusiastic references to him in the 1921 Report. Whereas Arnold had insisted upon the spiritually educative role of literature, Cook stressed the need for creative participation in the development of each individual boy. Drawing upon Continental and American theories of interest, play and self-expression, Cook concentrated upon the variety of richness of work in English in his reaction against the remoteness of classical studies. His methods, moreover, appeared to the Report's contributors to be helpfully relevant to the contemporary situation since they illustrated the way in which progressive ideas could be adapted to the education of young adolescents. Thus, his approaches were recommended to all teachers of English to children from every part of society.

Above all, children's self-expression in their own language and their personal response to literature were recommended as formative experiences by educators interested in the psychology of adolescence and critical of the repression of individual growth by the rigid methods employed by the public schools in teaching the classical curriculum. Stanley Hall, the American psychologist, repeatedly insisted upon the value of the child's native language and literature. Equally insistently, and more meaningfully to many teachers in this country after the First World War, Sir Percy Nunn, in *Education: Its Data and First Principles*, stressed the important role played by English in the fostering of individuality. These progressive educators, viewing childhood romantically, and optimistic about the benefits of school experiences designed to foster individual growth, were reacting sharply against the public school 'life-style' produced by teaching methods designed to encourage conformity and discipline. Expressing his anxieties in terms similar to E. M. Forster's about the upper-class Englishman's 'undeveloped heart', Sir Percy Nunn said, in 1920:

'Educational efforts must, it would seem, be limited to securing for everyone the conditions under which individuality is most completely developed—that is, to enable him to make his original contribution to the variegated whole of human life.'[26]

Throughout his book Nunn is concerned with the need for education to encourage the development of individuality, of personal uniqueness, of a child's potential for creativity. Like Hall, and like I. A. Richards and, later, David Holbrook, Nunn turned to the child's native language as the most accessible material for creativity. Denying that those who fail to compose, paint or invent are uncreative, Nunn drew attention to 'the facts of speech', pointing out that daily expressions of oneself in language 'are humble but veritable acts of creation'.[27] Referring approvingly to Caldwell Cook's books on English teaching, Nunn made it clear that he saw the Perse play methods as those most likely to call this potential for creativity in language into the fullest being. In the sections concerned with the curriculum he considered most likely to promote activities of the 'most permanent significance in the wider world',[28] Nunn said: 'Of school studies, literature is from the present standpoint the most important.'[29]

The originally broad, humanist, classical curriculum had, it seemed, degenerated into a narrow set of texts, mechanically analysed and memorised. Education was expanding now far beyond the privileged upper classes. Concern about this education's lack of emotional and moral content provoked, in the first decades of the twentieth century, interest in the possibilities of progressive theories about individuality, freedom, and growth and creativity. As the inspirational quality of classical studies diminished, and their practical relevance was increasingly questioned by critics concerned with our failure in competition with Germany, France and America, English studies were frequently recommended as a worthy replacement for ancient literature.

Most importantly, at a time when interest was intensifying in the role of creativity in individual growth, English appeared to offer abundant opportunities, hitherto limited to the most gifted in classical studies, for creative expression through composition in the native language. E. A. Greening Lamborn, in his preface to W. S. Tomkinson's book, *The Teaching of English: A New Approach* (1921), summarised the new ideal.

'What Greek literature did for the few of the past, English literature must do for the many of the future. The new ideal in the elementary schools is indeed the old ideal in the universities—an education not so much concerned with livelihood as with living. What is really new is the revelation of the importance of the emotional life and of the need to cultivate and enrich it by humanistic treatment of all our studies.'[30]

In his book Tomkinson takes us close to the concerns and recommendations of the government's 1921 Report. He bitterly criticised the mechanical methods of English teaching and deplored the low status of the subject in the school curriculum. Discussing literature, he referred to the 'possibilities of reading as a creative art',[31] and anticipated educators of the 1940s and 1950s when he likened the child's creative potential to the poet's.

'The creative instinct is as strong and abiding in the child as in the poet. They are both makers. The poet labours to make a piece of beautiful work which will have its chances for all time; and in his work finds the truest expression of himself, his highest human opportunity. The child strives after the expression of himself and does it in the same way as the poet—by creative work.'[32]

By the 1920s, in spite of the public schools' indifference and the universities' uncertainty, a range of educators was claiming that English studies should be central to most pupils' experience. Contributors to the 1921 Report, troubled about the discrepancy between what they were convinced could be achieved by sensitive enlightened teaching and the dismal results produced by most schools' methods, repeatedly related English to quality of living. The section of this Report concerned with composition indicates to what extent progressive theories had been responsible for bringing English from the periphery to the centre of the curriculum. The experience of literature and creative work in the native language had both come to be seen as being vitally important in the development of character. Indeed, contributors to this Report go so far as to measure the success or failure of a school by its pupils' capacity for self-expression.

As suggested earlier, the mood of post-war England seemed generally sympathetic to educational theories which were responsible for bringing literature and children's creative work to the centre of the curriculum. In 1918, at the University of Reading, Principal Childs asserted that:

'The moral of the war was, not that they should develop trade but that they should develop humanity. The chief burden in maintaining and keeping uppermost the spiritual element in man must rest, for a variety of reasons more upon the teaching of English and English literature than any other subject.'[33]

Although the most influential work on the nature of adolescence had come from America, and the keenest interest in the child as an artist had come from Germany, initiative for the foundation of the New Education Fellowship in 1921 came from this country. The ideas of educators like Edmund Holmes (*What Is and What Might Be*, 1917), Norman MacMunn (*The Child's Path to Freedom*, 1914) and Caldwell Cook (*The Play Way*, 1917) fused with a feeling of the need for a new ideal in education after the war to produce willingness to experiment. As Boyd and Rawson point out when commenting upon the optimistic idealism invested in education in the post-war years: 'The New Education Fellowship provided a centre round which all manner of ideals and experiments in new living could crystallise.'[34] The ideal in forming the Fellowship was the promotion of world peace through education, and in order to achieve this, the following decision was made:

'The New Era International Conference on Education will be held at the College Hall Sophie-Berthelot, Calais from 30 July to 12 August 1921. The theme of the principal series of lectures is "The Creative Self-Expression of the Child".'[35]

The themes of all the conferences in the early 1920s were related to 'educational and individual salvation by some kind of personal dynamic'. In their discussion of these meetings, Boyd and Rawson drew attention to the powerful influences of Freud, Jung and Adler upon educational thinking, concluding their summary of the most important papers presented by saying that, if there was one article of faith to emerge, it was 'that the arts contribute uniquely to the personality and its development'.[36] A comparison between H. Courthorpe Bowen's reports on Abbotsholme in 1895 and the 1927 Report on *The Education of the Adolescent* points to the change which had taken place in thinking about English in schools. As if expressing an unorthodox opinion, Courthorpe Bowen wrote of Reddie's curriculum:

'In my opinion English literature—studied as literature—should have a definite and honourable place in the curriculum, and should be taught in close connection with the Nature Study, Drawing and Painting and English Composition. It is the true centre and inspirer of aesthetic training and a most valuable help in moral teaching.'[37]

The Consultative Committee of 1927, confronting the problem of reconciling the needs of children between 11–15 and the 'industrial society into which, when their formal education has ceased, the majority of them will enter',[38] points out that at the time of writing 'the nature of the educational process is better and more widely understood.'[39] With that in mind, the Report states that English literature is 'clearly a subject of great importance'[40] but, moving beyond that, it urges 'dramatic work associated with good literature', debates, lectures and classroom discussion, stressing the importance of 'the children's own experiences'.[41] Clearly Herbart's 'interest' theories, Caldwell Cook's 'play' methods, Stanley Hall's and Percy Nunn's work upon the nature of adolescence and needs of the individual for development had combined with pressures from events in wider society to produce a very broad interpretation of children's experience of English in school. Literature is still considered to be of vital importance because of its humanising content, but to it have been added oral work, drama and creative writing in order that, through active participation in the learning process, children should achieve fuller individuality.

Although schools' practice lagged far behind progressive theory's interpretation of English, official statements about the subject's place in the curriculum underwent noticeable changes in the early years of this century. The 1921 Report's proposals show how readily its contributors had responded to European and American ideas about the need to consider the uniqueness of each pupil. The Report makes very clear that interpretation of English as a school subject had extended beyond the nineteenth-century notion of great literature as the civilising agency, to include the oral and written creations of pupils themselves. Anxieties about the expansion of popular education, dissatisfaction with what seemed to be the illiberalism of the classical curriculum, and post-war suspicion of Victorian values were beginning to create official sympathy for theories which placed the child at the classroom's centre.

Notes

1. Final Report of the Commissioners appointed to Inquire into the Elementary Education Acts, England and Wales, 1888 (Cross), p. 217.
2. S. J. Curtis and H. E. Boultwood, *A Short History of Educational Ideas* (London, University Tutorial Press, 1953), p. 366.
3. Report of the Committee of the Council on Education (1875), quoted by W. Mullins, in *A Study of Significant Changes in the Theory of the Teaching of English . . .*, unpublished MEd thesis, University of Leicester (January 1968), p. 67.
4. Board of Education *Handbook of Suggestions for the Consideration of Teachers* (1915).
5. *Suggestions* (1905), p. 35.
6. Report of a Conference on the *Teaching of English in London Elementary Schools* (1909).
7. *The Teaching of English in England* (London, HMSO, 1921), p. 75.
8. Cecil Reddie, *Abbotsholme* (London, George Allen, 1900).
9. Ibid., pp. 27 f.
10. G. S. Hall, *Adolescence* (New York, Appleton, 1905), Vol. 2, p. 453.
11. Ibid., p. 457.
12. Ibid., p. 456.
13. Ibid., p. 509.
14. Edmond Holmes, *What Is and What Might Be* (London, Constable, 1911), p. 86.
15. Ibid., p. 155
16. Ibid., p. 129.
17. Ibid., p. 232.
18. C. Norwood and A. H. Hope, *Higher Education of Boys in England* (London, Murray, 1909), p. 342.
19. Ibid., p. 553.
20. D. A. Beacock, *Play Way for English Today* (London, Nelson, 1943), p. 3.
21. Caldwell Cook, *The Play Way* (London, Heinemann, 1917), p. 3.
22. Ibid., pp. 3 f.
23. Ibid., p. 8.

24. Ibid., p. 38.
25. Secondary Education, with Special Reference to Grammar Schools and Technical High Schools, *The Spens Report* (HMSO, 1938), pp. 143, 156.
26. Sir P. Nunn, *Education. Its Data and First Principles* (London, Edward Arnold, 1920), p. 13.
27. Ibid., p. 34.
28. Ibid., p. 250.
29. Ibid., p. 266.
30. E. A. Greening Lamborn, Preface to W. S. Tomkinson, *The Teaching of English: A New Approach* (Oxford, Clarendon Press, 1921), p. 2.
31. Tomkinson, op. cit., p. 51.
32. Ibid., p. 81.
33. Principal Childs' 'The Teaching of English in Schools', English Association Pamphlet No. 43; papers edited by E. J. Morley (May 1919). Lecture delivered at University of Reading.
34. W. Boyd and W. Rawson, *The Story of the New Education* (London, Heinemann, 1965), p. 76.
35. Ibid., p. 69.
36. Ibid., pp. 166 ff.
37. H. Courthope Bowen; quoted by Cecil Reddie in *Abbotsholme*, op. cit., p. 231.
38. Report of the Consultative Committee, *The Education of the Adolescent* (London, HMSO, 1927), p. 42.
39. Ibid., p. 107.
40. Ibid., p. 110.
41. Ibid., p. 191.

Chapter 6

The Newbolt Report and
English for the English

'. . . literature is not just a subject for academic
study, but one of the chief temples of the human
spirit, in which all should worship.'
The Newbolt Report (1921)

The Newbolt Report and George Sampson's book, *English for the
English*, are landmarks on any survey of the subject's development
over the past one hundred and fifty years. They express all the major
anxieties about its treatment in universities, schools and teacher-
training establishments, as well as all the certainties about the value
of English which had been intensified since Arnold's analysis of his
'mechanical' and 'external' society. They reflect, too, the characteristic
mood of the period following the First World War, the sharp despair
and the faith in the power of education to improve the future. Both
documents have greatly influenced later discussion about English in
schools; they are still referred to with appreciation today. Most of all,
they anticipate future prescriptions about the qualities which seem
desirable in the subject's teachers. When their authors were faced with
the discoveries of widespread hostility to literature, bad conditions in
elementary schools and poorly trained, uncultivated teachers, they
responded, in the main, by calling for men and women with exceptional gifts to work in the classrooms. As we shall see, they
repeated the Victorian demands for 'apostles' and 'missionaries', thus
reinforcing the notion that English was the subject which needed
special people as its teachers.

   Chapter 5 has already suggested that the mood of post-war England
was very sympathetic to the need for educational reform. One of the
war's results was to produce not only a sense of the military and economic benefits enjoyed by Germany because of her educational
system's freedom from irrelevant traditionalism, but also an awareness of our working-class's cultural inferiority. In 1918, at Manchester,
Lloyd George voiced his dissatisfaction.

'The most formidable institution we had to fight in Germany was not the arsenals of Krupps or the yards in which they turned out submarines, but the schools of Germany. They were our most formidable competitors in business and our most terrible opponents in war. An educated man is a better worker, a more formidable warrior, and a better citizen. That was only half comprehended before the war.'[1]

And as one of their many pieces of evidence of the elementary schools' failure in this country to do more than, as H. G. Wells had expressed it, 'educate the lower classes for employment on lower-class lines',[2] the Newbolt Report quotes a chaplain on the personal qualities of the men in the trenches. In support of their case for the improved study of English in schools, the Report quotes him as saying:

'The only trouble is that their standard of general education is so low. Put the product of the old elementary schools side by side with the man from overseas, and his mental equipment is pitiful . . . .'[3]

The war uncovered the old problems of the elementary schools—large classes, poorly qualified staff, physically weak children, children in part-time employment, and continued use of outdated, discredited methods of mechanical rote-learning. Most importantly, the horrors of war produced a yearning for ways of improving the great majority's living conditions. The revelation of the wide differences between rich and poor produced a desire for reform, a response to which was the Report's plea for a more wide-spread liberal education in schools. H. A. L. Fisher expressed this general feeling when he said, in 1917 at Manchester, in preparation for his Bill to raise the school-leaving age:

'I conceive that it is part of the duty of our generation to provide some means for compensating the tragic loss which our nation is enduring, and that one means by which some compensation may be provided is by the creation of a system of education throughout the country which will increase the value of every human unit in the whole of society by giving all our children the best possible opportunity that we can afford to give them, and they can afford to turn to account.'[4]

As President of the Board of Education, he expressed also his unease about the division between the public and elementary schools' curricula, between the civilising, humanising subjects and the severely practical. At the above meeting in Manchester Fisher said on this matter (and it is a plea repeated in more specific terms by the 1921 Report's Committee and by George Sampson):

'The proposition for which I am contending is that youth is the period of life specially set apart for education. I venture to plead for a state of society in which learning comes first and earning comes second among the obligations of youth, not for one class only, but for all young people. At present the rich learn and the poor earn.'[5]

Expressions of national guilt and the need for greater social justice were now being made publicly at an official level, and it was becoming clear that recommendations for the replacement of the classics by English studies were having implications far beyond practical changes in the curriculum. As we shall see when we look at the Report's emotive language in its chapters on the cultural health of the nation, recommendations for improved English teaching in schools were made with religious passion because, for their supporters, they represented ways in which guilt could be assuaged and greater social justice achieved in a divided nation.

It is useful, firstly, to look briefly at the background to the 1921 Report. The national sense of inferiority to Europe in education, the rising demand for secondary school places, and the general feeling that reform was necessary, brought about the appointment of a number of committees to inquire into the state of certain subjects in this country's schools. Between 1918 and 1919, four such committees were set up, to report on the teaching of science, modern languages, classics and English. The context against which these investigations were made is clear from the Board of Education's Report for 1917–18, which conveys the national sense of need for improvement, and a vivid impression of the highly emotional sources from which it arose. This context, it can be argued, was particularly important in affecting the kind of Report made upon the teaching of English.

'The tension and suffering of the war have revealed many things which we had forgotten or to which we were indifferent, and we now know that the shattered temple of Peace has to be rebuilt more nobly and the fabric of society has to be reconstructed upon more generous lines.'[6]

About his period of office at the Board of Education during this time, Fisher wrote, in 1940:

'The vast expenditure and harrowing anxieties of the time . . . helped to promote a widespread feeling for improvement in the general lot of the people.'[7]

It is worth, also, looking at the terms of reference for his inquiry for the insight which they give into what was felt more and more acutely to be an educational crisis. The distinguished Committee, under the chairmanship of Sir Henry Newbolt, and including among its inspectors, principals and heads of schools, Sir Arthur Quiller-Couch, J. H. Fowler and Caroline Spurgeon, was asked:

'To inquire into the position occupied by English [Language and Literature] in the educational system of England, and to advise how its study may best be promoted in schools of all types, including Continuation Schools, and in Universities, and other Institutions of Higher Education, regard being had to:
'(1) the requirements of a liberal education;
'(2) the needs of business, the professions, and public services; and
'(3) the relation of English to other studies.'[8]

In its opening pages, where the Committee refers to the 'wide scope' given by the terms of reference to their 'consideration of English', its members described the breadth of the questions which they consider to have been raised by their assignment. On the first page, they stated:

'The inadequate conception of the teaching of English in this country is not a separate defect which can be separately remedied. It is due to a more far-reaching failure—the failure to conceive the full meaning and possibilities of national education as a whole, and that failure again is due to a misunderstanding of the educational values to be found in the different regions of mental activity, and especially to an underestimate of the importance of English language and literature.'[9]

Echoing Fisher's dissatisfaction with the injustice of two different kinds of education designed to prepare pupils for two different ways of life, the Committee deplores the system which has as its object that 'of equipping the young in some vague and little-understood way for the struggle of adult existence in a world of material interests'.[10] It, too, draws attention to the differences between those pupils who receive 'special treatment', the 'superior' education which has been 'the privilege of the minority only' and children in elementary schools, pointing out that 'no source of unity is to be found in the teaching provided by different types of schools'.[11] The existence of such widely differing schools, with differing goals and, hence, differing curricula has, the members claim, 'widened the mental distances between classes in England'.

From the opening, then, members of the Newbolt Committee make it clear that, like Matthew Arnold whose writings they frequently invoke, one of their main goals is the achievement of greater social unity. It is, in fact, the fusion of this Committee's anxiety about the evils of social divisiveness with its conviction about the totally educative value of literature which gives the document its arresting passion. Fundamental changes in society are considered desirable and since, in the Committee's view, improved teaching of English in all our schools is the means of achieving them, it is not surprising that the Report has made an important contribution to the subject's ideology of social and individual improvement.

The committee did not wish to undervalue the study of the classics. But, like the contributors to *Essays on a Liberal Education*, its members thought that their linguistic difficulties would prevent all but a very few from reaching an enjoyment of classical literature. They admitted that the classics, well taught, offered the finest education, but they insisted that the classics were not the means of bridging the all-too-obvious gulfs between social classes. Moreover, transfer of the classical curriculum's teaching methods to the elementary schools had already had disastrous effects upon English. In the Committee's view, the classics, as they had come to be taught in the nineteenth century, had actually held back liberal education in schools. In the historical section on the development of English, the Report states:

'The formalism which so often warped the public school idea of Education is seen setting its stamp upon the Elementary School so soon as it attempts to grow. English, indeed, makes an appearance, but only as a pale reflection of the discipline of classical studies.'[12]

Thus, a new approach was needed, one which would provide a truly humanising education for all pupils in public schools, one which would also offer opportunities for greater self-realisation to all pupils in elementary schools. The Report declares its members' convictions very emphatically:

'We have declared the necessity of what must be, in however elementary a form, a liberal education for all English children whatever their position or occupation of life . . . . We believe that in English literature we have a means of Education not less valuable than the classics and decidedly more suited to the necessities of a general and national education. . . . '[13]

The introduction of good English teaching into all of the nation's schools would, the Report asserts, do much to promote social unity. If the emphasis in the elementary schools upon memorising, rote-learning and irrelevant, arid composition writing and comprehension were to be replaced by a concentration upon good plain speech and writing, and practice given in talking and listening, a way would have been found of breaking down social barriers. Not only would 'command of his native language' give the working-class child the means of learning other subjects more successfully but it would enable him to be more confident and effective socially. Even more importantly, rich and poor would become united through their involvement in a common culture. The Report suggests that:

'An education of this kind is the greatest benefit which could be conferred upon any citizen of a great state, and that the common right to it, the common discipline and enjoyment of it, the common possession of the tastes and associations connected with it, would form a new element of national unity, linking together the mental life of all classes by experiences which have hitherto been the privileges of a limited section . . . . If we use English literature as a means of contact with great minds, a channel by which to draw upon their experience with profit and delight, and a bond of sympathy between the members of a human society, we shall succeed, as the best teachers of the classics have often succeeded in their more limited field.'[14]

The inclusion of literature in the elementary school curriculum would narrow the gap between those who were referred to by Fisher as 'educated to learn' and those 'educated to earn'. Literature in schools could, more than any other study, achieve the education of the whole child because of its deliberate and beneficial irrelevance to him as a future wage-earner. 'The literature lesson', the Committee says, 'is no mechanical matter'; it consists 'not in the imparting of information, but in the introduction of the student to great minds and new forms of experience'.[15] In the Committee's view it was imperative to include the non-vocational in the elementary school curriculum as a matter of social justice, while in George Sampson's view it appeared, in addition, to be politically realistic. In his Preface to the 1925 edition of *English for the English*, he says:

'Deny to working-class children any common share in the immaterial, and presently they will grow into the men who demand with menaces a communism of the material.'[16]

George Sampson insists, in a statement frequently quoted by educators in English, that it is the schools' responsibility to educate children for their occupations, but to prepare children against their environment. He says with a strength of emphasis which was to become characteristic of many recommendations made about the teaching of English:

'I am prepared to maintain, and indeed, do maintain, without reservation and perhapses, that it is the purpose of education, not to prepare children for their occupations, but to prepare children against their occupations.'[17]

His argument is that the elementary schools are the most important schools in the country and that English is 'by far the most important subject in the elementary schools'.[18] He repeats the convictions of Fisher and the Newbolt Committee when he describes their goal as being: 'to develop the mind and soul of the children and not merely to provide tame and acquiescent labour fodder'.[19]

With the introduction of English writers for study in all the nation's schools, the Newbolt Report expected a general raising of society's cultural level and its capacity to respond to great works of art. The Committee suggested that what its investigations had uncovered in the way of national philistinism and distrust of art might be counteracted by a changed approach to teaching in schools. It reported that rich and poor in England were inclined to misunderstand, undervalue and be bored by art, and it recommended that serious efforts should be made to substitute imaginatively chosen material in English for the dull routine followed in public and elementary schools. Children's experience of literature as material which is both comprehensible and enjoyable might do much, the Committee felt, to raise the country's level of cultural appreciation.

The powerfully emotional language of both *English for the English* and the Newbolt Report reflects their writers' strong commitment to their views. George Sampson and the contributors to the Report were desperately concerned about the state of the elementary schools. Clearly they believed wholeheartedly in the need for improved English teaching and in the benefits which would result.

George Sampson insisted that the situation in the schools was 'tragic', that 'English cannot wait' since 'the teacher of English is continuously assailed by powerful and almost insuperable hostile forces'.[20] In the closing pages of his book (its introduction refers to it as 'a tract for the times' written 'with the passion of a crusader'),[21] Sampson states that the forces of philistinism, triviality and vulgarity must be opposed in our society. He asks angrily, and his combative language anticipates the tones of Leavis and Thompson, 'but is not the power of the enemy due to the folly that has limited the warriors who might destroy it to the few who could utter the Shibboleth of the classics?'[22] Sampson's, and the Report's, religious imagery is highly suggestive. It obviously helps to convey the strength of these writers' convictions about the need for English studies to replace the classics. It suggests also that a point in the process of secularisation had now been reached where spiritual values were being invested in works of art. Bryan Wilson's discussion of this is illuminating. He says:

'. . . as the arts as such acquired autonomy as craftsmen and artists were employed for purposes not specifically religious, so the arts came to embody values and to evoke emotional responses which were not themselves in the service of religion.'[23]

The arts' embodiment of spiritual values, a process hastened during the Victorian period by artists' alienation from their society, meant that they came to be recommended with greater and greater fervour for the majority's well-being. Philanthropic liberals throughout the nineteenth century were deeply disturbed by what they saw as the masses' loss of religion. Although it seems unlikely that the majority of the working classes was much affected by institutionalised religion in the big cities, fear such as Arnold's about its decline sharpened insistence upon the desperate need for literature. Increasing scepticism among educated Victorians gave the impression that the whole population was losing the support of religious faith. The language of the Newbolt Report and *English for the English* certainly suggests that the responsibility for 'uplifting'—the traditional function of the classics and the Church— was, in time of crisis, being transferred to English.

Sampson refers to the 'class of young barbarians whose souls are to be touched by literature'[24] and to the 'pure religion' and 'creative reception'[25] of the literary experience, his tones echoing those of the Newbolt Report in its section on the high responsibilities of the future English teacher. The Report's members expressed their views thus on the university professor of literature:

'He has obligations not merely to the students who come to him to read for a degree, but still more towards the teeming population outside the University walls, most of whom have not so much as "heard whether there be any Holy Ghost". The fulfilment of these obligations means propaganda work, organisataion and the building up of a staff of assistant missionaries. But first, and above all, it means a right attitude of mind, a conviction that literature and life are inseparable, that literature is not just a subject for academic study, but one of the chief temples of the human spirit, in which all should worship.'[26]

The teaching of literature is often referred to as 'missionary work' in the Report, reminiscent, as D. J. Palmer notes, of the nineteenth-century mood of moral earnestness which caused educators to invoke the Bible and noble poetry as necessary defences against political discontent and the debased attractions of the popular press. The Report states that the teachers of English should have the kind of qualities which are more usually found in the charismatic preacher. For the difficult task of 'humanising the masses', it asks for passion, zeal and creativity, in addition to the humility with which unfamiliar cultural regions should be entered. The Committee acknowledges, with regret, that the working classes are likely to identify superior cultures with privilege. It says, therefore:

'The ambassadors of poetry must be humble, they must learn to call nothing common or unclean—not even the local dialect, the clatter of the factory, or the smoky pall of industrial centres.'[27]

The tone of desperation which characterised both the Report and Sampson's book arose from their writers' conviction about the moral and spiritual value of great literature. It becomes increasingly familiar, particularly in the writings of F. R. Leavis and the Cambridge School of English, as the cultural crisis is is defined as worsening. Calls will be made in the 1930s and 1940s for 'warriors', for teachers 'who will fight', more aggressive figures than the high-born ambassadors on their good-will missions. Even more depressing than the Newbolt Committee's discovery of mechanical teaching methods and poorly qualified teachers, at a time when so much depended upon the successful diffusion of liberal culture, was the news of working-class hostility to literature. This extract (from the section on 'Literature and the Nation') describes the way in which the Committee responded to the news that the working class, identifying the arts with leisure, viewed literature with distrust.

'We were told that the working classes, especially those belonging to organised labour movements, were antagonistic to, and contemptuous of, literature, that they regarded it "merely as an ornament, a polite accomplishment, a subject to be despised by really virile men". Litera-

ture, in fact, seems to be classed by a large number of thinking working men with antimacassars, fish knives and other unintelligible and
futile trivialities of "middle-class culture" and, as a subject of instruction, is suspect as an attempt to "side-track the working-class movement". We regard the prevalence of such opinions as a serious
matter, not merely because it means the alienation of an important
section of the population from the "confort" and "mirthe" of
literature, but chiefly because it points to a morbid condition of the
body politic which if not taken in hand may be followed by lamentable
consequences . . . the nation of which a considerable portion rejects
this [literature's] means of grace, and despises this great spiritual
influence, must assuredly to heading to disaster.'[28]

Solution of this problem, in the Committee's view, was to be found
in the schools, in the recruitment and education of teachers capable
of inspiring pupils with a sense of enjoyment in literature. If the goals
of the schools were changed and the teachers could be educated to
do more than just impart useful knowledge to their pupils, society, it
was suggested, would inevitably improve. Hearts and minds would be
changed because of the nature of the literary experience, the power
of which was to satisfy 'the love of truth, the love of beauty and the
love of righteousness'. The following passage illustrates the Committee members' version of the personal changes effected by literature,
and their faith in the teachers' power to bring them about in society
as a whole.

'. . . a realisation of what might be accomplished through English
literature to "awaken the mind from the lethargy of custom and direct
it to the loveliness and wonders of the world before us" would, if it
became general among teachers, transform the face of the schools.'[29]

Full consideration has been given to the Newbolt Report and George
Sampson's book, *English for the English*, because of their influence
upon the teaching of English in schools during the past fifty years, and
because of the way in which they illustrate how changes in education
and wider society affected the subject's importance in the curriculum.
Both works reflect the dissatisfaction with the exclusiveness and
aridity of the classical curriculum, dissatisfaction which had its
source in nineteenth-century utilitarian and philanthropic discontent.
Because of linguistic difficulties, classical studies were 'humanising'
only a privileged few; their accessibility to these few perpetuated undesirable social divisiveness; their identification with the leisured class
was responsible for the humble status of English and for the wide-

spread working-class suspicion of the arts in general. George Sampson added to all this his criticism of our tendency to admire only 'the exotic', and thus to despise the rich heritage of English and neglect ways in which both language and literature could be genuinely 'practical' in pupils' lives.

Both works embody attitudes which, together, have had the effect of strengthening the notion that English has the unique power to improve character and to transform society. The commercial world was viewed with distrust and hostility and, as its 'forces' seemed to be more threatening, men of letters, educated in the nineteenth-century traditions of service and commitment to social improvement, urged the acceptance of a subject which could defend the whole of society against such forces. To English studies they transferred the classics' and religion's traditional responsibilities for character development, their moral seriousness deepened by their desire for social justice.

Moreover, both works illustrated the extent to which progressive theories of education had gained acceptance at official level. Their authors' interest was in the education of the 'whole child', in his participation and creativity, in the 'education of the emotions'. Clearly, these professors, lecturers, principals and teachers had responded warmly to those progressive theories which had been responsible for producing dissatisfaction with a state of affairs in schools where 'faculty' psychology determined content and methods, and for directing attention to the opportunities within English studies for individual development.

The authors of the Newbolt Report and *English for the English* clearly wished to make liberal culture, aesthetic appreciation, and self-realisation through art and the native language available to the whole nation. The following summary, which the Newbolt Committee made of its views about the centrality of English, in the context of the country's educational and social needs, bears an interesting resemblance to recommendations made thirty years later by the Newsom Committee. Both see English studies in schools as the solution to cultural problems produced by mass literacy in an industrial society.

'On the one hand, our national education needs to be perfected by being scientifically refounded as a universal, reasonable and liberal process of development; on the other hand, we find coincidentally that for this purpose, of all the means available, there is only one which fulfils all the conditions of our problems . . . . We recognise fully, on the one side, the moral, practical, educational value of natural science, on the other side the moral, practical value of the arts and of all great literatures ancient and modern. But what we are looking for now is not merely a means of education, one chamber in the structure we are hoping to rebuild, but the true starting-point and foundation from which all the rest must spring. For this special purpose there is but one material. We make no comparison, we state what appears to us to be an incontrovertible primary fact, that for English children no form of knowledge can take precedence of a knowledge of English, no form of literature can take precedence of English literature: and that the two are so inextricably connected as to form the only basis possible for a national education.'[30]

The Newbolt Report's and George Sampson's recommendations for the teaching of English make it very clear that the subject was being defined as the curriculum's centrally humanising element. From *Essays on a Liberal Education* (1868) to the Newbolt Report (1921) convictions had been repeatedly expressed about the need for all children to receive more than a vocational education at school. By the early part of this century, fears about what seemed to be threats to quality of life from the cheap press and cinema had fused with progressive notions about the value of the arts in education to stimulate widespread interest in the potential of English literature and creative activity to protect children against commercial entertainment and to promote individual development through self-expression. Even more importantly, after the First World War hopes were being expressed that general acceptance of the new subject would bind together the divided social classes.

What has been noted is that by the time of the Newbolt Report's publication English teachers were beginning to be equated with Matthew Arnold's 'preachers' of culture; what was being viewed as a cultural crisis demanded teachers with outstanding personal qualities. If enthusiasm for literature, and readiness to engage in creative activity, were to become widespread, success depended upon the powers of exceptional people. George Sampson had this in mind when he wrote:

'I am thinking of . . . the class of young barbarians whose souls are to be touched by the magic of poetry and whose souls will certainly not be touched unless there is first a soul to teach them.'[31]

The Report's contributors fully realised, however, that at that time recruits to teaching were, in general, ill-equipped academically and culturally to undertake this assignment with great confidence. Their response to teachers' lack of academic qualifications and professional confidence consisted partly of demands for higher standards and improved training. But their vision of greater social unity and shared love of art drew from contributors fervent expressions of need, in the schools, for 'missionaries' with inspirational powers to overcome the discouraging every-day classroom realities.

Part II will argue that as even greater hopes have been invested in English to protect pupils against their environment and to encourage personal growth and social competence, the demands upon its teachers have grown correspondingly heavy. The main concerns of Part II, however, will be to identify the sources of optimism in this century, about what good English might achieve. It will look closely at the following influences: artists' and critics' persistent anti-industrialism; progressive theories about creativity; the Cambridge School of English; and finally, modern linguistics. We shall see how each tradition or theory has promoted interest in a certain aspect of English: how anti-industrialism and progressivism have encouraged creativity; how the Cambridge School has been closely linked with critical discrimination; and how linguistics have shifted the emphasis to children's classroom talk. But to separate each influence too precisely would be to over-simplify the account of the growth of English studies. Collectively, these developments represent educators' deep dissatisfactions with elements in modern urban society for which the schools appear to have failed to compensate. Their recommendations inevitably, therefore, overlap and interrelate with the various activities in English. As the final chapter in Part II will show, the proposals which assume the value of great literature, creative activity, critical discrimination and class talk, have all, in their different ways, grown out of the educators' conviction that there must be experiences in the curriculum which encourage children's emotional, moral and social development. Whether their vision of individual happiness and shared quality of life stemmed from regret for our lost agricultural past, or from progressive notions about childhood vision and personal growth, or from the desire for greater social justice by way of children's extended opportunities to use language, educators in these areas believed that their goals were most likely to be achieved through good English teaching. Part of their response to society's recalcitrance about being transformed has been, perhaps unhelpfully for the profession, to insist upon its even greater need of even better English teachers.

Notes

1. Lloyd George, speech given in Manchester, September 1918; quoted by G. Bernbaum, *Social Change and the Schools* (London, Routledge, 1967), p. 16.
2. H. G. Wells; quoted by G. A. N. Lowndes, *The Silent Social Revolution* (London, Oxford University Press, 1969), p. 4.
3. P. B. Clayton, Chaplain at Poperinghe 1914–18; quoted in *The Teaching of English in England* (London, HMSO, 1921), p. 17.
4. H. A. L. Fisher, speech given in Manchester, 1917.
5. Ibid.
6. Board of Education, *Report* for 1917–18, p. 1.
7. H. A. L. Fisher, *Unfinished Autobiography* (London, Oxford University Press, 1940), p. 94.
8. *The Teaching of English in England* (1921), op. cit., Preface, p. 1.
9. Ibid., pp. 4 f.
10. Ibid., p. 6.
11. Ibid., loc. cit.
12. Ibid., p. 45.
13. Ibid., pp.14 f.
14. Ibid., pp. 15 f.
15. Ibid., p. 24.
16. George Sampson, *English for the English* (Cambridge, Cambridge University Press, 1952), Preface to 1925 ed., p. xv.
17. Ibid., p. 11.
18. Ibid., p. 18.
19. Ibid., p. 34.
20. Ibid., p. 27.
21. S. C. Roberts, Introduction to *English for the English* (1925) (Cambridge, Cambridge University Press, 1952), p. viii.
22. Sampson, op. cit. (1952), p. 125.
23. Bryan Wilson, *Religion in Secular Society* (London, Watts, 1966), p. 45.
24. Sampson, op. cit. (1952), p. 90.
25. Ibid., p. 89.
26. *The Teaching of English in England*, op. cit., p. 259.
27. Ibid., p. 260.
28. Ibid., pp. 252 f.
29. Ibid., p. 106.
30. Ibid., p. 14.
31. Sampson, op. cit. (1952), p. 90.

Part II

CHANGING DEFINITIONS OF ENGLISH SINCE THE FIRST WORLD WAR

Chapter 7

Anti-Industrialism: The Claims for Literature and Creativity

'What we have lost is the organic community . . . and
a responsive adjustment growing out of immemorial
experience, to the natural environment and the rhythm
of the year.'

F. R. Leavis and Denys Thompson, *Culture and Environment*

The anti-industrialism of Victorian headmasters, coupled with their
attachment to the ideals of classical civilisations, had mixed effects
upon the growth of English in schools. While their distaste for modern
urban society hindered the progress of English into high-status
schools and universities, their commitment to the notion of a humane
core of the curriculum meant that, finally, this powerful ideal was
transferred to English when the classics lost their central position.
The effects upon English this century of artists', critics' and educators'
regret for the loss of our own previous 'civilisation' have been much
less ambiguous. That anti-industrialism which has been inspired by
the ideal of the small, rural, organic community has played a very
important role in the strengthening investment made both in literature
and creative work. Most of all, it has led teachers to stress the need
for children to create, because this has been seen as a form of compensation for the great majority's stultifying conditions of mechanical
labour and escapist leisure. After reviewing the key expressions of
Victorian revulsion from their society, this chapter looks in some
detail at the critical responses of George Bourne and D. H. Lawrence,
two writers who have had the most far-reaching influence upon the
educators concerned with English in schools. Although F. R. Leavis,
and his pupils who are teaching in colleges and universities are clearly
important here, we shall leave an examination of the Cambridge
School's role until later in Part II.

Firstly, however, it is useful to recall briefly some evidence of the
way in which the educators' and literary critics' fears about the evil
effects of industrial society were related to their recommendations
for work in schools. Matthew Arnold's criticism of Victorian society

as being 'external' and 'mechanical', his anxiety lest a tide of almost 'American vulgarity' should wash over us, contained his distrust of industry's growing domination of the nineteenth century. His recommendations for the inclusion of literature in the elementary schools' curriculum grew out of his sense of the need for culture in a materialistic society. Others who proposed the inclusion of English literature in all schools did so by reference to what they viewed as the pernicious features of the cheap press. Misgivings arose about the quality of life for the majority of young people entering industry as labourers, and efforts were made to create a curriculum which compensated for unsatisfactory elements in wider society. Norwood and Hope supported a curriculum which they believed would foster 'mental and moral growth' before the nation's adolescents became factory workers. Contributors to the Newbolt Report conveyed their attitudes to modern urban society through references to 'starved existences' and the 'clatter of the factory', in the face of which they urged the ambassadors of poetry to call nothing 'common or unclean'. George Sampson, campaigning strenuously for an education of the nation's children *against* their environment, argued that industrialism reduced boys and girls to 'tame and acquiescent labour fodder', while Caldwell Cook, earliest exponent of creative activity in English, believed that without this and similar opportunities for self-expression, 'our people will continue to live as a race of petty and exploited town dwellers'.[1] Thus from the first, when considered as anything more than the basic skills of reading and writing, English was proposed as an important school subject by reference to the threatening forces of industrialism.

Regret for the loss of what were believed to have been the satisfactions of the past explains the increased emphasis placed on the value of creative work in English. In so far as the agricultural, 'organic' past has been contemplated with a sense of loss by artists, critics and educators, the creative experience, in particular in English, has come to be seen as complementary to the protective power of literature.

Central to Raymond William's argument in *Culture and Society* (where he discusses English anti-industrialism in rigorous detail), is the contrast drawn by nineteenth-century writers between the 'mechanical' nature of their society and the 'organic' communities of pre-industrial England. He quotes from 'Signs of the Times' published in the *Edinburgh Review* in 1829.

'It is the age of Machinery, in every inward sense of the word. . . . Nothing is now done directly, or by hand; all is by rule and calculated contrivance . . . men are grown mechanical in head and in heart, as well as in hand.'[2]

Two central works on this theme are *Contrasts* by A. W. Pugin and *Past and Present* by Thomas Carlyle. Each writer, provoked by his distaste for the debased artistic products of Victorian England, moves from his criticism of bad art to the society responsible for it. Pugin, for example, is quite explicit on his opening page:

'On comparing the architectural works of the last three centuries with those of the Middle Ages, the wonderful superiority of the latter must strike every attentive observer.'[3]

In order to explain this difference, he asserts the moral superiority of the Middle Ages; like other nineteenth-century writers he insists that bad art is the product of an inadequate civilisation:

'. . . it was, indeed, the faith, the zeal, and above all, the unity, of our ancestors, that enabled them to conceive and raise these wonderful fabrics that still remain to excite our wonder and admiration.'[4]

Williams argues that these artists' opposition to the laissez-faire attitude of nineteenth-century society produced a powerful alternative conception of an organic society which existed in our pre-industrial past. Repelled by the contemporary industrial scene, the division of labour's reduction of men to mere machines, they revered what they thought of as having been the cohesive, organic, interrelated and interdependent nature of the small medieval community. Having found medieval art superior to the products of their own society, these writers affirmed the virtues of the past which had created it. Convinced that it was impossible for the artist to be great in a corrupt society, they argued that the future appeared disastrous without a return to an improved way of life. Ruskin expressed it thus:

'The art of any country is the exponent of its social and political virtues. The art, or general productive or formative energy, of any country, is an exact exponent of its ethical life. You can have noble art only from noble persons, associated under laws fitted to their time and circumstance.'[5]

Convinced that the quality of life had been debased by machinery and the profit motive, nineteenth-century critics argued that men's happiness depended on their engagement in relations more fundamental and inspirational of respect than the acquisition of wealth. It is not, Ruskin said:

'. . . that men are ill fed, but that they have no pleasure in the work by which they make their bread, and therefore look to wealth as the only means of pleasure. It is not that men are pained by the scorn of the upper classes, but they cannot endure their own, for they feel that the kind of labour to which they are condemned is verily a degrading one, and makes them less than men.'[6]

Central to these writers' anti-industrialism was the notion that delight in work had been destroyed by the machine system of production. Carlyle, Ruskin and Pugin found their 'organic' alternative in the medieval past, while Morris, blaming capitalism more than machinery, looked forward to a socialist future, 'so that men could decide for themselves how their work should be arranged, and where machinery was appropriate'.[7] The intensity of Morris's response anticipates contemporary reaction against urban society. He says:

'Apart from the desire to produce beautiful things, the leading passion of my life has been and is, hatred of modern civilisation.'[8]

There is, moreover, particularly in *Past and Present*, anxiety about society's fragmentation, a fear to be expressed later in the Newbolt Report and other works recommending English for its unifying potential. In *Past and Present*, Carlyle, disillusioned with the democratic process, the religious institutions, the mobility of the new rich and, above all, the 'cash-payment nexus', concentrated upon the effects of the Corn Laws. In the following extract he attacks his society's degeneration and disintegration:

'Occurring simultaneously with the decline of genuine religious faith with its cohesive force, the ascendancy of industrialism and utilitarianism had fragmented the "brotherhood of man" into millions of atoms, each person a faceless, nameless nullity . . . . Nothing short of society's ethical and religious regeneration, a return to thè serene faith, obedience and values of Abbot Sampson's time, will offer any promise of a genuine cure.'[9]

Carlyle contemplated mid-Victorian England with considerable despair. Since 1836 the country had suffered poor harvests, high prices and increasing pauperism, and this culminated in the summer of 1842 in strikes and riots. In *Past and Present*, in a detailed recreation of Abbot Sampson and his medieval community, Carlyle presented what Williams calls 'the most substantial, as it is the most literal, of all visions of medieval order which the critics of nineteenth-century society characteristically attempted'.[10] Although conceding that many people had led miserable lives in the past, Carlyle asserts:

'And yet I will venture to believe that in no time, since the beginnings of society, was the lot of those same dumb millions of toilers so entirely unbearable as it is even in the days now passing over us . . . it is to live miserable . . . isolated . . . unrelated, girt in with a cold universal laissez-faire.'[11]

William's argument is that out of these critics' dissatisfaction with their society, 'Culture came to be defined as a separate entity and a critical idea'.[12] Explaining these artists' and literary critics' alienation from an indifferent or hostile public and an unsympathetic commercial world, Williams describes how they fashioned a conception of the artist who had access to a special imaginative truth.

' "Culture", the "embodied spirit of a People", the true standard of excellence, became available, in the progress of the century, as the court of appeal in which the real values were determined, usually in opposition to the "factitious" values thrown up by the market and similar operations of society . . . the positive consequence of the idea of art as a superior reality was that it offered an immediate basis for an important criticism of industrialisation.'[13]

From Williams's analysis, the implications for English studies are obvious. 'The idea of art as a superior reality' produced a sense of need for a body of men capable of sustaining tradition and of responding to new works of art. When this sense of need was strengthened by hostility to science and to conditions in wider society, it produced the desperate tones in which so many proposals for literature were made. The main argument of this chapter is, however, that anti-industrialism has had an equally strong influence upon opinions about the value of creativity. We shall see, later, the extent to which their dissatisfaction with modern urban conditions influenced the progressives' notions about creativity. At this point, though, because of their direct impact upon lecturers and teachers in English, we shall look at some of the writings of George Bourne and D. H. Lawrence. Their regret for our loss of the 'organic' rural community and for the disappearance of satisfying labour reappears and is developed in so much contemporary argument about the role of English.

Like Lawrence, George Bourne witnessed the transition from what he viewed as the integrated, organic, small rural community, its labour indivisible from pleasure, its relationships founded upon profound knowledge of a traditional craft, to the disintegrating, modern, commercial situation. The opening pages of *Change in the Village*, written in 1912, are suffused with regret.

'The old life is being swiftly obliterated . . . they are yielding to the dominion of new ideas themselves . . . in another ten years time there will be not much left of the traditional life whose crumbling away I have been witnessing during the twenty years that are gone.'[14]

Like the Hammonds whose work, *The Village Labourer*, influenced Fabian thinking on social reform and informed many progressive educators' vehement expressions of anti-industrialism after the First World War, George Bourne regretted the effects of enclosure upon the lives of country people. He argued that before the loss of common land, labourers had knowledge and skills covering every aspect of their lives, changes in seasonal demands providing sufficient variety and satisfaction. After listing a wide range of cottage activities and crafts involved in peasant life, Bourne refers to the interest of each day.

'Not one of the pursuits I have mentioned failed to make its pleasant demand on the labourer for skill and knowledge; so that after his day's wage-earning he turned to his wine-making or the management of his pigs with the zest that men put into their hobbies.'[15]

Enclosures had had the effect of removing all these activities and had 'left the people helpless against influences which have sapped away their interests . . . the peasant outlook gave way . . . to that of the modern labourer and the old attachment to the countryside was weakened'.[16] Relationships, because of the new system of payment by cash, and division of labour, had become strained and competitive, and leisure time had become a search for diversion. In former times, he maintained, work and leisure were indivisible; like Morris, George Bourne claimed that pleasant work gave delight in labour. In a passage frequently quoted as evidence of the superiority of an age when time was filled with meaningful activity instead of stultifying mechanical labour and manufactured, purchased entertainment, George Bourne describes the village day:

'Their leisure was of no use to them for recreation—for "making themselves anew", that is—or for giving play to faculties which had lain quiet during the day's work . . . . Leisure, and the problem of using it, are new things there. . . . So lightly was it valued that most villagers cut it short by the simple expedient of going to bed at 6 or 7 o'clock. But then, in their peasant way, they enjoyed interesting days. The work they did, although it left their reasoning and imaginative powers undeveloped, called into play enough subtle knowledge and skill to make their whole day's industry gratifying.'[17]

George Bourne's experience of life in a village community, his vivid recreations of the wheelwright's shop and the variety of crafts and knowledge involved in the felling and preparation of timber have added persuasive force to later opponents's attacks on industrial society. His appreciation of craftsmanship, affection for the taciturn labourers, and conviction that in spite of poverty and physical discomfort, theirs was a life of profound satisfaction and quality in contrast to the urban labourer's, have had the effect of sharpening contemporary critics' powerful sense of loss. Like the nineteenth-century critics, like the Hammonds and many progressive educators whom they influenced, like F. R. Leavis and his students, George Bourne regretted our loss of the small, organic interdependent, cohesive community of our pre-industrial past, 'very different from the organised effects of commerce'.[18] Although, inescapably, these losses have been viewed as having serious implications for education, George Bourne drew specific attention to the lost 'education' of the rural craft. Here he seemed to give strong support to teachers who wished to encourage pupils' creativity. He stated that a rural craft was, truly, an education, in that it embodied both discipline and opportunity for expression of individuality; it demanded experience, matured by an informed critical sense of one's materials and tools. His descriptions of experienced craftsmen at work, using all their senses to select and organise, have often been quoted as evidence against cheap elementary education, crammed full of facts and figures and remote from most children's daily lives.

'Truly it was a liberal education to work under Cook's guidance. I never could get axe or plane or chisel sharp enough to satisfy him; but I never doubted then or since that his tiresome fastidiousness over tools and handiwork sprang from a knowledge as valid as any artist's. He knew, not by theory, but delicately, in his eyes and fingers ... two things are notable about these men ... it is, that in them was stored all the local lore of what a good wheelwright's work should be like. The century-old tradition was still vigorous in them. They knew each customer and his needs; understood his carters and his horses and the nature of his land; and finally took a pride in providing exactly what was wanted in every case.'[19]

Like Lawrence, George Bourne criticised the education offered by the village school. It failed, he claimed, 'to initiate him [the pupil] into the inner significance of information in general [it was] . . . sterile of results . . . [its] simple items of information were too scrappy'.[20] This elementary education, together with the Church, politics and news-papers, was, he argued, 'largely abortive because they have not got into touch with the spontaneous movement of village life'. Suspicious of technical education for village children in the skills of ploughing and fruit pruning, he says of these activities that:

'they lived in the popular tastes and habits, and they passed on spon-taneously from generation to generation, as a sort of rural civilisation . . . the life of it is gone, not to be restored. . . . The old rural outlook of England is dead, and the rural English, waiting for something to take its place, for some new tradition to grow up amongst them, are in a state of stagnation.'[21]

Bourne's descriptions of work and leisure in a small rural com-munity and his passionate tones of regret have spoken eloquently to many artists and critics this century. Deeply concerned about the inadequacy of state education today, with its exclusive stress on cog-nitive skills, G. H. Bantock and David Holbrook have argued for a much richer education of the senses and emotions, particularly for working-class children. English teachers they insist, should be responsible for encouraging their pupils through mime, drama, art, music, story-telling in poetry and prose, for touching again the vital centres of the vast majority, for whom rural satisfactions have been replaced by the mechanical, disintegrative routines of industrial labour and the trivial irrelevances of manufactured entertainment.

Of even greater influence this century upon educators concerned with literature and creativity in schools has been the work of D. H. Lawrence. Few writers have described with his insight the nature of the gains and losses of industrialised England. His persuasiveness comes from several sources: the authenticity of his experiences as the son of a miner, the complexity of his treatment of this theme, and the intensity of his despair about the quality of working-class life as he observed it. Influenced by this writer who had known both worlds, educators and critics in the field of English have reflected deeply upon the implications of Lawrence's attacks on industrialism for a society committed to mass literacy. His exploration of the quality of men's lives is inevitably close to disturbing educational issues and has provoked serious argument about responsibility for the great majority who have been affected by industrial change.

In *Women in Love*, in 'The Industrial Magnate', Lawrence, like Carlyle, bitterly criticises mechanisation for its effects of atomisation and incoherence. Describing Gerald Crich's legacy from his father, the nineteenth-century philanthropic mine-owner, Lawrence says:

'He did not inherit an established order and a living idea. The whole unifying idea of mankind seemed to be dying with his father, the centralising force that had held the whole together seemed to collapse with his father, the parts were ready to go asunder in terrible disintegration.'[22]

Gerald sees the folly and unreality of continuing to run the mines along his father's philanthropic lines. Embodying Lawrence's hated modern 'will', the son determines to draw the 'sword of mechanical necessity'.

'The working of the pits was thoroughly changed, all the control was taken out of the hands of the miners, the butty system was abolished. Everything was run on the most accurate and delicate scientific method, educated and expert men in control everywhere, the miners were reduced to mere mechanical instruments. They had to work hard, much harder than before, the work was terrible and heartbreaking in its mechanicalness. But they submitted to it all. The joy went out of their lives . . . . It was the first great steps in undoing, the first great phase of chaos, the substitution of the mechanical principle for the organic, the destruction of the organic purpose, the organic unity, and the subordination of every organic unit to the great mechanical purpose. It was pure organic disintegration and pure mechanical organisation. This is the first and finest state of chaos.'[23]

Throughout this complex work, in which Lawrence contemplates Thomas Crich's philanthropy and the miners' submission to Gerald's steely strength entirely without sentimentality, he conveys his hatred of the power of machines to impose inhuman rhythms and false patterns of numerical equality upon men who should be responding to their environment, work and fellow men with individual spontaneity. In 'Nottinghamshire and the Mining Country', he writes about his father's life as a miner in terms reminiscent of George Bourne's descriptions of his villagers.

'Under the butty system, the miners worked underground as a sort of intimate community . . . . My father loved the pit . . . he loved the contact, the intimacy . . . . He was happy, or more than happy, he was fulfilled.'[24]

George Bourne, Lawrence, and others like F. R. Leavis, G. H. Bantock and David Holbrook, share the conviction that, in spite of harsh physical conditions and poverty, men were happier in the pre-industrial past. These writers' hostility to modern urban society, their convictions about the superiority of art at every level in the past, explain their repeated claim that the agricultural life was more sustaining and satisfying to men than the industrial life. Mechanisation, they claim, has wrenched men away from working to natural rhythms, from close physical contact with others, and from their own deepest instincts. Much of Lawrence's writing persuasively criticises developments which have moved men away from the work and environment which, he believed, provided the profoundest satisfactions. In *The Rainbow*, more fully than in any other novel, he describes the deep, unconscious fulfilment of living in intimate relationship with nature. The early Brangwens of agricultural England have much in common with George Bourne's pre-enclosure villagers; in their lives, work and pleasure are indivisible, their needs inseparable from the rotating demands of the season. Rich with natural imagery drawn from the elements, crops, animal life and sexual experience, this passage's biblical rhythms insist, above all, upon the interrelatedness of rural life, upon the depth of its 'knowing' far beneath the modern schools' cognitive skills.

'But heaven and earth was teeming around them, and how should this cease? They felt the rush of the sap in spring, they knew the wave which cannot halt, but every year throws forward the seed to begetting, and, falling back, leaves the young born on the earth. They knew the intercourse between heaven and earth, sunshine drawn into the breast and bowels, the rain sucked up in the daytime, nakedness that comes under the wind in autumn, showing the birds' nests no longer worth hiding. Their life and interrelations were such, feeling the pulse and body of the soil, that opened to the furrow for the grain, and became smooth and supple after their ploughing, and clung to their feet with a weight that pulled like desire, lying hard and unresponsive when the crops were to be shorn away. The young corn waved and was silken, and the lustre slid along the limbs of the men who saw it. They took the udder of the cows, the cows yielded milk and pulse against the hands of the men, the pulse of the blood of the teats of the cows beat into the pulse of the hands of the men. They mounted their horses, and held life between the grip of their knees, they harnessed their horses at the wagon, and, with hand on the bridle-rings, drew the heaving of the horses after their will.'[25]

Lawrence's recreations of fulfilled lives in agricultural England have stimulated concern among educators about the diminished opportunities in industrial society for personal satisfaction. Three books, *Culture and Environment* and *Mass Civilisation and Minority Culture* by F. R. Leavis, and *Fiction and the Reading Public* by Mrs Q. Leavis, illustrate the extent to which these key figures in English teaching responded sympathetically to George Bourne and D. H. Lawrence. They, too, argue that the old ways of life have been destroyed by machinery, standardisation and suburbanism, and regret bitterly that commercially produced mass entertainment which encourage cheap, stereotyped emotional responses have replaced the varied, sustaining life of the rural community. Leavis's central concern in *Culture and Environment* is with the debasing effects of the mass media. It is essential, in his view, to encourage the powers of discrimination of students and children. The strength of his anti-industrialism is relevant here because of its relationship with his life's efforts to promote the serious and engaged study of English literature. The position of Leavis and his colleague, Denys Thompson, is clearly the same as that of Lawrence. Like him, they insist that:

'What we have lost is the organic community . . . and a responsive adjustment growing out of immemorial experience, to the natural environment and the rhythm of the year.'[26]

Drawing upon George Bourne's and Lawrence's descriptions of the indivisibility of work and leisure before industrialisation, they regret the modern habit of living for leisure instead of getting the satisfactions derived from work.

'The modern labourer, the modern clerk, the modern factory hand live only for their leisure, and the result is that they are unable to live in their leisure when they get it.'[27]

Thirty years later, Leavis expressed the same view in an article in the *Times Literary Supplement*. Referring to urban man's 'work', he wrote (in 1968): 'something to be got behind him so that he can get away to live—before the telly, over the pools form, in the bingo hall, in the car.'[28] Mrs Leavis, too, draws upon the testimony of George Bourne and D. H. Lawrence. In *Fiction and the Reading Public*, where she argues that tastes have been steadily degenerating with the coincidence of mass literacy and disintegration of the folk culture, she writes that George Bourne's notes 'go a good way towards explaining this'.

'The old order made reading to prevent boredom unnecessary, whereas the narrowing down of labour that specialisation has produced has changed the working day from a sequence of interests to a repetition of mechanical movement of both body and mind. . . . But these had a real social life, they had a way of living that obeyed the natural rhythm and furnished them with genuine or what might be called, to borrow a word from the copy writer, "creative" interests—country arts, traditional crafts and games and singing, not substitute or kill-time interests like listening to radio or gramophone, looking through newspapers and magazines, watching films and commercial football, and the activities connected with motor cars and bicycles, the only way of using leisure known to the modern city dweller . . . .[29]

For the past forty years, Leavis has written and lectured on this theme of cultural disintegration, engaging his students in the rigorously detailed analysis of literature in order to keep alive our last remaining tradition of the use of language. In *Culture and Environment*, in which he contrasts our cultural debasement with the fine, discriminating responses of the wheelwright's world, he said: 'At the centre of our culture is language, and while we have our language tradition is, in some essential sense, still alive.'[30] Leavis has been primarily concerned with the establishment of English as a central university discipline, his aim being to create the conditions under which an élite could be educated to continue the tradition of discrimination and fine response to language. Many of his pupils, however, have concerned themselves with English in the school curriculum, and it is here that the strength of his antagonism to urban society has been most influential. Those involved in teaching English to able children, as will be discussed later, have responded to Leavis's convictions by investing great value in their pupils' capacity to respond sensitively to great literature. Those involved with less able pupils, particularly from working-class backgrounds, have turned to pupils' creativity to compensate for the inadequacies of industrial society. At every level, Leavis's view of technological progress as a transition entailing profound loss has had a powerful influence upon the emergent ideology of the redemptive power of English. In 1969, in *Lectures in America*, Leavis said again what he had been saying since the thirties, 'A general impoverishment of life—that is the threat that, ironically, accompanies the technological advance and the rising standard of living, and we are all involved.'[31] William Walsh, a student of Leavis's and a Professor of Education at Leeds, wrote in 1964 in *Literature and Humanity* in similar tones:

'As for the people huddled in enormous urban areas, they seem to have lost their task for the flavour of colloquial salt, they seem no longer able to produce that verve and variety of dialect or that energy of phrase and image with which they used to replenish the potency of the word. Language as it is used today exhibits a progressive dehumanisation.'[32]

Closely bound up with his hostility to industrialism was Lawrence's fear lest the physical life be diminished or destroyed by the intellectual. Lawrence believed, firstly, in the value of the life of the body, and expressed his fears about its destruction by the intellect. The great majority, he believed, were unfitted to be brought to 'mental consciousness' and were unhappily confused and burdened by the political decision-making which egalitarianism had imposed upon them. Imprisoned by mental concepts which were only half understood during their cheap, mechanical schooling, they were losing, Lawrence believed, the capacity to respond to their environment and to each other from the most vital sources of being. He described modern England, in which men are losing keen awareness of their physical selves in industry's reduction of individuals to units operating vast numbers of identical machines, as 'a tomb', 'something broken', and its people as 'grubby', 'shabby', like corpses deadened by relentless machines. In characteristically passionate language he wrote:

'My great religion is a belief in the blood, the flesh, as being wiser than the intellect. We can go wrong in our minds. But what our blood feels and believes and says, is always true. The intellect is only a bit and a bridle. What do I care about knowledge. All I want is to answer to my own blood, direct, without fribbling intervention of mind, or moral or what not. I conceive a man's body as a kind of flame, like a candle flame, forever upright and yet flowing: and the intellect is just the light that is shed on to the things around.'[33]

Like George Bourne, and later G. H. Bantock and David Holbrook, Lawrence was deeply critical of education's failure to replace what had been lost through England's transition to industrialisation. Sounds of children's tuneless singing from the ugly board school feature in Connie Chatterly's deadly, ugly journey through Tattershall; the Harbys's authoritarian régime into which Ursula enters as a teacher in *The Rainbow* conveys vividly Lawrence's antipathy to utilitarianism in state education—the grim buildings, severe rows, withered plants, chanted facts and inflexible harsh discipline reflect industrial conditions in mines, factories, and cheaply built communities of the world outside. Lawrence, like other critics, insisted that the knowledge of the schools failed to touch the deepest selves of working men's children.

'In my father's generation, with the old wild England behind them, and the lack of education, the man was not beaten down. But in my generation, the boys I went to school with, colliers now, have all been beaten down, what with the din-din-dinnings of board schools, books, cinemas, clergymen, the whole national and human consciousness hammering on the fact of material prosperity above all things.'[34]

Machine labour, submission before the false god of equality, education remote from men's deepest 'knowing', the unreal images of the increasingly popular cinema, were, in Lawrence's view, all formidable obstacles to achievement of individuality. His poems, particularly, cry out in angry despair. 'Vivid', 'living', 'flowing' are the descriptive words for men who are flesh and need touch; modern industrial society, with what he claims are its false gods of equality and material prosperity, has made 'hooked fishes' of them, turned them into 'white-faced millions mewed and mangled in the mills of man',[35] whose only hope in the face of mechanical death is to 'touch one another'.[36] In Lawrence's writing, hostility and regret fuse into concentrated distrust of modern civilisation. Industrialism means the domination of man by machines, the natural, seasonal and dynamic[37] replaced by the driving, destructive forces of the mechanical. Instead of the inevitable, instinctive responses to seasonal change moving men to their pleasant labours, restless desires for material comfort and distracting entertainment motivate them to drudgery in mine and factory. And, depressingly, this great change from the agricultural to the industrial has condemned England to ugliness—the living and beautiful sprawled over by cheaply built rows of mean houses and factory smoke. His values, his sympathies and his anger converge in this poem which depicts working men as the victims of industrialism.

WHAT HAVE THEY DONE TO YOU?

What have they done to you, men of the masses, creeping
back and forth to work?
What have they done to you, saviours of the people, oh

what have they saved you from, while they pocketed
the money?
Alas, they have saved you from yourself, from your own
frail dangers
and devoured you with the machine, the vast maw of iron.
They saved you from your squalid cottages and poverty of
hand to mouth
and embedded you in workmen's dwellings, where
your wage is the dole of work, and the dole is your
wage of nullity.
They took away, oh they took away your man's native
instincts and intuitions
and gave a board-school education, newspapers, and the
cinema.
They stole your body from you, and left you an animated
carcass
to work with, and nothing else:
unless goggling eyes, to goggle at the film
and a board-school brain, stuffed with the ha'penny
press.
Your instincts gone, your intuition gone, your passions
dead
Oh carcass with a board-school mind and a ha'penny
newspaper intelligence
what have they done to you, what have they done to you,
Oh what have they done to you?
Oh look at my fellow-men, oh look at them
the masses! Oh what has been done to them?[38]

What has been suggested throughout this chapter is that current
definitions of English in schools have been powerfully affected by the
anti-industrial tradition in literature and criticism. Writers' certainty
about the superiority of the past has produced bitter criticism of
modern urban society and idealised recreations of the 'organic' communities of agricultural England. Their sense of loss, their lack of
sympathy with working people's material aspirations, have driven
educators to seek experiences within the school curriculum which will
compensate for those which, they are convinced, used to provide personal satisfaction and contentment. Thus, upon English literature and,
more crucially in this area of personal fulfilment, upon creativity,
have been placed the burden of responsibility previously carried by
the traditional organic community. Literature and, particularly for
working-class pupils, creative work, it is argued, can bring children
into touch with their native traditions and can affect these living
centres of being hitherto neglected in state education.

As concern has deepened about the content of the curriculum for working-class pupils, educators in English who have been influenced by Bourne, Lawrence and Leavis have tended to express their dissatisfaction with modern urban life with increasing hostility. As despair has intensified, recommendations for what might be achieved by sensitive English teaching have tended to become more and more insistent. This chapter ends by looking at those figures who are still making important contributions to ideas about the role of English in schools.

The work of G. H. Bantock, once a pupil of Leavis, and also a Professor of Education, is of particular importance in this area of industrialisation and mass literacy. Deeply concerned, like Arnold, Bourne, Lawrence and Leavis, about the quality of life for the majority in our society for whom literacy, as taught in schools, had failed utterly to be a humanising experience, he asks what he calls the 'real question' when he says: 'Can we in the schools do anything towards the evolving of a new folk culture?'[39] Apart from the progressives' curricula which, as we have noted, affected the lives of a tiny, privileged minority, the schools of the nineteenth and twentieth centuries have been characterised by an 'almost complete abstraction from any full and coherent way of folk life'. Sharing Leavis's pessimistic view of modern society's failure to sustain its citizens uprooted from small, rural communities of close intimacy, relationship with nature and pride in knowledge of their craft, Bantock discusses what the role of education should be. In common with Lawrence, he thinks that it is bewildering, unsatisfying and uncongenial to many of our pupils to be brought to 'mental consciousness', to be educated in the traditional, academic way. He asserts:

'Education, indeed, stepped in as the folk environment collapsed—and failed precisely because it neglected what the folk environment had provided in moral and cultural strength.'[40]

He suggests that for the majority of our children education should concern itself with the affective subjects. Opposed to egalitarianism in education, because failure to benefit from the academic leaves many pupils ill-equipped to resist commercial culture, he proposes that much more of the syllabus should be given to dance, mime, music, drama and poetry.

'. . . we ought to seek some more affectively based, some less self-consciously elaborated, methods of inducing literary appreciation for the majority—the stress, perhaps should be on participation through speech, mime and movement.'[41]

Like Leavis, Bantock values the engagement with literature because, acknowledging English teaching's debt to Leavis, this is a
'training in moral awareness and sensitivity which reacts centrally
on the problems of living'.[42] He contends that the role of the arts has
been too small in the education of able children, regretting that
science and technology which 'do not provide that moral insight, that
degree of affective control, that ordering of the emotional life through
intelligence, that self-awareness through psychological insight, that
sensitising to the life situations which great literature can afford'[43]
have become so important. But he is even more concerned about its
neglect in the curriculum of the vast majority. Bantock argues that
an academic education for children of lower ability from working-
class homes—the heirs of England's rural communities—leads to
boredom and their readier susceptibility to the trivia of the mass
media. The following passage shows how sympathetically he responds
to Bourne's and Lawrence's views about England's cultural state.

'What, in fact, is required, is a new folk culture—to replace the one
whose strength lay precisely in its mature acceptance of the conditions of human existence, which displayed remarkable subtleties
and beauties within the various media in which it expressed itself and
which was, therefore, at the opposite pole to that which so often passes
for popular culture today.'[44]

The extent to which convictions like these have contributed to the
uncertainty of purpose which some English teachers are very conscious of today is discussed in Part III. They are, obviously, at odds
with the hope which many hold about the upward mobility of
working-class children through experience of a common curriculum.
Within the last ten years, the most influential figure in English
teaching has probably been David Holbrook, whose book, *English
for Maturity*, has transformed approaches to the subject at the
secondary modern ability levels. Like Leavis, whose student he was at
Cambridge, and like Bantock, Holbrook laments the lost organic
community, drawing, as they do, upon Bourne's and Lawrence's
recreations of its intimacies, variety and fine discriminations. Like
them, he expresses hostility to modern conditions of labour and the
bromides of escapist leisure but, unlike them has, in his work about
English teaching, concerned himself exclusively with 'the sensibilities
of three-quarters of the population',[45] the secondary modern children
of average or low ability, and based much of his writing upon his
classroom experience with them. The theme of *English for Maturity*,
and of *The Exploring Word* (in which he proposes a creative rather

than an academic education for college of education students), is that 'it is the task of the school . . . to begin to help re-establish a popular culture . . . to develop . . . the very culture of the feelings'.[46] Modern popular culture is 'a disabling culture', to counteract the trivialising, brutalising effects of which the school must stimulate acting, writing, singing and painting, as well, whenever possible, as involvement with great literature.

The numerous anthologies of children's writing, the course books with selected passages for stimulating creativity, testify to the effectiveness of these views in promoting encouragement of original work in schools. As is discussed in other chapters, several powerful forces in education and wider society have been responsible for shifting our interest from the established artist to the spontaneous responses of the child. A major factor, however, has been the persistent tradition of anti-industrialism with its undertow of a profound sense of loss. Convinced about the superior quality of life in pre-industrial communities, and repelled by urban squalor, mechanical work routines and mass-produced commercial art, educators have invested hope in the personal recreations of experience, mainly in language. In 1969, writing in Holbrook's tones, Fred Inglis expressed his distaste for our modern environment in *The Englishness of English Teaching*.

'Mostly, we simply do not recognise in any conscious way that the places we live in have only a brutalised identity, and we do not know what spiritual impoverishment our loveless, placeless homes make for.'[47]

Like his nineteenth-century predecessors, Inglis makes the move from bad art to impoverished quality of life and, in his role of training English students in a university department to teach in schools, his views are surely being transmitted to the classroom. So too are those of Raymond O'Malley of Cambridge who writes that 'a paper stall, taken seriously, stirs feelings not easily kept short of despair'.[48] And both subscribe to Leavis's view that it is the responsibility of English teachers to remedy this cultural sickness. Uncompromisingly, Fred Inglis calls for 'militancy against all that is hateful in contemporaneity and for a brave access of energy to build on those things which are worth the holding'.[49]

Many educators concerned with English in schools have accepted Lawrence's profoundly pessimistic diagnosis of modern industrial society and his distrust of egalitarianism. They share his regret for what they believe to have been satisfactions yielded by agricultural labour, closeness to nature and to fellow men. Mechanisation is thus not to be welcomed for its removal of desperate poverty, provision of more widespread good health and increased leisure, and opportunities for upward social mobility. It is to be feared for its sprawling ugliness, its reduction of men to mere extensions of machinery, its stimulation of material greed, its introduction of cheap, standardised education. These views have had important consequences for the ideology of English teaching. The cultural condition of advanced industrial society, from a standpoint like Lawrence's, can only deteriorate; and it is clearly impossible to return to a pre-industrial situation. Revival of 'genuine folk culture' is defined as the schools' responsibility and its achievement is possible only through the inspirational qualities of teachers. As the 'cultural crisis' is seen as worsening, it is likely that demands for exceptional teachers will become more insistent. English teachers, Holbrook asserts, are responsible for training 'the sensibilities of three-quarters of the population'. This is a view which, it will be argued throughout Part II, although expressed in a variety of different ways, appears to be held by every group supporting the subject's centrality in schools.

Notes

1. Caldwell Cook, *The Play Way* (London, Heinemann, 1917), p. 356.
2. Thomas Carlyle, *Works of Thomas Carlyle*, Vol. 2, p. 233; quoted by Raymond Williams *Culture and Society, 1780–1950* (New York, Anchor Books, 1960), p. 78.
3. A. W. Pugin, *Contrasts* (Leicester University Press, 1969), p. 1.
4. Ibid., p. 6.
5. J. Ruskin, *Lectures on Art*, Library edition, Vol. 20, p. 39.
6. J. Ruskin, *Stones of Venice* (1899 edn), Vol. 2, Ch. 6, 'The Nature of Gothic', pp. 163 ff.
7. Williams, op. cit., p. 167.
8. William Morris, 'How I Became a Socialist', (Nonesuch Morris, 1934), pp. 657 f.
9. Thomas Carlyle, *Past and Present* (1843 edn) (Boston, Richard D. Altick, 1915), p. xi.
10. Williams, op. cit., p. 89.
11. Carlyle, *Past and Present*, op. cit., p. 210.
12. Williams, op. cit., p. 93.
13. Ibid., pp. 37, 47.
14. George Bourne, *Change in the Village* (1912) (London, Duckworth, 1955), p. 11.
15. Ibid., p. 79.
16. Ibid., pp. 87 ff.

17. Ibid., pp. 136 f.
18. George Bourne, *The Wheelwright's Shop* (1923) (Cambridge, Cambridge University Press, 1963), p. 33.
19. Ibid., p. 54.
20. Bourne, *Change in the Village*, op. cit., pp. 150 f.
21. Ibid., p. 194.
22. D. H. Lawrence, *Women in Love* (Harmondsworth, Penguin, 1960), p. 248.
23. Ibid., pp. 259 f.
24. D. H. Lawrence, 'Nottinghamshire and the Mining Country' (1929), in *Selected Essays* (Harmondsworth, Penguin, 1950), p. 117.
25. D. H. Lawrence, *The Rainbow*, Phoenix edn (London, Heinemann, 1955), p. 2.
26. F. R. Leavis and D. Thompson, *Culture and Environment* (London, Chatto & Windus, 1933), pp. 1 f.
27. Ibid., p. 68.
28. F. R. Leavis in the *Times Literary Supplement* (1968).
29. Q. D. Leavis, *Fiction and the Reading Public* (London, Chatto & Windus, 1965), pp. 48, 209.
30. Leavis and Thompson, op. cit., p. 81.
31. F. R. Leavis, 'Luddites? Or is There Only One Culture?', *Lectures in America* (London, Chatto & Windus, 1964), p. 13.
32. William Walsh, *A Human Idiom. Literature and Humanity* (London, Chatto & Windus, 1964), pp. 12 f.
33. D. H. Lawrence, letter to E. Collins (17 Jan. 1913), *The Portable D. H. Lawrence* (New York, Viking Press, 1947), p. 563.
34. D. H. Lawrence, 'Nottingham and the Mining Country', op. cit., p. 119.
35. D. H. Lawrence, 'Dark Satanic Mills', 'More Pansies', *The Complete Poems of D. H. Lawrence* (London, Heinemann, 1964), Vol. 2, p. 628.
36. D. H. Lawrence, 'Future States', 'More Pansies', in *The Complete Poems of D. H. Lawrence*, op. cit., p. 611.
37. See earlier extract from *The Rainbow*.
38. D. H. Lawrence, 'What Have They Done To You?', 'More Pansies', *The Complete Poems of D. H. Lawrence*, op. cit., p. 630.
39. G. H. Bantock, *Education in an Industrial Society* (London, Faber, 1963), p. 117.
40. Ibid., p. 82.
41. Ibid., p. 167.
42. Ibid., p. 153.
43. Ibid., pp. 168 f.
44. Ibid., p. 210.
45. David Holbrook, *English for Maturity* (Cambridge, Cambridge University Press, 1965), p. 9.
46. Ibid., p. 56.
47. Fred Inglis, *The Englishness of English Teaching* (London, Longman, 1969), p. 22.

48. Raymond O'Malley, 'Creative Writing in Schools', in *English in Education: Writing*, Vol. 3, No. 3 (Autumn 1969) (Oxford University Press, NATE), pp. 72 f.
49. Inglis, op. cit., pp. 186 f.

Chapter 8

Progressive Theories
Since the 1920s

'Perhaps the most important asset for a teacher
engaged upon creative work of any kind is the capacity
to wait upon the moment, and sometimes to wait and
wait. It is, of course, a gift essential to the psycho-analyst.'

Marjorie Hourd, *Coming into Their Own*

Before the First World War progressive theories were already making
an impact upon discussion about English in schools. The notion of
growth had changed, in particular, descriptions of children's composition; to satisfy their need for enjoyable activity it had come to be
seen as work which should be related to their experiences and interests. Educators' profound dissatisfaction with their society after
the war led, with their distrust of the traditional curriculum, to
changes which raised 'composition' onto the much higher plane of
creativity. The development of a fervently optimistic, reverential
attitude towards children's expression, as we shall see, has had far-
reaching effects upon the role of the teacher. His image, no longer
drawn from the public worlds of ambassadors and missionaries, has
come to be created from the private areas of experience. The good
teacher, though more suggestively described, has become an elusive
figure—the psycho-analyst or, sometimes called upon to be creative
himself, the artist.

In common with others who have been responsible for the movement of English to the centre of the curriculum (those hostile to the
dehumanising effects of too much science in our schools, and those
fearful of the forces of industrialism) progressive educators' long-
experienced sense of being under threat, and of offering unheeded
remedies for society's ills, produced claims made in tones of almost
desperate insistence. Educational innovators were few in this country.
They were, moreover, identified either with small, somewhat eccentric
schools or with the low-status infant and junior stages of the system.
Prolonged neglect or misinterpretation, until events combined to pro-

duce a mood sympathetic to progressivism, had tended to make its supporters defensively extravagant in their claims.

R. J. W. Selleck draws attention both to the religious fervour with which these claims were made and to the intensity of the progressives' hostility to the old system of class learning and promotion of cognitive skills.

'. . . not only were they right but they were right about something important. Through all they said and did, there runs the belief that great things were at stake—the salvation of the world, they sometimes say, without any embarrassed sense of disproportion.'[1]

He explains the gradual official acceptance of progressive theories by reference to conditions in society in the 1920s. The war itself produced a feeling of need for a new start. Unemployment after the war sharpened intellectual philanthropic despair and distaste for modern urban conditions.

'At a time of mass slaughter, and rationing, the progressives promised a new world in which the *individual* mattered . . . . This, after huge losses, suggested hope.'[2]

Post-war conditions confirmed progressive educators' anti-industrialism and strengthened their belief in the value of personal responses, personal participation and personal creativity as resistance against stultifying industrial labour. Caldwell Cook's recommendations about play, delight in school work, and the spontaneity of the child response showed his deep disgust for the modern urban scene.

'Our people will continue to live as a race of petty and exploited town-dwellers, having their homes in tenements, slums and villas, seeking their amusement in the music hall, and the cinema palace and the gramophone, their sport in the vicarious football of hirelings, their food in tins and packets, and their literature and politics in halfpenny newspapers bribed by the advertising manufacturers of soap, drink, tobacco, underwear and patent medicines.'[3]

In the face of these perceived evils—the war, unemployment, squalid urban housing, mechanised work and leisure—the progressives placed their hopes in the child. Victorian rationality had obviously led us to disaster; distrusting this, henceforth the stresses would be upon the emotions and the instincts of childhood. Hearts and not heads, A. S. Neill suggested, should be our concern in school, while Sir Percy

Nunn who, as Selleck says, 'gave the progressives a textbook', insisted that:

'the comparative fruitlessness of so much educational effort is mainly due to neglect of the feelings which are the proximate sources of human energy, the real springs of educational progress whether in learning or conduct.'[4]

Thus, they proposed a romantic, optimistic view of the child who, in a loving relationship with his teacher who encouraged him to develop his uniqueness through involvement with the arts, would grow best without adult interference. Margaret McMillan's preface written in 1923 for *Education through the Imagination* (1904), helpfully conveys this mood of romantic optimism which embraced the children and the unsophisticated in hopefulness for the future.

'When we first set up the nursery school we builded better than we knew, for we began to learn how much of the inward light in a child is already all but quenched when it comes to school age. The nursery school taught us the same lesson as we learned in the trenches—the intrinsic beauty and heroism of the 'common' folk. And by contrast between what is and what—as our new experience taught us—might be, we begin to see our need of a new rational education, an education new in kind as well as in scope . . . . The child has what many grown-up folk have lost, the sense of beauty, which is, as it were, a short cut to the kingdom.'[5]

The 1920s saw the development of child study as a field of research, the setting up of annual conferences, and the establishment of many more experimental schools. Out of all this arose a powerful conviction about the necessity of educating the emotions and the indispensable role of the arts in promoting individuality. Faced with the need for reconsidering the curriculum, and anxious about the needs of adolescents before entry into industrial labour, educators placed considerable hope in a broader definition of the arts. From the Montreux Conference (1923) came this assertion:

'Education in the future must be regarded as the process of calling out the best that is in the child, whatever that be called—soul or spirit, or the divine spark of creative ability.'[6]

The Handbook of Suggestions (1927), accepted these progressive theories when it stated that literature was 'not merely a means of escaping from practical life, but . . . a means of coping with it' and when it emphasised the encouragement of 'both creation and appreciation' in the arts as a 'means of spiritual enlargement'.[7] Teachers of the traditional type were criticised by Finch and Kimmins in *The Teaching of English* and *Handwriting* (1923), for neglecting children's 'creative activities and expression'. If, they said, the 'life of inner experience and feeling . . . the source of creative effort' were neglected, 'expression in undesirable ways' could result.[8] Contributors to the Spens Report (1939) reminded readers that in 1931 they had recommended that the curriculum 'should be thought of in terms of activity and experience rather than of knowledge to be acquired and facts to be stored'.[9] References to children's growth and individual development recur throughout this Report. In order that this should be achieved, the contributors recommend that 'a larger place than hitherto must be found for those activities which we believe opinion would generally call creative'.[10] In its thinking about English in schools, the Report appears to have been influenced by Stanley Hall's studies of the adolescent.

'The reading, discussion and reflection which this study [English] provides and stimulates are capable of exercising a wide influence upon the life and outlook of the adolescent, more generally and lasting in its effects than that normally exercised by any other subject in the curriculum.'[11]

The Report suggests that encouragement of 'and some insistence on, the writing of original verse' be given and, tempering the rather unprogressive compelling tones, goes on to refer to the experience of literature in characteristically exalted terms: 'It has been said that a man who has learnt to love either a poem or a person he at first disliked has gone far on the road to salvation.'[12] Later, when discussing the demands which this experience in schools makes on the teacher in the way of 'sincerity' and 'love', the Report notes that:

'this love can, like religion, be 'caught' but not taught . . . not by easy raptures or didactic exhortation, but by a kind of inward glow which warms all those who come in contact with it.'[13]

'Divine spark', 'glow', 'tenderness', 'love' whether attributed to the teacher or the child, are all suggestive of that new hope which progressive theories offered in a bleak modern world. Wars, industrialism and increased power of the mass media can explain the educators' sympathy with theories investing hope in the child and distrustful of adult authority. In 1937, in *The Education of the Emotions*, Margaret Phillips quotes T. F. Coade from *Education for Today*:

'The world needs a new kind of citizen, citizens with a new outlook and a new heart. And that result can be achieved, in modern conditions, by education alone. It is the task of education to produce . . . men and women who are emotionally as well as intellectually free.'[14]

And in 1946, referring to the Second World War, Sir Herbert Read made much the same point: '. . . the secret of our collective ills is to be traced to the suppression of spontaneous creative ability in the individual.'[15] *Education through Art* and Marjorie Hourd's *Education of the Poetic Spirit* (1949) expressed and developed most of the progressive ideas relating to the affective subjects. Until the writings of David Holbrook and the supporters of children's creative work in the 1960s, these two books represented the dominant progressive notions about education of the emotions through art and literature and the need for special qualities in the teacher if this was to be achieved. Read, like Marjorie Hourd, takes a romantic view of childhood in insisting upon the value of the child artist. He says:

'What the child writes, or draws, might best be described as an act of poetic intuition, and it is a mystery beyond our logical analysis . . . . I can only say [before children's drawings] with Frank Cizek: "The teacher must be the most modest and humble of persons who sees in a child a miracle of God, and not pupil material." '[16]

In the field of children's art, Marion Richardson, a teacher of acknowledged gifts, refers likewise to 'the artist's vision within the child'[17] and, at the end of her book, *Art and the Child*, where she describes an exhibition of children's paintings, says, in approval of inexperienced spontaneity: 'How little the children know, and how right they are'.[18] Marjorie Hourd, noting her indebtedness to Herbert Read and agreeing with his notions about art providing 'better persons and better societies', suggests that the same principles should hold for drama. After claiming that drama serves the double purpose of releasing fantasy and acting as a means of grasping reality, Miss Hourd turns to a consideration of children's visionary power. Like Herbert Read, she asserts the close similarity of the child to the adult artist, saying:

'I do not want us to regard children as lesser poets as we do when mature writers fail, but as young poets—poets in embryo. . . . Instead of there being a great gulf fixed between the mature and immature artist, their worlds lie very close together, their meanings are akin, and the process by which they reach them is the same.'[19]

Today there are many published anthologies of children's work, the enthusiastic introductions to which convey a sense of the high value placed on their ability to recreate experience through language. There are noticeably few critical commentaries or discussions of problems of progress, omissions which imply success of the children's achievements and adult belief in the attitude of non-interference. In *English for Diversity* Peter Abbs writes that 'the teacher must accept what the children write. There should be no marking, no assessing. . . . This is essential if the teacher is to create an atmosphere in which imagination thrives.'[20] The American educators who surveyed a number of English schools in 1968 commented upon the way in which our teachers value children's writing; they noted the serious treatment given to 'creative pieces written by children as literary documents for reading and study by the whole class . . . [it] reflects a British tendency to place a high premium on the artistic creations of young people'.[21] They also noted the teachers' deliberate policy of non-interference:

'Technical errors in the writing of the lower forms are accepted because teachers set their sights on more basic, longer range goals in personal development . . . never did she [the teacher] give any advice or any concrete suggestion for improving the poems.'[22]

The stress is placed either upon the power of this work to promote a child's personal development—education through art—or upon the rich artistic potential of the child himself who, it is argued, needs creative work for this to find its fullest realisation. Michael Baldwin, poet and editor of the anthology, *Billy the Kid*, writes in his introduction to a group of children's poems submitted in a competition that 'they are all of them good poems', and 'they have all been part of my growth these last months no less than the works of the mature poets I have been able to come to freshly during the same period'.[23] Upon this aspect of English the American educators commented thus, in their attempt to draw a comparison between teaching in their country and ours: 'While the end product of the American system is the critic, the end product of the emerging British system is the artist.'[24]

Until now, attention has been paid almost exclusively to progressive theory's role in promoting interest in children's creations in prose, poetry and art. This has been immensely important for the development of English in schools as it is now defined. An additional contribution, however, has been the introduction and encouragement of children's dramatic activity. Perhaps in this, more than in other apsects of work in English, the major influences upon the subject noticeably converge, and within this work, descriptions of the ideal teacher's responsibilities become most extravagant. Romantic perceptions of children's visions have fused with a desire for the revival of genuine folk culture; and these have coincided with a growing concern about a suitable curriculum for average and below-average pupils. Mime, improvisation and scripted drama have been introduced into work in English, or as separate activities with specialist staff, because they seem to meet so many of what have come to be defined as children's needs. They offer liberating physical activity, popular with progressive educators from Cecil Reddie through Caldwell Cook to Peter Slade as part of their shared reaction to the passive, academic, 'mechanical' routine of the Victorian curriculum. Unlike the public schools' team games, drama satisfies the individual's emotions and senses, and offers scope for individual response and interpretation. Progressives, anxious to build a better world through changed educational methods, viewed drama as an activity inside which children could be encouraged to co-operate unselfishly and sociably, motivated by enjoyment and interest rather than compelled by regimentation. Moreover, it was argued, their anti-social impulses would be therapeutically released through acting out a wide variety of roles. Even more attractively, drama has been viewed as the most egalitarian art form, and thus has much to recommend it during a period of reaction against élitism and traditional standards in the arts. It is proposed as an activity suitable for children of all abilities:

'. . . there is not a child born anywhere in the world, in any physical or intellectual circumstances or conditions, who cannot do drama. The moment the development of people becomes our aim, this factor becomes clearly apparent.'[25]

Something of this century's reaction against Victorian rationalism and distrust of élitism in the arts is conveyed in Brian Way's consideration of the value of drama in every child's development.

'They [the arts] are concerned with the development of intuition, which is no less important than intellect, and is part of the essence of full enrichment of life both for those who have intellectual gifts and those who have not. . . .'[26]

Brian Way and his teacher, Peter Slade, are Viola's and Cizek's heirs, with their almost religious conviction about art's essential role in the 'development of full personality'. Slade quotes also from Herbert Read, indicating the strength of the progressive line on education through art from the conferences in the 1920s to drama teachers today. In 1949 Read wrote:

'Drama is absolutely essential in all stages of education. Indeed I regard it as that form of activity which best co-ordinates all other forms of education through art. Since, in my view, education through art should be the basic method in all education whatsoever, it can be seen that too high a value cannot be placed upon Child Drama.'[27]

Possibly because it appears to meet so many needs which are defined as essential and urgent in the current situation, drama has had the most extravagant claims made for it. There is, as has been noted, a sense of impending crisis about most progressivist recommendations—'essential responsibilities to a democratic society'; 'we are fighting to give meaning to our lives'; 'the threat of a world crisis which has never been experienced in the history of mankind is upon us.'[28] Most educators, convinced about the regenerative power of the arts, believed that developments this century provided irrefutable evidence of a cultural crisis. Two World Wars, the disintegration of rural communities, and the spread of the mass media had produced a situation for which inspired teaching of literature, drama, music and art appeared to be the only remedy. As we have seen, one of the important results of this conviction has been an insistence upon the desperate need for outstanding teachers. Progressive educators have added to the growing burdens of English teachers by making some extraordinary assertions about the redemptive powers of drama. Because of drama's emotional, physical and social potential, its apparent reflection of real life, it has tended to become equated with the quality of life itself. Recently, as anxiety has deepened about the school experiences of the less-able pupil, supporters of drama (like those writers nostalgic for past ages whose superior art suggested, to them, superior ways of life) assume that good drama teaching is the direct equivalent of admirable living. The following passage illustrates how drama's supporters, doubtless wishing to match claims for the classical curriculum, justified a hitherto low-status activity by reference to all the virtues which a school might wish to promote.

'The lad who has had little drama at school is, quite frankly, in many instances, a lout. He cannot move, and does not want to. . . . The adolescent of either sex who has had a sensible training in drama at

school can be recognised almost at once. . . . I would say without hesi-
tation that cleanliness, tidiness, gracefulness, politeness, cheerfulness,
confidence, ability to mix, thoughtfulness for others, discrimination,
moral discernment, honesty and and loyalty, ability to lead com-
panions, reliability, and a readiness to remain steadfast under difficulties, appear to be the result of correct and prolonged drama training.'[29]

An important result of acceptance of progressive theories has been
the redefinition of the teacher's role. Distrust of adult authority, and
romantic optimism about the child's qualities, have produced attempts
to describe the ideal relationship between teacher and pupil. Discussing this aspect of progressivism, Selleck says:

'The progressives were heirs to that gradual destruction of certainties
that had been a part of nineteenth-century England . . . . "Dark Coun-
cils", the tyranny of adulthood", "adult interference", knowledge
that was "desiccated", "minced and peptonised", "adults who were un-
worthy models" or "grey-beard loons" responsible for the sorry state
of Western civilisation—so the progressives wrote, and betrayed their
own uncertainties, and disenchantment with the world they and their
fathers had made.'[30]

Consequently, the new hopes for the child's vision to create a better
world entailed the need for teachers capable of fostering his fullest
development, ideally through the arts. We have noted already the
Spens Report's requirements of 'love' and 'sincerity' in teachers of
literature. Inevitably, the requirements for teachers of creativity were
equally high. For Herbert Read, they must be capable of establishing
relationships that encourage the development of child art: 'Whatever
aspect of education we take . . . rapport established between the
teacher and the child is the all-important factor'.[31]

Both Herbert Read and Marjorie Hourd have been influenced by
Martin Buber's work on the relationship between teacher and pupil
in their discussions about the delicate balance required between
involvement and detachment. Each of them draws heavily on
Buber's exploration of the teacher's role in *Between Man and Man*;
recognising the opportunities in the progressive educational situation
for personal domination and self-gratification, Buber recommended
control of the 'personal' by a disciplined impersonal context.

'. . . when authority begins to decay, that is when magical validity of
tradition disappears . . . the moment comes near when the teacher no

longer faces the pupil as an ambassador but only as an individual, as a static atom to a whirling atom . . . . Eros appears . . . finds employment in the new situation.'[32]

The teacher, he says, can, ideally, be seen as 'a representative of the true God' and his responsibility in relationship with his pupil as that of 'giving and withholding', 'intimacy and distance, which of course must not be controlled by reflection but must arise from the living tact of the natural and spiritual man'.[33] Although the educator can, and should, imaginatively project himself into the experience of his pupil, he must realise that he is not, as an educator, understood by the child. Thus, the educator must exercise unselfishness and control if he is to avoid changing the teacher-pupil relationship to friendship. He knows himself, and, imaginatively, he knows his pupils' experiences; he must, in the teacher-pupil relationship, accept withdrawal of his own concerns. If the child is to enter into really worthwhile experience during his relations with the educator, his involvement must be with something he can acknowledge as 'other' than himself. Inescapably, the demand here is for a mature educator seeking little personal gratification and accepting subordination of himself in the teacher-pupil relationship.

In Buber's exploration Herbert Read and Marjorie Hourd found definitions of the teacher's role which admirably matched their own view of the adult qualities most likely to encourage children's art and poetry. Herbert Read lays heaviest emphasis upon the love needed by the child, while Marjorie Hourd is interested in Buber's insistence upon loving detachment. Although her affinities with the progressives are evident in her assertion that 'The aim of the literature lesson is . . . to provide a means towards a fuller development of personality',[34] unlike many, she sees the teacher's role as one of disciplined responsibility. Her views are much like Buber's. Agreeing that 'there can be no education of any value unless a relationship is set up between teacher and child',[35] she recognises the complexity of what she is recommending, saying, that it is 'difficult to describe'.

'The technique of knowing and yet appearing not to know, of consciousness in unconsciousness, action in non-action, is the one recommended in this book.'[36]

Martin Buber, Herbert Read and Marjorie Hourd all place upon the teacher a responsibility that is almost religious in nature. To the Newbolt Report's call for 'missionaries', they add the qualities of affection, imaginative sympathy, intuition and emotional maturity.

The teacher is described as 'whispering', suggesting how children should 'plant . . . on upturned soil', encouraging children to 'plant something of their own'.[37] In her section on adolescence and the teacher's role in the promotion of social sympathy, Marjorie Hourd, anticipating criticism of some of her recommendations, says:

'To give scope to this "creative sensibility" is not to sacrifice children to . . . ceaseless mind-wandering and endless phantasy, but it is to provide them with an opportunity to realise their affinity with the universe.'[38]

'Opportunities to realise their affinity with the universe', like many similar assertions about the nature of children's creativity, introduces a different kind of religious note from that struck in the Newbolt Report's recommendations. Its call for 'missionaries' was for men of action who, with fervour and energy, would struggle to inspire love of literature and to promote social unity in spite of misunderstanding and hostile conditions. Theirs was a public mission, to preach the gospel of high culture and to succeed through convincing sincerity and force of personality. During the 1920s, however, widespread acceptance of progressive theories produced new versions of the ideal teachers. This acceptance involved embracing the romantic view of childhood, a high valuation of individuality, and hostility to conformity and standardisation. In wider society, moreover, developments in art, music and literature which challenged established traditions were reinforcing progressive educators' emphasis on spontaneity, the personal and the unconscious. Thus, the somewhat muscular notion of missionaries propounded in 1921 gave way, during the 1930s, to the elusive image of the 'whisperers'. This in no way, however, meant a decline in the English teacher's importance; accompanying the developing notion of the validity of the child's vision are different but weightier definitions of the good teacher's responsibility. For the child to fulfil his visionary creative potential, thus playing a vital part in our achievement of a brighter future, his teacher needed special spiritual qualities.

'His help is needed in reaching those instinctive forces of the personality; and further in bringing the child into touch with the past and future of the ages, with what Jung called " the collective unconscious", and Wordsworth "the ghostly language of the ancient earth".'[39]

Throughout recommendations like this, it is assumed that English teachers must be special people; they must be able, through personal attractiveness, to draw a creative response from the widely differing personalities of their pupils, and they must be sufficiently mature to resist self-gratification through exercise of their personal powers.

In books published since the war much evidence can be found of the persistence of these ideals. In *The Exploring Word*, in which he is critical of over-intellectualising teacher-training, David Holbrook argues about the need for personal maturity in the teaching situation. In his, and in later proposals, the influence of progressivism upon redefinitions of the teacher's role is very clear.

'Education, especially the education of literacy, creativity and response to works of the imagination, is a natural subjective process, largely intuitive. It is also a process to do with love, with giving and receiving, and with sympathy and insight . . . as teachers, we must uphold the significance of intuition and "touch", and resist ignorance, misunderstanding and such impulses of intellectual hostility as threaten the great creative movement in English teaching. . . .'[40]

In his plea for the achievement of 'balance', Holbrook comes close to Buber's interpretation of the teacher-pupil relationship. Teaching, in Holbrook's view, is a 'creative process' which, to be effective, depends heavily upon 'intuition'. His discussion of English teaching is largely in terms of personal relationships, 'the meeting place between the imperfect struggling personality of the English teacher, and the incomplete and wrestling personality of the child',[41] the religious element in Buber having changed into its contemporary form of empathy, or affinity.

Similarly, Fred Inglis in *The Englishness of English Teaching* claims that an indefinable personal quality, an arresting life-style, characterise the outstanding English teacher. His critical comments on a number of teachers in schools where he made surveys of attitudes in English indicate his positive values. Of one teacher he says, as a reservation, 'He is not disposed to reach a long way down into his pupils',[42] and of another that 'His teaching, one might guess, is exceedingly competent, without reaching far down into them',[43] and of a third that 'There is little restlessness in DV, not a search to extend his responsibilities . . . not looking for more . . . but is tremendously thorough'.[44] By implication, thoroughness, competence and capacity for hard work are insufficiently inspirational qualities for the good English teacher. Writers like David Holbrook and Fred Inglis are continuing to ask for a special sort of person to teach English, to inspire enthusiasm for literature and, more importantly, to reach the child's inner being and draw out his creativity. The contemporary missionary is seen as a complex, intense, introspective personality who, in the classroom, has the charismatic power to stimulate his pupils' sincere self-expression. Fred Inglis, like other writers in this field since the Newbolt Report, asks much of the English teacher. After all, the artist is likely to be a more complicated character than the missionary.

'His responsibility is to the experience of his children, their minds, emotions and spirits, and to the value of his age, his history and the moral sense of his race. He needs a peculiar responsiveness to his children—almost, one is tempted to say, the responsiveness of the artist to his art—and they need to know this in him. It is a matter of knowing the right sort of magic to lead one child from a closed alley of experience into an open one.'[45]

The decline of religion in wider society, the process of secularisation, has had important effects on artists, and on other groups of people like the psycho-analysts, counsellors and teachers, all of whom in their different ways are concerned with the improvement of their fellow men. To them, it is frequently suggested, have been transferred the hopes which previously were invested in religion for the bringing about of a better world. Whereas it was natural for philanthropic liberals educated in the classical-Christian tradition of the public schools to refer to good English teachers as 'apostles' and 'missionaries', today's references are to the artist and the psycho-analyst. In the 1969 Autumn edition of *English in Education*, Raymond O'Malley, a lecturer responsible for preparing English graduates for teaching, wrote:

'It is of the utmost importance for the teacher to perceive the possibility of unconscious meanings, to respect them, and to leave them alone. A sympathetic intuitive adult reader is what the child most needs, and not an amateur psychologist. . . . The good teacher develops an acute sense of the presence of deeper meanings. He knows what not to remark upon. He knows how to give oblique reinforcement, but he is scrupulous not to know to much. This extra sense gives the necessary blend of reticence and warmth that makes for good teaching.'[46]

'Unconscious meanings', 'sympathetic intuitive adult' and 'acute sense of the presence of deeper meanings' convey assumptions similar to those made by the early progressive educators. What this statement about the good teacher suggests is that, in common with the progressives of the 1920s, O'Malley believes that children's creative work is supremely important; that there are 'deeper meanings'. In addition, he shares the view that the teacher's role is to be taken very seriously in this context because it carries responsibility for the personal development of the child. The teacher himself is seen as a creator, someone involved in a delicate, growing relationship. It is hoped that he will be unusually sensitive in his relations with children, fully understanding the symbolic meanings of their writing and sufficiently tactful to absorb these meanings for enrichment of later relationships. The implication is that the teacher—almost the God-like figure of Buber's description—will interact with the developing child over a period which covers his maturation. A number of progressive notions inform these recommendations: reverence for childhood's activities; a sense of need for adult responsibility; the supremacy of the inner, the implicit, private and intuitive over the public and explicit. Noticeably, Martin Buber's recommendation that the teacher's approach should blend reticence and warmth remains a central concern for educators in English. As long as they hold a romantic view of the child and continue to invest hope in him for a better world, they continue to call upon some semblance of a deity to foster his development.

What this discussion is primarily concerned about is the increasingly heavy burden which, from the late nineteenth century, has come to be placed upon English teachers. Responsibility for reviving a genuine folk culture has, this century, been added to the Newbolt Report's insistence that they should offer liberal education throughout all classes of society. Growing acceptance of progressive theories of education, with their emphasis upon children as artists, has added further force to the developing ideology of English in schools. Contemporary reverence for children's creative work, the romantic conviction that the deepest truths rest within its artlessness, have contributed to this already powerful ideology a new and highly problematical dimension. The notion has been introduced that the teacher who fails to stimulate artistic creations is, in some indefinable but serious way, a failure as a person; he lacks either style, or maturity, or more dismally both and, therefore, is failing the child and the larger cause of education's achievement of a better future. Progressivism's contribution to what, in his analysis of counselling, Paul Halmos calls 'the ideology of progress at the heart of Western Man's social thinking'.[47] has been its faith in the vision and achievements of the child. As this affects English in schools, with its predominantly personal and aesthetic content, it has meant a significant redefinition of the teacher's role. His authority as an instructor has been reduced, while his responsibility as childhood's guide has been increased. Because the relationship between adult and child has come to be defined as a subtle, intimate affair, independent of, or transcending the workings of the school as an institution, recommendations for its conduct tend to invoke mysteries, making a virtue of their vagueness, 'working the upturned soil'. They have much in common with the literature of counselling which teems, Paul Halmos, says, 'with declarations of faith in the virtues of empathy'.[48] This following extract from Marjorie Hourd's writing about creativity illustrates how progressive theories have drawn the activity of English teaching close to therapeutic activities in wider society. It illustrates, also, in its reference to the 'gift', the writer's belief that the qualities of the good teacher are inescapably elusive; they cannot be worked for, or trained. In *Coming into Their Own*, she says:

'Perhaps the most important asset for a teacher engaged upon creative work of any kind is the capacity to wait upon the moment, and sometimes to wait and wait. It is, of course, a gift essential to the psychoanalyst.'[49]

Notes

1. R. W. J. Selleck, *English Primary Education and the Progressives, 1914–1939* (London, Routledge, 1972), pp. 66 f.
2. Ibid., p. 87.
3. Caldwell Cook, *The Play Way* (London, Heinemann, 1971), p. 356.
4. Sir P. Nunn, *Education: Its Data and First Principles* (London, Edward Arnold, 1920).
5. Margaret McMillan, *Education through the Imagination* (London, Dent, 1923), Preface.
6. Quoted by W. Boyd and W. Rawsome, *The Story of the New Education* (London, Heinemann, 1965), p. 78.
7. *Handbook of Suggestions* (1927), p. 18.
8. R. Finch and C. W. Kimmins, *The Teaching of English and Handwriting* (London and Glasgow, Blackie, 1932), Chap. 5, *passim*.
9. Spens Report (1929), p. 152.
10. Ibid., p. 156.
11. Ibid., p. 218.
12. Ibid., p. 226.
13. Ibid., p. 228.
14. Margaret Phillips, *Education of the Emotions through Sentiment Development* (London, Allen & Unwin, 1937), p. 14.
15. Sir H. Read, *Education through Art* (London, Faber, 1943), p. 202.

16. Ibid., p. 209.
17. Marion Richardson, *Art and the Child* (London, University of London Press, 1948), p. 60.
18. Ibid., p. 82.
19. Marjorie Hourd, *The Education of the Poetic Spirit* (London, Heinemann, 1949), pp. 90, 98.
20. Peter Abbs, *English for Diversity* (London, Heinemann, 1969), pp. 66 f.
21. J. R. Squire and R. K. Applebee, *Teaching English in the United Kingdom* (USA, National Council of Teachers of English, 1969), p. 92.
22. Ibid., p. 120.
23. Michael Baldwin, compiler of *Poems by Children* (London, Routledge, 1962), Introduction.
24. Squire and Applebee, op. cit., p. 43.
25. Brian Way, *Development through Drama* (London, Longman, 1967), p. 3.
26. Ibid., p. 4.
27. Sir H. Read; quoted by Peter Slade, *Child Drama* (London, University of London Press, 1954), p. 122.
28. M. F. Andrews (ed.), *Aesthetic Form and Education* (Syracuse University Press, 1958), pp. 22, 55.
29. Slade, op. cit., pp. 124 f.
30. Selleck, op. cit., p. 98.
31. Read, op. cit., p. 230.
32. M. Buber, *Between Man and Man* (London, Kegan Paul, 1947), 1926, pp. 93 f.
33. Ibid., p. 95.
34. Hourd, op. cit., p. 13.
35. Ibid., p. 17.
36. Ibid., p. 19.
37. Ibid., p. 96.
38. Ibid., pp. 108 f.
39. Ibid., p. 120.
40. David Holbrook, *The Exploring Word* (Cambridge, Cambridge University Press, 1967), pp. 40 ff.
41. Ibid., p. 151.
42. Fred Inglis, *The Englishness of English Teaching* (London, Longman, 1969), p. 40.
43. Ibid., p. 43.
44. Ibid., p. 54.
45. Ibid., p. 42.
46. Raymond O'Malley, 'Creative Writing in Schools', in *English in Education: Writing*, Vol. 3, No. 3 (Autumn 1969) (Oxford University Press, NATE), pp. 75 f.
47. Paul Halmos, *The Faith of the Counsellors* (London, Constable, 1965), p. 190.
48. Ibid., p. 117.
49. Marjorie Hourd and Gertrude Cooper, *Coming Into Their Own* (London, Heinemann, 1959), p. 19.

Chapter 9

F. R. Leavis and Cambridge English

'We cannot, as we might in a healthy state of culture,
leave the citizen to be formed unconsciously by his
environment; if anything like a worthy idea of
satisfactory living is to be saved, he must, he must
be trained to discriminate and to resist.'

F. R. Leavis and D. Thompson, *Culture and Environment*

A discussion of the most important influences upon English in schools
since the First World War must include a separate consideration of
the work of F. R. Leavis. Although, as we shall see, there was already
a tradition within Cambridge English to engage in wider educational
issues, it was Leavis who tightened the link between English studies
at university level and the school teacher's responsibility in the outside world. Believing in the central value of great literature, and in
the need for critical discrimination in our debased cultural environment, Leavis gave English teachers the responsibility for training
pupils, and hence citizens, 'to resist'. Bringing rigour and purpose to
English studies at Downing, Leavis inspired many graduates to enter
teaching, to introduce his critical methods into schools, colleges and
university education departments. They envisaged the exercise of
critical discrimination as a form of continuous warfare against hostile
forces in the environment. Leavis demanded men 'who would fight',
and many graduates responded to the battle cry by entering schools
to teach English as he had taught them. They adopted his aggressive
stance, his military imagery and his combative tones; and as the
cultural crisis was viewed as increasingly desperate, they became
'warriors' in the place of the 'preachers', 'missionaries' and 'ambassadors'. Men who have become very influential in the field of English
teaching—Denys Thompson (*Reading and Discrimination*, 1943), who
has edited *English in Schools* and *Use of English* over a period of
twenty-five years; Boris Ford (*Young Readers, Young Writers*, 1960),
who has held three chairs of education; G. H. Bantock (*Education in
an Industrial Society*, 1963), who has a chair of education; Frank
Whitehead (*The Disappearing Dais*, 1961), who is on the editorial

board of *Use of English* and the National Association of Teachers of English (NATE); and David Holbrook *English for Maturity* (1965)—have all drawn their enthusiasm, their commitment to literature and criticism from the Cambridge English School. They have, as have many of their students, taught, lectured and written on the role of English in schools. Several members of this group have co-operated to edit *English in Schools* (1939–49) and *Use of English* (1949–   ). In addition, when the professional organisation, the National Association of Teachers of English, was established in 1963, Boris Ford, Frank Whitehead, and Esmoor Jones who had studied at Downing, held its main offices. With far-reaching effects upon the strengthening ideology of English in schools, each of these figures has undertaken his work in Leavis's spirit of serious dedication. Denys Thompson summarises their shared viewpoint in characteristic terms in an article in *Scrutiny*: 'In an ordinary school, all the time a literary education is striving to sharpen percipience and to provide standards, it is fighting a running engagement against the environment.'[1] All of this group, and now several younger men like Fred Inglis, share Leavis's certainty about the imminence of cultural catastrophe unless English teachers, in sufficient numbers, join their crusade for encouraging pupils' discriminating response to all aspects of their environment.

Leavis and his first disciples were deeply worried in the 1930s about what they saw as severe threats to quality of life at every level: communism and fascism; the conditions of work and leisure in advanced industrial society; university indifference to their 'serious' approach to literature. Their response was to put their faith in the teacher's power to encourage the spirit of criticism. Their proposed solution to problems of 'false' living produced by commercial culture was the development of pupil's ability to respond individually to great literature. Through the critical method they would learn, it was hoped, to reject the persuasive appeals of the media.

Firstly, however, it is necessary to make a brief survey of English studies in the universities in order to explain the desperate tones of Leavis's recommendations for the subject. During the nineteenth century, lectures on literature at the college level had been given mainly in the proliferating Mechanics' Institutes, of which about five hundred had been founded by 1850. Literature, it was hoped, would, by its enriching nature, act as a protection against the students' corruption by seditious political material. Palmer suggests that the widespread popularity of inspirational informal lectures on literature played an important part in the ultimate introduction of English studies into Oxford and Cambridge.

Its inclusion as a subject by London had certainly done little to hasten its acceptance by the ancient universities. As Stephen Potter observes:

'Because the London degree was likely to be suspect from the start, in order to "keep up the standard", examinations were made a more rigid test here than anywhere else. . . . London, wanting both the necessary type of tutor for individual teaching, and actuated by utilitarian principles, made its first contribution to the New Subject in these early days a codification, an examinification, a disciplining, a chastening.'[2]

Although English studies were well established in Scottish universities (chairs of English language and literature were established at Glasgow in 1862, Edinburgh in 1865, Aberdeen in 1893 and St Andrew's in 1897) where English literature was studied in classes of rhetoric and logic under a system much like the Dissenting Academies, here, in late nineteenth-century England, its status was extremely low. In the 1880s, English studies 'were expanding rapidly, but the expansion was only lateral',[3] that is, in elementary schools, girls' schools and Mechanics' Institutes, but not in public schools and universities.

The sole study of English at Oxford and Cambridge, until the mid-nineteenth century when scholarship turned its interest to Middle English, was the study of English language, in its earliest form of Anglo-Saxon. The work of James Ingram on the *Anglo-Saxon Chronicle* and J. J. Conybeare on Anglo-Saxon poetry (both occupants of the Rawlinson Chair of Anglo-Saxon founded at Oxford in the late eighteenth century) had helped greatly to advance the subject. Until 1904, when its linguistic studies were transferred to the Rawlinson Chair of Anglo-Saxon, the Merton Chair of English Literature and Language at Oxford was identified exclusively with language teaching. And it was unfortunate for the supporters of English literature at universities that during the nineteenth century English language scholars had concentrated their attention more and more upon philology and phonetics. Generally trained in Germany and influenced by the German conviction that a speech which had lost its inflexions was in a state of decay, language scholars tended to resist the entry of English literature at university level; their tendency was to despise the language of Shakespeare, Milton and Wordsworth as degenerate. Chadwick expressed his regrets about this to the Newbolt Committee.

'At the time when the first Honours Schools in English were established, philology was regarded as their main object. This was due to the fact that German influence was paramount.'[4]

Oxford's tutors, believing that the function of universities was to advance knowledge at the highest level, opposed the introduction of a subject which, from their almost scientific standpoint, lacked rigorous mental discipline. Like the public school headmasters, who despised English for its association with the education of girls and the working classes and who rejected it for its lack of difficulty, Oxford's tutors insisted that its acceptance would threaten their high academic standards. While the supporters of English literature at university level attacked the narrowness and sterility of philological studies, their opponents maintained that its entry would endanger the contemporary quality of education. J. S. Collins, a brilliant lecturer on literature with the London Society for the Extension of University Teaching, criticised philology in these terms:

'It certainly contributes nothing to the cultivation of taste. It as certainly contributes nothing to the education of the emotions. The mind it neither enlarges, stimulates nor refines.'[5]

E. A. Freeman, Regius Professor of History, in direct opposition insisted upon the addition of Slavonic to language study; attacking Collins in 1887, he said:

'It is surely allowable that some studies are undesirable because they are not solid enough, and others because they are in a certain sense too solid, that is, because they are too technical . . . all things cannot be taught . . . the crammer cannot teach taste.'[6]

The feeling, therefore, persisted at Oxford that English was insufficiently demanding as an academic discipline. As Palmer shows in his detailed discussion of the situation, Oxford's attitude is represented by Grose, a member of the Hebdomadal Council's Committee, who assured the House that the English School 'would harmonise, not interfere with the Literae Humaniores School, though it would be really advantageous, if it drew off the weaker candidates from that',[7] and by the theologian, Professor Sanday, who said 'the women should be considered and the second- and third-rate men who were to become schoolmasters'.[8] Thus, at Oxford, English developed more or less as a study of philology, its 'scientific coolness' supplying the discipline which the reading of novels and poetry obviously lacked.

At Cambridge, however, the situation was different. On the surface, certainly, Cambridge appeared unimpressed by the claims which were being made for the new subject's educative value. In his account of the development of English studies at Cambridge, E. M. W. Tillyard refers to the 'meagre and haphazard provision for the teaching of English before 1919'.[9] English, as an independent Tripos, consisted of two sections—Modern and Medieval, and Old English. Students were allowed to combine one of these with a part of any other Tripos, few choosing to take both parts. Tillyard claims that, before the war, English was thoroughly despised by Cambridge, and that Medieval and Modern Languages were known as the 'Courier's Tripos' and English as the 'Novel-Reading Tripos'. Nevertheless, before the war much thought was being given by some scholars at Cambridge to the establishment of an English Tripos concentrating mainly on the critical study of literature as defined by Matthew Arnold. In 1913, deeply influenced by Arnold, A. C. Benson, Fellow of Magdalene, proposed a 'School of English' which 'might set a mark upon the education of this country'.[10] Arnold, Benson, and Quiller-Couch in his *Lectures on English* ('On the Art of Writing', 1916; and 'On the Art of Reading', 1920) linked the notion of founding an English School concentrating on literature with the cultural health of the country, a link which was also made by the Newbolt Committee and again later by Leavis in the 1930s. In Cambridge, before the First World War, several scholars were at work preparing the English Tripos of 1917, and were concerned to promote the critical study of English literature at the highest level of the education system. Insisting on the historical rather than on the literary value of Anglo-Saxon, and opposing compulsory philology, H. M. Chadwick and H. F. Stewart (who did most of the shaping of the Tripos) and Quiller-Couch (its main apologist) played a vital preparatory role for Leavis. These figures shared a vision of a better future in which the foundation of their new English Tripos, which finally became independent of the Modern Languages Board in 1926, was to play a central part. These scholars had a strong sense of responsibility to education. In 1914 Benson said, in reply to an attack on his proposals for an English School, 'I believe that English is very shortly going to become an integral part of every school curriculum . . . and teachers for this purpose will have to be found and trained'.[11] And in his Preface to *On the Art of Reading*, Quiller-Couch wrote: 'The real battle for English lies in our Elementary Schools, and in the training of our Elementary Teachers.'[12] When Leavis, drawing on the different critical powers of T. S. Eliot (*The Sacred Wood*, 1920), I. A. Richards (*Practical Criticism*, 1926) and W. Empson (*Seven Types of Ambiguity*, 1930), evolved what came to be recognisable as 'Cambridge English', he retained these earlier scholars' sense of mission, 'this sense of obligation' to all levels of education and society, as well as to the furtherance of knowledge, and 'faith in the saving effects of literature'.[13] The two main characteristics of the men responsible for shaping the English Tripos, their belief in the critical method and their concern with the responsibility of education, have distinguished Cambridge English from 1913, through Leavis, to the contemporary work of disciples like David Holbrook and Fred Inglis.

The Newbolt Report's chapter on English at the universities conveys widespread confusion about the subject. It describes the situation in 1921, gives the various opinions expressed about existent proposals for English courses, and makes its own recommendations. The contributors to this Report, who were in the main very sympathetic to the Cambridge scholars' hopes for English, write persuasively about raising the subject's status at university level. Convinced of its humanising value, and optimistic about its likely bonding effects between different classes in society, the members of the Committee argue for its recognition by the ancient universities. Their fear is lest English continue to be viewed as a soft option by the classicists, and their problem is, while making a strong case for its humanising power, to fend off Oxford's recommendations that it should be primarily a philological study. Although the Committee acknowledges the desirability of movement outwards from literature into history and philosophy, and movement inwards from knowledge of Anglo-Saxon and Middle English into modern literature, it is anxious lest the new subject become submerged beneath all those added by professors keen to raise its academic respectability. The reader gets the impression of a Committee almost overwhelmed by witnesses' anxieties about the dire consequences for university studies if English courses were encouraged to be separate from the classics.

'The University teachers of English who have given evidence before us are very nearly unanimous in desiring that a candidate for English Honours should have some acquaintance with Greek and Latin literature and if possible with both. It has indeed been contended by a distinguished authority that English literature without such an acquaintance is "not very profitable".'[14]

Although the majority of witnesses were clearly in favour of linking English with the classics, the Newbolt Committee members were much less enthusiastic. Where the Committee was prepared to extend outwards from English literature, it was into Anglo-Saxon and pre-Chaucerian texts. Another serious problem was the consideration of the claims of philological studies in university English courses. In the section, 'The Study of Language in the Universities', the precarious state of English becomes even clearer. While the classicists disdained the new subject from outside, deeming it appropriate only for women and less-able men, the linguists considered that theirs was the only acceptable version of the subject at a university level. And linguistics had already established itself as a respectable discipline with the Rawlinson Chair of Anglo-Saxon at Oxford, and the Elrington and Bosworth Chair at Cambridge. The Report indicates the strength of the linguists' position.

'The scholars who chiefly influenced the examinations in English of the University of London and the Cambridge Modern and Medieval Tripos, and somewhat later the Oxford Final Honours School of English Language and Literature, had either been trained in Germany or were under the influence of German educational ideals and methods . . . . At a time when the first Honours Schools in English were established, philology was regarded as their main object. In our Tripos English and German were run on parallel lines, and the course was based on the courses pursued in German universities.'[15]

Strong opposition to this monopoly of English studies by the linguists was expressed by Professors Chadwick, Raleigh and Ker, and the Committee, clearly impressed by the force with which numbers of witnesses objected to the 'scientific' approach to literary studies, moved towards this conclusion:

'. . . before the post-graduate period, in the teaching of the English language in the pre-Chaucerian stages, philology and phonetics should be given a subordinate place, and that the chief aims should be to enable students to read our earlier literature with understanding and enjoyment. . . .'[16]

The Report employs the term 'humane' throughout these discussions. The Committee is keenly aware of its dilemma; concentration upon the humane to the exclusion of the classics, history, philology, modern languages and philology, was to incur contempt for the 'soft option', while inclusion of other subjects could diminish the humanising potential of the central humane study. Professor Chadwick opposed compulsory philology with considerable bitterness; believing that English literature owed more to 'Mediterranean' and French influences than to Teutonic, he argued that 'it cannot be too clearly recognised that compulsory philology is the natural and mortal enemy of humanistic studies.'[17] The Committee members suggest, finally, a compromise; they propose that candidates should, with the study of modern writers, be allowed to choose their complementary course from Anglo-Saxon, Middle French and Medieval Latin. Thus, while accepting that English students should take a second course, they do not insist that it should be Anglo-Saxon. Their fears lest the English School becomes 'overloaded with primitive literature' are very clear; their concern is primarily with recommendation for the establishment of English Schools which would become 'true Schools of the Humanities'. At every stage of the argument, while concessions are made to the claims of other languages, convictions are expressed firmly about the educative power of English studies at the very highest academic level.

At the end of their discussion, care is shown for practical matters such as numbers of university scholarships and endowments for fellowships, doubtless in response to Chadwick's assertation that 'Cambridge has abundance of endowments for post-graduate work in classics, but practically nothing for English studies'. And there is also concern about provision of teaching staff. It is strongly recommended that the growth of teaching posts in English in the past twenty years should continue. The chapter's conclusion, which is about professors' salaries, usefully indicates the precarious status of the new subject and its vulnerability in the face of the traditionally established disciplines.

'The endowment of an English Chair should at least be equal to that of any other humanistic Chair in the particular institution. It should be impossible in the future for a modern provincial university to advertise side by side vacant Chairs of Greek and English in which a substantially higher salary was attached to the former than to the latter, though the students taking Greek would necessarily be far fewer than those concerned with English.'[18]

The following is a summary of the situation as far as English at universities was taught after the First World War. At London, where courses could be taken in Language and Literature, the stress, because of the dominant role of examinations, was upon facts and the history of literature. At Oxford, English studies were primarily linguistic, while at Cambridge, although two English courses were available, it was unusual for students to take both and more acceptable for one English course to be linked with another discipline. Supporters of English studies were preoccupied with the subject's central problems of the relative merits of facts about literature, or good taste in literature. Although facts could be taught, this would fall far short of the subject's highest humanising potential; although the training of taste was undeniably attractive, professors asked each other whether it could be done. Some supporters looked to the addition of other easily taught subjects to support the fragile new undertaking, while others fought for the establishment of a new, humane, central study as disciplined and ennobling as the classics had once been.

In 1967, remembering the early days of the 'Cambridge School', Leavis dedicated his lecture to H. Munro Chadwick, and Mansfield D. Forbes, 'to whom the world owes more than it knows'. He recalled warmly the contribution which they both made to the foundation of an English School liberated from linguistics and classics; they had, he said, the foresight to leave 'Oxford in the nineteenth century with London and strike boldly out with the institution of a distinctly literary English course'.[19] This, he said, was a 'creative response' to the society's needs after the First World War, to which the ' "classical" tradition of Form, Latin versifier's taste, conventional externality and *belles-lettres*'[20] was utterly irrelevant. Acclaiming the brilliance of Mansfield Forbes, he referred to Forbe's contrivance of I. A. Richards's association with the Cambridge School, an involvement which introduced a critical rigour into English studies, sharpened by his antagonism to the bad art of the mass media. He said this about Richards's *Principles of Literary Criticism*:

'The benefit it conferred was liberation. To be released from the thought-frustrating spell of "Form", "pure sound value", prosody and the other time-honoured, quasi-critical futilities had a positively vitalising effect that can hardly be done justice to today.'[21]

Like Leavis, E. M. Tillyard pays tribute to Cambridge's response to the depressed mood of the post First World War period. He suggests that this depression gave the main impetus there to the creation of a new course designed to provide resistance against the evils of modern industrial society. Palmer and Tillyard agree that the fusion of Freudian psychology, G. Moore's linguistic philosophy, and I. A. Richards's critical method gave Cambridge's modern English School its unique 'astringency and discipline'. Palmer says that Richards must be acclaimed as 'the main instrument in this country, and perhaps anywhere, of developing in literature the seminal ideas of G. Moore in philosophy',[22] out of these, he says, developed the practice of analytical criticism. This absorption of other disciplines had the effect of immeasurably strengthening English studies and liberating them from their burdens of classics and philology.

I. A. Richards's work is dominated by two main ideas, both of which are central to Leavis's critical approach and evident in the work of teachers and critics trained in the Cambridge tradition. One was that art and the rest of human activity are continuous and not contrasting. He denied vigorously the notion of the isolated, aesthetic experience, the separate and essentially different nature of artistic creation, asserting, consequently, the normality of the artist.

'The fashion in which the experience is caused in us is different, and as a rule the experience is more complex and, if we are successful, more unified. But our activity is not of a fundamentally different kind . . . . The world of poetry has in no sense any different reality from the rest of the world and it has no special laws and no other worldly peculiarities. It is made up of experiences of exactly the same kinds as those that come to us in other ways . . . . It is more highly and delicately organised than ordinary experiences. . . .'[23]

The second important idea was that art is the most valuable of all activities because it encourages what Richards described as the balancing and ordering of our impulses. Although Richards has been severely criticised for the vagueness and elusiveness of his theory of impulses, his belief which developed from it about the 'improving' power of great art has been extremely influential. His argument gained considerable persuasiveness from his analysis of contemporary popular culture which, he claimed, hindered personal balance and integration by its power to 'dis-organise' through its continual stimulation of 'stock responses'. Gloom about the post-war years' industrial squalor, despair about the growth of the popular press and cinema, and defensiveness against classicists' and linguists' contempt for literary studies accelerated acceptance of Richards's critical views. His analysis of popular culture was convincing to supporters of English literature. His evolution of critical principles for English which competed convincingly with science, and confounded the traditional charges of 'soft option', was of immense help to the foundation of a new academic School. D. W. Harding suggests that it is the understandable uneasiness of the English specialist in the face of classical confidence and scientific objectivity which partly accounts for Richards's employment of psychology in his critical work; he refers to it as 'a means of shaking the complacency of practical people who are more uneasy at the hints of psycho-analysts than they are at the gibes and fury of artists'.[24]

Richards thought that art's confinement to the special, rarefied realm of the aesthetic could have pernicious effects upon the cultural health of society.

'For many reasons standards are much more in need of defence than they used to be. It is perhaps premature to envisage a collapse of values, a transvaluation by which popular taste replaces trained discrimination. Yet commercialism has done stranger things .... Sinister potentialities of cinema and loud speaker . . . best sellers, magazine verses . . . music hall songs . . . are decreasing in merit .... At present bad literature, bad art, the cinema, etc. are an influence of the first importance in fixing immature and actually inapplicable attitudes to most things. Even the decision as to what constitutes a pretty girl or a handsome young man, an affair apparently natural or personal enough, is largely determined by magazine covers and movie stars. The quite common opinion that the arts have after all very little effect upon the community shows only that too little attention is being paid to the effects of bad art.'[25]

More emphatically, making the move from bad art and the individual's inability to reject it, to a debased society, he argues the need for a critically discriminating and subtly appreciative public. Unequivocally, Richards equates 'fine conduct of life' with 'fine ordering of responses'. As Leavis and his students were to suggest or imply, Richards asserts: 'Bad taste and crude responses are not mere flaws in an otherwise admirable person. They are actually a root evil from which other defects follow. No life can be excellent in which the elementary responses are confused and disorganised.'[26] Given Richards's influence upon Leavis, and his upon succeeding generations of students, their role in giving English in schools a special significance is clearly of great importance. Raymond Williams writes that: 'It is not too much to say that *Principles of Literary Criticism* . . . contained a programme of critical work for a generation . . . on this attitude to good and bad literature a whole subsequent critical and educational programme has been based.'[27]

In *Culture and Society*, Raymond Williams links Richards and Leavis in his section 'Two Literary Critics'. He draws attention to their likeness to Arnold in their equation of 'culture' with 'criticism', and notes their powerful influence upon English education. Of Leavis he says, in his discussion of *Mass Civilisation and Minority Culture*:

'. . . given its reference to Richards. [it] is the effective origin of that practical criticism . . . which has been of growing importance in the last quarter century . . . it is not neglible to have instituted a practical method of training in discrimination—a method which has been widely applied and yet can be greatly extended in our whole education system.'[28]

Like Richards, Leavis believed that modern urban society was in a state of cultural disintegration. Ugly environments, mechanical work rhythms and the trivialising media had, in his view, replaced the small organic agricultural communities, their traditional values, daily intimacies and traditional crafts. Even more seriously for the cultural health of society, he has always argued that standards are declining at the highest levels. The liberal education of the past which the classics had offered had degenerated into a pedantic study bearing no reference to real life conduct. Leavis felt with immense conviction that English literature should now replace the classics as the humane centre of academic study, not as a 'soft option', but as a discipline characterised by a critical rigour as demanding as the sciences. Classics, Anglo-Saxon and Bloomsbury *belles-lettrism* were, in their different ways, too remote from life and its need for fine and discriminating use of language—our one remaining tradition—and too effete in contrast with science to be the humane centre of university study. In 1934, he wrote:

'We know that, in such a time of disintegration as the present, formulae, credos, abstractions are extremely evasive of unambiguous and effective meaning and that, whatever else may be necessary, no effort at integration can achieve anything real without a centre of real consensus—such a centre as is presupposed in the possibility of literary criticism and is tested in particular judgements. But "tested" does not say enough; criticism, when it performs its function, not merely expresses and defines the "contemporary sensibility", it helps to form it. . . . It is the modern disintegration that makes it urgent in our day to get a real literary criticism decisively functioning.'[29]

Leavis insisted upon the centrality of English studies at university because of the opportunities they contained for sustaining tradition and providing continuity. Troubled by current disintegration of cultural standards, Leavis valued study of our literature because of its fusion of the traditional and the living. He hoped that the universities would take responsibility for the education of an intelligent, sensitive minority capable of appreciating the great works of the past and responding critically to contemporary literature, thereby sustaining and perpetuating a valuable tradition. Referring to university students, he proposed:

'At the centre of their work, in a way and under conditions to be discussed, would be a study of the literature of their own language and country—the most intimate kind of study, that is of a concrete tradi-

tion. And a study of tradition in literature involves a great deal more
than the literary.'[30]

Rejecting philology to provide the discipline necessary for English
study's academic respectability, Leavis proposed the literary-critical
discipline because, he claimed:

'It trains, in a way no other discipline can, intelligence and sensitivity
together, cultivating a sensitiveness and precision of response and a
delicate integrity of intelligence that integrates as well as analyses and
must have pertinacity as well as delicacy.'[31]

The act of discrimination, as defined by Richards and Leavis, demanded a finely judged response to a writer's use of language which
involved the reader's intelligence and feelings. Undertaken in order
to appreciate, with reasons, the precise nature of a writer's quality, it
involved the critic in an activity they defined as moral. Language, they
argued, is employed by the artist to recreate experience in such a way
as to affect our reactions to it. In discriminating between the supremely
accurate and sensitive and the banal or gross, Richards and Leavis
claimed that the reader was training himself to respond more
delicately to life itself. In 'A Sketch for an "English School" ', Leavis
wrote:

'The kind of work advocated entails, in its implacable discipline, a
most independent and responsible exercise of intelligence and judgement on the part of the student. The more advanced the work the
more unmistakably is the judgement that is concerned inseparably
from that profoundest sense of relative value which determines, or
should determine, the important choices of actual life. . . .'[32]

To the claims made for English by the progressives, hostile to industrialism and anxious about children's emotional development, the
Cambridge School added assertions about personal improvement
through critical engagement with literature. Richards and Leavis, like
the progressives, made their claims in tones of desperate urgency.
Deeply troubled by what they defined as cultural disintegration,
declining standards—'I have a more difficult task than Arnold had'[33]
(Leavis wrote in 'Literature and the University')—the exigencies of
our time, they were making their case for what they believed was
truly educative against the context of post-war depression and the
threat of mass-media control as exercised by the Nazis. In the March
editorial to *Scrutiny* (1934), Leavis wrote:

'The social and cultural disintegration that has accompanied the development of the vast modern machine is destroying what should have been the control, and leaves a terrifying apparatus of propaganda ready to the hands of the more or less subtle, more or less conscious, more or less direct, emulators of Hitler and his accomplices. What is to forestall or check them? . . . without an intelligent, educated and morally responsible public, political programmes can do nothing to arrest the process of disintegration— though they can do something to hasten it. . . . *Scrutiny* stands for co-operation in the work of rallying and strengthening such a public. . . .'[34]

Leavis, moreover, saw himself as fighting not only against the forces of cultural disintegration but also against academic indifference. Evidence of the anger and frustration experienced by those supporting English studies in the face of traditional classical and philological superiority exists in 'The Discipline of Letters' by Q. D. Leavis in *Scrutiny* (1943). Discussing Raleigh's and Gordon's refusal to take literature seriously at Oxford, she says that this 'shows what happens to ability when it is exposed to the atmosphere of classical studies pursued without any standards other than those of scholarship and of social snobbishness'.[35] Her anxieties about the status of English studies in the universities appear not to have been without foundation. Gibes about 'soft options', 'novelist's degree', and 'chatter about Harriet', which reflected academic concern about the subject's lack of discipline—and entrenched privilege's hostility to the middle-class entrants from grammar schools, and the increasing number of women students—appeared not to have died away completely by the 1960s. When V. W. Robson gave the F. R. Leavis lecture, 'English as a University Subject' in 1965, he said:

'The cutting away of English studies from the classical tradition, for which Mrs Leavis called in 1943, has now been accomplished. Faculties of English are not now staffed from classical departments. Even at Oxford, where the classics still retain a powerful social and intellectual prestige, the "English" don feels himself less on the defensive. True, there are still traces of the old snobberies; intellectual and social snobbery, as is often the English way, are curiously intermingled. Of the English school a classical don remarked to me recently that an intelligent man could read it in his bath. It is noteworthy that All Souls offers no fellowships in English or Modern Languages, and one can still hear the view expressed, or implied, that a gentleman does not need to study English Literature—or for that matter French:

English, like Modern Languages, is a somewhat plebean subject, read mainly by grammar school boys. And of course many of those who read English are women.'[36]

Leavis and his students marshalled themselves against all they disapproved of in the world of privilege, especially the way of life which they felt was represented by the Bloomsbury group. They were convinced that its *belles-lettrism* threatened their claims for the rigour of English studies in the face of established scientific objectivity. What Cambridge English saw as the Bloomsbury group's hedonistic, effete, sexually complicated life-style represented to them a deplorable, self-indulgent decadence. These literary figures fell far short of Leavis's ideal of moral improvement through engagement with literature. Lionel Trilling, commenting upon 'Dr Leavis and the Moral Tradition,' notes his strictness with Bloomsbury; he 'seeks to scotch the ideas of a privileged class represented by such writers as Lord David Cecil, Lytton Strachey, Clive Bell and Virginia Woolf. The Cromwellian revolution never really came to an end in England, and we can say of Dr Leavis that he has organised the lofty intellectual expression of its late endemic form'.[37] Leavisite certainty about the morally educative value of engagement with literature was sharpened into stridency by an apparently unimpressed opposition, the 'Academic English Club' to which Mrs Leavis referred so bitterly in 1943. 'It will', she said, 'go on recruiting its kind so long as it has a stranglehold on appointments in every university, and will continue to put up "à la mode" Gordons to maintain its supremacy'.[38] The need, she insisted, was for recruitment of 'new blood', for introduction of 'the living' to oppose 'the dead' into university English, in political terms, an attack on outworn, irresponsible privilege. The militant, crusading language of this article, like Leavis's lectures on the issue of university English studies, seems likely to have been provoked by his frustration. There is a similarly strong combative note in the work of many of his supporters who have felt threatened and ignored by the academic world and wider society.

'What English studies need then is not more scholarships but fresh contacts, cross fertilisation—Besides being educational in the real sense, so that English studies would be freed from that sense of futility so widely complained of by university students, it would give post-graduate and "research" students a real field of useful work. And other studies would profit. But can anyone be so optimistic as to believe that any university reform less violent than a bloody revolution would make such a prospect possible.'[39]

Disappointment about unrealised hopes for the establishment of an English School at Cambridge conceived and structured as the centre of humane studies, his and his wife's neglect by the Faculty, a disgust with the 'mediocrities' who had achieved high university appointment have, it appears in the 1960s and 1970s, added to Leavis's despairing contemplation of modern urban society. The new Tripos as he had designed it would have been 'a creative response to change —change in society and civilisation that had been made unignorable by the war'. This Tripos, with its potential for the production of a sensitively responsive minority capable of maintaining and continuing tradition, supported by teachers encouraging discrimination in schools, would have gone a long way, he believed, towards repelling the assaults being made on cultural standards by forces in wider society. The language of the following extract conveys the strength of his feelings.

' "This battle, desperate as the odds look, must not—shall not—be lost." What threatens us, the alternative to successful resistance, is too unspeakably repellent—the hope is the recognition of that. What we face in immediate view is a nightmare intensification of what Arnold feared.'[40]

Primarily, Leavis was concerned with the establishment of an English School at Cambridge, and most of his time has been spent teaching there, editing and writing for *Scrutiny*, and producing books on English literature demonstrating his disciplined critical method. In several places, however, he made clear his views about the relevance of his approach to work at school level.

'. . . what has been said has obvious applications at the school level, and much might be done if it were permitted, if there were teachers educated to do it, and if the examination system were not allowed to get in the way . . . the training of sensibility . . . might profitably begin at an early age. . . . Practical criticism of literature must be associated with training in awareness of the environment—advertising, the cinema, the press, architecture, and so on, for, clearly, to the pervasive counter-influence of this environment the literary training of sensibility in school is an inadequate reply.'[41]

In 1933 Leavis and Denys Thompson wrote *Culture and Environment* as a basis for work on discrimination in schools. The chapter headings indicate unmistakably the authors' hostility to the modern urban scene: mass production; advertising; fiction and the currency of national life; the loss of the organic community; substitute living; education. More intensely and precisely than the progressives, who wanted creativity to strengthen the individual's personal life against threatening external pressures, Leavis and Thompson reacted against the debasement of language in modern society because of its inevitable debasement of our emotions. Referring to I. A. Richards's work on the 'stock responses' stimulated by the mass media, Leavis and Thompson said:

'Those who in school are offered [perhaps] the beginnings of education in taste are exposed, out of school, to the competing exploitation of the cheapest emotional responses . . . . We cannot, as we might in a healthy state of culture, leave the citizen to be formed unconsciously by his environment; if anything like a worthy idea of satisfactory living is to be saved, he must be trained to discriminate and to resist.'[42]

As has been noted earlier, these calls have not been ignored. The Cambridge English School has, since the 1930s, produced not only professors and senior lecturers in university English and Education departments throughout the country, but authors of many influential books and articles, editors and chairmen of professional journals, and many secondary school teachers passionately committed to Leavis's literary critical approach to English. *Culture and Environment* has been reprinted many times since 1933 and its convictions restated throughout works like *The Disappearing Dais, The Englishness of English Teaching* and contributions to the quarterly *Use of English.* Those of Leavis's students who have considered English for the average and below-average pupils have made few concessions to recent proposals for the 'richness' of working-class culture to be included in the curriculum. G. H. Bantock and David Holbrook, both of whom have written fully about the curriculum of the less able, though they demand much more time spent upon affective subjects, define these by reference to high culture or the folk culture of our agricultural past. Their wish is to provoke pupils' critical response through their engagement with whatever music, art, drama and poetry can be related to their own lives, and through their own creative work. Whether concerning themselves with English throughout all abilities, or paying special attention to its purpose in the education of the less able, Leavis's supporters share his commitment to the view of literature as the central humanising experience of the curriculum and to critical discrimination as a morally educative activity. In the opening editorial of *Use of English*, Denys Thompson wrote:

'English is more than a subject. Its particular value (or "use") is that it can create and heighten that critical attitude to our civilisation which current affairs teaching should strive after. And thus, in formal education it can give unity and purpose to our syllabus . . . . It is a common place that education must educate against the environment. And yet, after eighty years of compulsory education the environment seems to be winning. Even while at school the child is falling into the grip of the entertainment industry and by the time he is an adult the quality of his reading suggests that the environment has won.'[43]

If the teacher is to 'win' he must be, not only thoroughly committed to the value of literature and hostile, too, to 'the environment', but also ready to engage in continuous battle for the well-being of his pupils. As the environment has become defined as worsening in cultural quality—the Cambridge English teachers, David Holbrook in particular, make persistent attacks upon current permissiveness in television and cinema—teachers are urged to strengthen their opposition to its products. Repelled by most contemporary culture, finding its sophisticated elements devoid of 'vision', writers like Holbrook remain true to the spirit of Sir Arthur Quiller-Couch's Preface of 1917. 'Can you not give them also', he asked, 'in their short years at school, something to sustain their souls in the long Valley of Humiliation?'[44] From Matthew Arnold to David Holbrook the response to this kind of question, with its strong indictment of the modern industrial environment, has been to recommend good teaching of great literature. In the period when religious imagery had lost its power, these teachers, once 'preachers', were redefined in military terms; 'the battle, desperate as the odds look, must not—shall not—be lost. . . .'

Throughout Parts I and II it has been suggested that the aims of English today have their origins in several convergent ideologies of personal and social improvement through the arts. The progressives' contribution was their theory of education of the emotions through creativity. Progressives, in common with students of the Cambridge School, distrusted industrialism; like Leavis, they looked back regretfully to England's lost organic rural community. Their response to the threatening forces in modern society was to suggest the promotion of personal development through craft, music, dance, drama and the composition of poetry and prose under the guidance of sympathetic and mature teachers. Leavis's response was to campaign for the establishment of an English School which, he believed, would ensure the education of an élite to salvage a disintegrating civilisation, and to promote the activity of critical discrimination which would 'train citizens to resist'. Progressive educators and the Cambridge School of

English believe that nothing less than society's quality of life is a stake, and they make their recommendations in similar tones of combative, religious commitment.

Since publication of the Newsom Report, and widespread accept-ance of its identification of children's linguistic competence as the major factor responsible for achievement at school, new developments have taken place within English which have seriously challenged the Leavisite assumptions. Since the war, for several reasons which will be discussed in the next chapter, interest has moved to the curriculum of the average and below-average pupil. While many educators, in-cluding the Newsom Committee, support the continued teaching of literature and discrimination, sharp reaction has been expressed by the New Left in English against the Leavisite exclusive concentration upon élite culture in schools. Great literature, it is now being argued, is not only inappropriate and inaccessible to the majority of our pupils whose time should first be spent on extension of their linguistic com-petence; its inclusion in all pupils' curricula, with the inevitable ex-clusion of working-class culture, implicitly supports the present social structure with all its inequalities. Thus, educators suspicious of Leavisite élitism are seeking to undermine the *status quo* by re-arrangement of the traditional 'middle-class' grammar school cur-riculum, dismantling literature into themes and projects, and trans-ferring interest from high art to their pupils' personal experiences. The New Left in education, unlike the Cambridge School, who un-hestitatingly defined its enemy as exploitative commercial culture, express their goals in much more precise political terms. From their standpoint, the Cambridge School's insistence upon the value of great literature and disparagement of commercial culture represents en-dorsement of middle-class values. Thus, radical educators wishing to promote all children's independence, confidence and personal fulfil-ment, have attacked Leavisite English for its role in perpetuating social divisions and injustices along with the tripartite school system, the traditional curriculum and authoritarian teaching methods. Wish-ing to achieve their goals with a sense of purpose equally strong as Leavis's or David Holbrook's, the New Left propose several major shifts of emphasis—from the school's values to the pupils', from the teacher's talk to the pupils', and from the subjects, high art in particular, to the experiences of the pupils' everyday lives.

Notes

1. D. Thompson, 'What Shall We Teach?', *Scrutiny*, Vol. 2, No. 4 (March 1934), p. 384.

2. S. Potter, *The Muse in Chains* (London, Cape, 1937), pp. 141, 154.
3. D. J. Palmer, *The Rise of English Studies* (London, Oxford Univeristy Press for the University of Hull, 1965), p. 64.
4. Munro Chadwick; quoted in *The Teaching of English in England* (London, HMSO, 1921), p. 217.
5. J. C. Collins, *The Study of English Literature* (1891); quoted by Palmer, op. cit., pp. 83 f.
6. E. A. Freeman, 'Literature and Language', in *Contemporary Review*, Vol. 52 (October 1887), pp. 540 ff; quoted by Palmer, op. cit., p. 99.
7. Grose; quoted by Palmer, op. cit., p. 111.
8. Sanday; quoted by Palmer, op. cit., p. 111.
9. E. M. Tillyard, *The Muse Unchained* (London, Bowes & Bowes, 1958), p. 64.
10. A. C. Benson, letter to the *Cambridge Magazine* (6 December 1913).
11. A. C. Benson, 'Rejoinder', in the *Cambridge Magazine* (31 January 1914).
12. Sir A. Quiller-Couch, *On the Art of Reading* (Cambridge, Cambridge University Press, 1920), Preface.
13. R. C. Townsend, 'The Idea of an English School: Cambridge English', in *The Critical Survey*, Vol. 3, No. 3 (Winter 1967), p. 132.
14. *The Teaching of English in England* (1921), op. cit., p. 210.
15. Ibid., pp. 216 f.
16. Ibid., p. 219.
17. Chadwick, op. cit., p. 225.
18. *The Teaching of English in England* (1921), op. cit., p. 250.
19. F. R. Leavis, *English Literature in Our Time and the University* (London, Chatto & Windus, 1967), Introduction, p. 12.
20. Ibid., p. 13.
21. Ibid., p.17.
22. Palmer, op. cit., p. 154.
23. I. A. Richards, *Principles of Literary Criticism* (1924) (London, Kegan Paul, Trench, Truber, 1935), pp. 17, 78.
24. D. W. Harding, 'I. A. Richards', in F. R. Leavis, *Determinations* (London, Chatto & Windus, 1934), p. 229.
25. Richards, op. cit., pp. 36, 202 f.
26. Ibid., p. 62.
27. Raymond Williams, *Culture and Society 1780–1950* (New York, Anchor Books, 1960), p. 261.
28. Ibid., p. 265.
29. F. R. Leavis, *Determinations*, op. cit., Introduction, pp. 1 f.
30. F. R. Leavis, 'A Sketch for an "English School"', in *Education and the University* (London, Chatto & Windus, 1943), p. 19.
31. Ibid., p. 34.
32. Ibid., p. 35.
33. F. R. Leavis, 'Literature and the University: The Wrong Question', in *English Literature in Our Time and the University*, op. cit., p. 44.
34. F. R. Leavis, 'Why Universities?', in *Education and the University* (London, Chatto & Windus, 1943), pp. 118 f.

35. Q. Leavis, 'The Discipline of Letters', in *Scrutiny*, Vol. 12, No. 1 (Winter 1943), p. 16.
36. W. W. Robson, 'English as a University Subject', F. R. Leavis Lecture (1965) (Cambridge University Press), pp. 21 f.
37. L. Trilling, 'Dr Leavis and the Moral Tradition' (1949), in *A Gathering of Fugitives* (London, Secker & Warburg, 1957), p. 143.
38. Q. Leavis, op. cit., p. 22.
39. Ibid., p. 26.
40. F. R. Leavis, 'English Literature in Our Time and the University', op. cit., Introduction, p. 33.
41. F. R. Leavis, 'How to Teach Reading', in *Education and the University*, op. cit., pp. 137 f.
42. F. R. Leavis and D. Thompson, *Culture and Environment* (London, Chatto & Windus, 1942), pp. 3 ff.
43. D. Thompson, editorial in *Use of English*, Vol. 1, No. 1 (Autumn 1949).
44. Quiller-Couch, op. cit., p. 73.

Chapter 10

Socio-Linguistics:
English and Social Justice

'A speaker who is made ashamed of his own language
habits suffers a basic injury as a human being: to
make anyone, especially a child, feel so ashamed is as
indefensible as to make him feel ashamed of the
colour of his skin.'

M. A. K. Halliday, A. McIntosh and P. Strevens,
The Linguistic Sciences and Language Teaching

English in schools, as currently defined, consists of four highly valued
classroom activities: the experience of literature; creativity; critical
discrimination; and classroom talk. Paying attention almost exclusively to the first three, we have been considering them in relation
to relevant developments in education and wider society. Anti-
industrialism in literature, criticism and educational writing, progressive theories about activity and growth, and the Cambridge School
of English have been selected as the major influences upon English in
schools. The very recent enthusiasm for encouragement of children's
classroom talk has its main origins, however, in other developments.
Progressive theories, particularly about the value of activity and
child-directed learning, have certainly made some contribution to
this enthusiasm. In addition, scholars of the Cambridge School have
opposed passivity by giving support to personal engagement with
literature. These groups, though, have not been centrally concerned
with children's oral work, nor have they been primarily motivated by
a sense of social justice. Progressive theories which have brought
dramatic activity into the classroom have placed stress upon its role
in promoting personal development. Unlike many educators associated with the growing importance of oral work, however, these
groups were not specifically concerned about the transfer of power
from teachers to pupils.

   This chapter discusses the recent high value invested in children's
oral participation, linking its supporters' strong sense of social justice

with the relativism of modern linguistics. It describes the recommendation being made to English teachers for promoting 'oracy', noting the kind of responsibility which they are being given for children's 'personal development and social competence'.[1] It suggests that, to a very great extent, this new language teaching has drawn its sense of social justice from widespread anxiety during the past ten years about working-class children's underachievement in the schools. Its goals, often expressed in very emotional language, are adding, now, more new hopes to an already highly ambitious ideology.

The 1944 Education Act and the movement, during the past twenty years, towards comprehensive schools have indicated government interest in removing some of the inequalities of this country's social structure. However, in spite of the removal of financial barriers to extended education, and the expansion in higher education, research has revealed that the great majority of working-class children are failing at school. Committees set up in response to concern about social justice and wastage of the nation's talent have, until recently, focussed attention upon working-class children's poor physical backgrounds and their parents' unsympathetic attitudes towards education. It was not until 1963 that official acknowledgement was made of the central responsibility of children's retarded linguistic development for educational failure. The Newsom Report, drawing upon research in psychology and socio-linguistics into children's acquisition of language and its relationship with social class, said:

'The evidence of research increasingly suggests that linguistic inadequacy, disadvantages in social and physical background, and the poor attainments in school, are closely associated. Because the forms of speech for all they ever require for daily use in their homes and the neighbourhoods in which they live are restricted, some boys and girls may never acquire the basic means of learning and their intellectual potential is therefore masked.'[2]

Although the Report echoes the Newbolt Committee's assertion that 'until a child has acquired a certain command of the native language, no other educational development is even possible',[3] its proposals to teachers show some significant differences from those made in 1921; and its recommendations for further research into causes and remedial techniques have been much more far-reaching. While the Newbolt Committee was critical of the 'grammar book' concept of English, suggesting the pursuit of linguistic competence through drama, talks, discussion and writing about personal experience, it supported the practices of persistent correction by teachers, and children's imitations of their teacher's good pronunciation. Eager to propose English teaching which would produce social unity, the Committee said:

'It is emphatically the business of the Elementary School to teach all its pupils who either speak a definite dialect or whose speech is disfigured by vulgarisms, to speak standard English, and to speak it clearly, and with expression.'[4]

The Newsom Report places its heaviest stress upon classroom discussion. It asks the teacher to seize every opportunity in lessons 'to provide material for discussion—genuine discussion—not mere testing by teacher's question and pupil's answer',[5] and asks him to question, when he teaches, whether 'it is all monologue, or a reasonably balanced dialogue in which the pupils get a fair chance; is he interested in what they have to say?'[6] What the Newsom Report is advocating derives principally from developments in educational theory which support children's activity and the reduction of teachers' authority in the classroom. Throughout this century, from the important German Art Conference in 1901, through Sir Percy Nunn's work on individuality and Sir Herbert Read's *Education through Art* (1943), up to Carl Rogers's recommendations for encouragement of creativity (1961), convictions have been expressed by progressive educators about the value of children's activity and participation. Their increasing dissatisfaction with the mechanisation of men in advanced industrial society has deepened their hostility to the traditional academic curriculum and its teacher-directed methods of learning. In reference to the Second World War, Sir Herbert Read wrote: '. . . the secret of our collective ills is to be traced to the suppression of spontaneous creative ability in the individual. . . .'[7] Within the particular context of oral work, however, the Report's proposals derive also from the relativism of modern linguistics, findings in psychology about language acquisition, and in sociology about the relationship between language acquisition and social class.

This century, in reaction against earlier scholars' concentration upon the written language and traditional grammarians' perception of speech as an 'incorrect version of standard literary English', linguists have asserted the primacy of speech. Consistent with their subject's standing as a descriptive science, they have rejected making qualitative judgements about human communication. In his evidence to the 1921 Report, Professor Wyld expressed the modern linguists' disapproval of prescriptive grammar teaching. It is a point of view which, as interest in linguistics has grown this century, has become more and more widely accepted.

'A grammar book does not attempt to teach people how they ought to speak, but, on the contrary, unless it is a very bad or very old work, it merely states how, as a matter of fact, certain people *do* speak at the time when it is written.'[8]

Modern scholars reject utterly the commonly held notion that children from working-class backgrounds can 'hardly speak their own language' on arrival at school. They assert that, unless suffering from brain damage, all our pupils are communicating with their family and friends very efficiently. What working-class pupils lack, in order to succeed on the schools' terms, are the opportunities available among the middle classes to practise communicating in a wide range of social situations. Attacking the unscientific nature of society's folk-linguistics, twentieth-century scholars are drawing our attention to the socially determined origins of our value judgements about children's speech. Halliday, McIntosh and Strevens say, in *The Linguistic Sciences and Language Teaching*: 'There is actually no such thing as a slovenly dialect or accent'[9] and that 'wrong is a social judgement'.[10] The convergence, here, of progressive theories and modern linguistics has severely threatened both traditional adult authority in the classroom and conviction about the value of great literature. Progressives' and linguists' insistence upon the validity of children's experience and expression, and their hostility to adult imposition of standards of correctness have been responsible for radical changes of emphasis in English in schools. Drama, poetry, novels and essays have been re-arranged into 'relevant' themes and topics, and interest has been transferred from the work of established artists to the children's own creations. The assertion that 'There is actually no such thing as a slovenly dialect or accent' can be viewed as the modern linguist's version of the following characteristically progressive statement from *The Dynamics of Aesthetic Form* by Michael Andrews.

'In the truly creative arts there is no teaching: only growing, learning and becoming . . . . Freedom is extended in the most paramount sense. The learner is considered the measure of all things.'[11]

Against the context of developing interest in linguistics in this country and research in sociology into the relationship between social class and academic achievement, the Newsom Committee made the following recommendation:

'Such work as has been done in the study of social and environmental influences suggests that the learning difficulties, including the linguistic, of many of the pupils with whom we are concerned can be related to home backgrounds .... Much investigation remains to be done, both in establishing the nature of the educational difficulties and in developing teaching techniques for dealing with them ....'[12]

After publication of the Newsom Report in 1963, money was granted to the Sociological Research Unit at the University of London Institute of Education. Its project, directed by Basil Bernstein, was designed to:

'(1) investigate the exact nature of linguistic differences and their educational consequences among children from a lower working-class background;
(2) relate these language differences to differences in family structure and interaction;
(3) mount an experimental intervention programme to extend the range of communication of these children in the first three years of their school life.'[13]

Bernstein's subsequent work upon restricted and elaborated codes, with its obvious implications for the schools, has had a profound effect upon proposals for ways in which English should be more broadly interpreted. In addition, and lending persuasive support to these redefinitions of a subject, two influential books on the effects of home background upon pupils' achievement at school were published during the same period. *The Home and the School* (1964) and *Education and the Working Class* (1962) have raised, in a more general fashion, the problems of discontinuity for working-class children entering the predominantly middle-class world of the secondary school. Apart from Bernstein, the most influential figure in the field of linguistics and language teaching has been M. A. K. Halliday, Director of the Nuffield Programme in Linguistics and English Teaching from 1964 to 1970. Under his guidance, Doughty, Pearce and Thornton worked upon the *Language in Use* Project, now widely used in schools. Since Newsom's recommendations, Bernstein's and Halliday's work has influenced several important books in the field of English language work. Drawing, in particular, upon Bernstein's concepts of the restricted and elaborated codes and upon Halliday's contribution to *The Linguistic Sciences and Language Teaching* (1964), the following works have made several radical recommendations for a changed approach to English in schools: *Language and*

Education (1966); *Talking and Writing* (1967); *Programme in Linguistics and English Teaching* (1968); *Language, the Learner and the School* (1969); *Lost for Words* (1972).

Taking their lead from the Newsom Report's proposals, all of these books insist upon the necessity for much greater pupil participation in lessons. Rejecting the notion of correctness, they replace it by the concept of appropriateness. Severely critical of the 'monolithic concept of correct English' which, it is asserted, is nothing more reliable than accumulated social prejudice, their authors indicate the destructive results of teachers' disapproval of working-class communication. In *Exploring Language*, Peter Doughty points out that:

'A study of teachers' attitudes in primary schools has shown that the child's ability to use the linguistic table-manners his teacher expects is a key element in determining not only the teacher's attitude to the child, but his assessment of his potential as a learner.'[14]

Modern linguistics' interest in 'how we use language to live' has led to a denial of the validity of judgements upon speech as 'wrong' or 'slovenly', consigning them to the realms of social prejudice and folk-linguistics. Scholars are particularly anxious to attack ignorance and prejudice in teachers as a preliminary to the important business of promoting pupil talk in the classroom. Doughty continues:

'Much common-room demand for a "clear, concise and intelligent English" is an expression of the wish that students' experience of language should coincide with that of the teachers' . . . . The linguistic table-manners that are thought to reveal the presence of this universally applicable "plain English" define and delimit the social group who are thought best suited to the staffing of the key institutions in our society, the Law, the Civil Service, Education, Company Administration, and so on.'[15]

Reaction against the schools' low expectations for performance of working-class pupils because of their inability to conform to 'standards" derived from social prejudice is often sharply expressed. The following statements usefully illustrate the sense of social purpose which underlies proposals for a changed approach to language teaching. The implication here is that the interested, tolerant and encouraging teacher in the discussion situation is engaged upon work for greater social justice.

'A speaker who is made ashamed of his own language habits suffers a basic injury as a human being: to make anyone, especially a child, feel so ashamed is as indefensible as to make him feel ashamed of the colour of his skin.'[16]

Here, once again, we are reminded of the progressive educators' support for the democratic concept of individual worth. The relativism of modern linguistics, which has led to recommendations for greater pupil participation in lessons and distrust of schools' and teachers' judgements, gives persuasive scientific support to the psychotherapists' statements of faith about the conditions necessary for encouragement of creativity. Halliday's emotive references to 'injury as a human being' and the 'colour of his skin' bring his redefinitions of the teacher's role close to Carl Rogers's description in *On Becoming a Person*. Two essentials which Rogers cites for the 'psychological safety' needed to foster creativity are 'unconditional acceptance of worth'[17] and 'absence of external evaluation'. Emphasis, therefore, appears to have been shifted from the teacher to the taught, and from 'standards' to the child's performance, by both progressive educators and scholars in linguistics for reasons which, sometimes, are very similar.

Recent work in socio-linguistics suggests that the traditional school situation has been extremely unhelpful in promoting working-class children's 'personal development and social competence'. Their lack of access to the elaborated code because of the unavailability of social situations which demand it in working-class life appears to explain, in some measure, many working-class children's failure to manipulate the language of the school. The schools' almost exclusive concentration upon the 'representational' model of language, in spite of its irrelevance to the majority of their pupils, has had the effect of making this majority appear unresponsive and unpromising. In addition, the combination of teachers' social prejudices and their domination of most lessons, relieved only by questions demanding preconceived answers has, it is argued, hindered working-class children's academic progress and exacerbated their inarticulteness within the school situation. In Part 3 of *Language, the Learner and the School*, Harold Rosen quotes Flanders (1962) to open his argument against the teacher-dominated classroom.

'In the average classroom someone is talking for two-thirds of the time, two-thirds of the talk is teacher-talk, and two-thirds of the teacher-talk is direct-influence.'[18]

Similarly, Douglas Barnes draws our attention to the scarcity of open-ended questions in the lessons he observed, while Andrew

Wilkinson, who gave this area of English the term 'oracy', protests against the pupils' passivity in most schools. He says:

'The conventional educational situation imposes a receptive not a productive linguistic role on the pupil. It has given one-way communication, from the teacher to the taught. Many forces are combining to bring about changes here, particularly the psychologists' insistence upon the essential activity of the learner, though the changes have gone further at a primary level than others.'[19]

In addition to the teachers' tendency to dominate their classroom and their inflexibile attitude towards working-class pupils' speech, their allegiance to correction through traditional grammar books comes in for severe criticism. Although frequent attacks—as early as the 1921 Report and the English Association's 1923 Pamphlet (No. 56)—have been made against formal grammar teaching, this has persisted in schools and continues in many now. Lest official thinking appeared to be neglecting standards, the Board's *Suggestions for Teachers* supported it, even in 1933, when the desirability of freedom and creativity was generally accepted. In the *Year Book of Education* the following summary appeared: 'Without a groundwork of grammar, a child is left without a standard whereby he can correct his errors.'[20] To many teachers, too, formal grammar teaching offered some sort of safeguard against the 'inaccuracy' of the new, spontaneous, unsupervised original writing which, it was being argued, was essential to children's emotional growth. Also, since that situation persisted (which was deplored in the 1921 Report) of frequently unwilling non-specialist staff being given responsibility for English, they approached the task through the methods with which they felt safe. Today, even though grammar questions have disappeared from examinations in English, anxiety lest 'prescriptive' teaching continues— because of its irrelevance to the growth of linguistic competence and its underlying assumption of one, unassailable standard of correctness—draws bitter hostility from recent writers in this field. Halliday, McIntosh and Strevens write:

'Prescriptive teaching therefore means selecting those patterns, at any level, which are favoured by some, including some of the more influential, members of the language community, and using standard teaching practices to persuade the children to conform to them. . . . Is our language so poor and uninteresting a thing that we put it in the school curriculum only in order to fight for its lost causes, to pass pathetic judgements on some of its marginal features?'[21]

Although supporters of a new approach in English teaching through oral work are not, in general, hostile to the current emphasis on literature and creativity, reservations are expressed about exclusive concentration upon these for working-class pupils. Halliday criticises teachers' ignorance of linguistics and of the ways in which the discipline can make classroom English more profitable, saying that the university study of literature is 'not very closely related to teaching English in schools'.[22] He is, though, as much concerned about their neglect of other uses of English apart from the literary which, if given exclusive concentration, is likely to prohibit most pupils' enjoyment through lack of understanding. Without undervaluing the literary experience, supporters of oral work justify it partly on the grounds that the experience and confidence which it will give might make the literary use of language more comprehensible. He says:

'. . . if the English teacher does not teach the non-literary uses of English, there is no one else to do so. . . . Moreover, the pupil is more likely to appreciate English literature if he can also understand and get the most out of English in its non-literary uses. Literature is only literature against the background of the language as a whole.'[23]

This century's romantic view of children's creativity has been strengthened both by psychologists' finding about language acquisition and growth, and linguists' rejection of the superiority of adult communication. Critical of the schools' habitual tendency to employ an exclusively representational model of language, linguists have, like the progressives, proposed increased encouragement of the personal. In children's use of language across the curriculum, encouragement of the personal, particularly if this were to be reflected in a radically altered approach to the use of language in textbooks, would increase their enjoyment of experience at school. Halliday suggests that the danger in separating the written and spoken language in children's work is that it 'puts a brake on children's self-expression and leads ultimately to the listlessness of some classroom essays'.[24] Thus, progressive theorists, supporters of creativity in English and linguists appear, in general, to concur about the value of encouraging children's creativity, of starting with their experiences, of 'keeping the flow going',[25] without 'fussing about grammar and spelling'.

What must be noted, however, because of its likely responsibility for conflict between 'new' English teaching as interpreted by supporters of David Holbrook's approaches (the literary and creative) and as interpreted by the *Language in Use* team, is the team's criticism of an exclusively literary definition of the 'personal'. In 1968, in his introductory article to the *Language in Use* Project, Doughty drew attention to the disadvantages of teachers' basically literary training. He explains current uncertainty and bitterness about the appropriate role for English in schools by reference to the 'exuberant diversity of descriptive terms currently available . . . "creativity", "free writing", "theme", "project", "experience", "need", "maturity", "rich", and so on'.[26] Suspicious of the terms used for 'the critical discussion of literature, especially when the aim of the discussion is to assess the moral weight of a work for use in the classroom',[27] he makes the following attack on literary and creative English teaching:

'The major fact so often overlooked is the degree to which habitual notions about the value and function of all varieties of written English are derived from notions about the language of literature . . . . The only kind of written work acceptable to many teachers at present is written work that is recognisable as one variety of the language of literature, that is, the intensely autobiographic, densely metamorphic, syntactically highly informal, and devoted to the accurate reporting of personal response to experience. From the point of view of the pupils' needs as a whole . . . the limitations of this assumption should be apparent. One of the most unfortunate effects is the degree to which it ignored the nature and function of technical varieties of English, that is the working language of a complex industrial society.'[28]

Doughty asserts that the present stress upon literature and creativity is the contemporary version of the nineteenth century's approach to the classics. He argues that the majority of English teachers are working on the principle that if a pupil reads the best literature, it will 'rub off' on him and enable him to write the 'best English'. In his argument, the degree to which changes in approach to English teaching reflect developments in wider society is particularly noticeable. In reaction against what they perceived as the remoteness of the classics, reformers proposed study of the native literature. This, they hoped in 1921, would eventually succeed in binding together the divided social classes. Since then, research has revealed an immense wastage of working-class talent, and a reaction has set in against the élitism of a literary approach to English which, it is argued, is irrelevant and inhibiting to those who have insufficient competence to benefit from it.

  The real educational cultural problem of working-class children's academic failure is, Denis Lawton points out, 'essentially a question of range within a language, that is, that restriction in the control over a language involves a restricted view of the universe, a restricted mode of thinking, a restricted ability to benefit from educational processes'.[29] For language to be meaningful, it must, sociologists insist, be related to a meaningful social context. Since language learning is closely associated with role playing, working-class children need opportunities, in school, to practise a wide variety of roles which make specific linguistic demands upon them. Since working-class boys, research evidence reveals, produced the elaborated code inside a structured discussion, it is proposed that pupils from working-class backgrounds be given abundant opportunities for similar experiences. As Lawton says, 'they do have the potentiality available for utterances of a elaborated code kind, but they lack practice, and therefore facility . . . . If Bernstein's view of context, role, culture and language is accepted, then code learning, or extending pupils' range of control over language, must be achieved through changes in social structure of the school through extended possibilities of developing new role relations'.[30] To replace the old 'prescriptive' language teaching through grammar book exercises, Halliday recommends what he calls 'descriptive' and 'productive' language teaching, two proposals accepted by the authors of *Language in Use*. Halliday summarises his suggestions thus:

'Descriptive language teaching aims to show the pupil how English works; this includes making him aware of his own use of English. Productive language teaching is concerned to help him—to extend the use of his native language in the most effective way. Unlike prescriptive teaching, productive teaching is designed not to alter patterns he has already acquired but to add to his resources; and to do so in such a way that he has the greatest possible range of the potentialities of his language available to him for appropriate use, in all the varied situations in which he needs them.'[31]

Drawing on Halliday's views of the school's responsibilities, and Bernstein's recommendations for provision of those opportunities which demand 'inventiveness', 'the equivalence of competence', and their insistence that pupils possess 'meaning potential' but lack experience, the authors of *Language in Use* have constructed a series of situations for the classroom inside which 'the required growth of competence can take place'. Compiled for teachers of adolescents and pupils in further education, the project consists of 110 units, each built round a topic concerned with the way in which we use language. Part One explores 'Language—Its Nature and Function', Part Two explores 'Language and Individual Man', and Part Three is concerned with 'Language and Social Man'. The project sets out to relate 'the findings of Linguistic Science to what is feasible and desirable for pupils to explore in the classrooms',[32] expressing two goals: that children extend their repertoire of language codes through the schools' provision of opportunities to adopt a variety of roles (improvisations and sketches are suggested); and that they develop 'awareness' of the nature and function of language. These coincide with James Britton's aims, expressed in *Language and Learning*, in 1970:

'I see the beginning of school . . . not as the closing in of the workaday, but as the development of difference in language usage, a continuation and refinement, on the one hand, of language in the role of spectator, preserving the delight in utterance, providing for the contemplation of things in all their concrete particularity; and on the other hand the development by gradual evolution of language in the role of participant—language to get things done, the language of recipes and orders to the poultry-monger and of other more intellectual transactions.'[33]

Language in Use fills a gap between the discredited formal grammar and the highly technical structural linguistics, as yet unsuitable for adaptation below the sixth form. It provides teachers with a programme of work designed to improve linguistic competence and to introduce continuity into what its authors see as the potential chaos of 'imaginative' English. In so far as the project is practical and comprehensible in the confused area of English language work, it appears to be a welcome development for teachers. Nevertheless, its insistence upon the concept of 'appropriateness' to replace 'correctness', inside the context of encouraging greater social justice, creates a new kind of difficulty which the teacher must resolve. Ability to manipulate the elaborated code is assumed to be a desirable goal from the situations structured to encourage its use; but the teacher must not give the impression that this code is superior to the working-class child's everyday speech. Denis Lawton says:

'If the extension of the range of role relationships and opportunities for code learning are accepted as educational aims, a great deal of attention will have to be paid to appropriate methods of role learning and code learning, but in all cases the important factor should be that teachers should never give the impression to a working-class child that his culture in general, or his form of speech in particular is in any way inferior to the culture of the school. The concept of appropriateness rather than right or wrong speech and behaviour should become the desired end.'[34]

All recent proposals in this area insist upon reduction of the teacher's traditional authoritarian role. Non-standard working-class speech must be accepted in the classroom if children are to be successfully guided to participate in unfamiliar social situations offering them practice in switching language codes. The teacher will make the pupils' personal experience his starting-point, deliberately seeking information about which he has no authority to create their confidence in the value of their contribution to discussion. Much classroom work, it is suggested, should take place in pairs and 'mutually supportive' groups, instead of in the more traditional context of 'teacher-directed' discussion.

Concern about the value of the school experience of the average and below-average pupil, conviction about the need for greater pupil participation in what are acceptably 'real' situations, and insistence upon a radically altered relationship between teachers and children are common elements in the new language proposals and the recently conceived Humanities Programme. Harold Rosen draws attention to this in *Language, the Learner and the School*, suggesting that innovations in the curriculum have played an important part in focussing interest upon children's use of language. By reference to 'real situations', Peter Doughty and Geoffrey Thornton suggest that the interdisciplinary approach is inevitably the most suitable for language work.

'. . . questions about language activity in real situations, like homes and shops and factories and classrooms, do not readily yield to inquiries conducted exclusively within the boundaries of a single discipline. An appropriate form for Language Study is therefore going to have to be interdisciplinary.'[35]

Referring approvingly to Neil Postman's proposals in *Teaching as a Subversive Activity*, these authors claim that learners are facing 'a society in a process of continuous changes'.[36] Taking this as their central conviction, reinforced by their expressed hopes for society's movement towards reintegration of thought and feeling, they fuse the new approaches to language teaching with the teaching methods of interdisciplinary work. As has been noted, supporters of the new language methods wish to reduce teacher authority as part of their campaign to assert the primacy of speech, and to destroy the notion of the superiority of middle-class speaking habits. Supporters of the Humanities Project, a development with its origins also in concern about an appropriate curriculum for average and below-average pupils, are equally insistent upon a radically altered classroom situation. The project's goals—to 'encourage tolerance and the ability to think humbly'[37] and to 'assist the development of a capacity to make value judgements which are based on more than prejudice'[38]—are to be achieved through abundant classroom discussion. Its Director, Lawrence Stenhouse, says 'that if we wish students to be able adequately to meet important issues, these issues must be the stuff of the curriculum'.[39] Thus, it follows that the teacher cannot possibly be an 'expert' in these areas. His role, it is proposed, should be that of neutral chairman, not instructor. Stenhouse states firmly:

'Our strategy must renounce the position of teacher as "expert", capable of solving by authority all issues about values that arise in discussion—because the position cannot be logically justified. Yet it must be disciplined, so that the teacher understands his purely procedural authority in the classroom—his authority as "chairman" and can maintain it. Teaching must be based on discussion and inquiry.'[40]

Both the *Language in Use* Project and the Humanities Project have, as their goals, the promotion of what their supporters perceive as qualities in pupils' characters. The teachers, however, are strongly discouraged against any overt display of confidence in these qualities —ability to manipulate the elaborated code, and to make mature, liberal judgements—lest this inhibit the classroom involvement of children for whom they are unfamiliar. In spite of the acknowledged difficulties which these new approaches create for the teacher, both have been given the support of the Schools Council. Mounting dissatisfaction with the traditional school situation—prescriptive teaching, passive children, separated subject disciplines—expressed by progressive theorists appears, in the light of findings about working-class children's linguistic disadvantages, to be justified against the context of their failure to achieve in that situation.

It is mainly this sense of social injustice which gives recommendations for classroom change their urgency. Knowledge that 'a tiny percentage of the population has been given access to the principles of intellectual change, whereas the rest have been denied such access',[41] has led to proposals about teachers' changed attitudes towards working-class speech being made as if it is upon these that greater social justice depends. The tone is set by the Newsom Report.

'The overriding aim of English teaching must be the personal development and social competence of the pupil. And of all the different aspects of English, speech has by far the most significant contribution to make towards that development.'[42]

Halliday says that 'it is the teachers who exert the most influence on the social environment . . . by playing a major part in the process whereby a human being becomes a social man . . . . In the development of the child as a social being, language has the central role.'[43] This being so, there is considerable bitterness expressed about the persistence of folk-linguistics in schools and higher education, and anxiety to indicate its power to perpetuate the self-fulfilling prophecy about working-class children's inability to profit from school. There is, in his writing, a strong sense of the heavy price to be paid if the case for improved language work in schools is ignored.

'If it [English language] is left in the hands of amateurs—and the English Literature specialist is almost as much of an amateur in this context as is the scientist or mathematician—we can expect the result to be a nation of inarticulates.'[44]

Linguists are urged to think of themselves as 'missionaries in a new way' to their colleagues, and teachers aware of the crucial importance of classroom language as 'missionaries trying to forge in the school where they serve a language environment which makes sense'.[45]
A further dimension is added to the teacher's responsibility by what is implied by James Britton's use of 'sense'. Supporters of oral work share the Humanities Project's assumption about our need to consider an education which takes account of change. Both express concern about pupils' capacity to survive in what they see as society's state of flux; it rests, they claim, upon pupils' increased range of linguistic control and ability to confront controversial issues. Thus, on these grounds, rigidity in teachers' approach to language and values limits pupils' capacity to cope with the changing world outside; unless they abandon the notions of 'correctness' and 'right or wrong' answers, they will be failing to provide education which is preparation for life. It is useful, bearing in mind Postman's choice of title, *Teaching as a Subversive Activity*, to compare his assumptions with Harold Rosen's in *Language Study, the Teacher and the Learner*. Postman says, criticising conventional teaching:

'While they [students] have to understand psychology and psychedelics, anthropology and anthropomorphism, birth control and biochemistry, their teachers are teaching "subjects" that mostly do not exist any more. While they need to find new roles for themselves as social, political and religious organisms, their teachers . . . are shaping them up to be functionaries in one bureaucracy or another.

'Unless our schools can switch to the right business, their clientele will either go elsewhere (as many are doing) or go into a severe case of "future shock" . . . when you are confronted by the fact that the world you were educated to believe in does not exist.'[46]

Harold Rosen, making similar assumptions about change, places his emphasis upon the central role of language acquisition. He too, has his argument turn on the issue of the pupil's survival which, when viewed in conjunction with the demands for greater social justice, involves the teacher in a role which is as heavily responsible as that defined for him by the supporters of literature and creativity.

'If we have a climate of continuous change in society, then the struggle to make meanings out of a continuous flux of new experience demands an ability to perform rapidly and successfully a whole range of symbol exchanges . . . . As language plays so central a part in the autonomy and operational effectiveness of individual human beings, then their capacity for survival is seriously affected, in so far as they find themselves continuously in a situation where their attempts to make sense of new experiences frustrated by their lack of the necessary language for learning or language for living.'[47]

References to 'pupils' needs to find new roles for themselves', 'severe cases of future shock', 'capacity for survival is seriously affected' indicate the extent to which recent reformers believe that teachers have the power to affect society's quality of life. Halliday, indicting amateurism in English teaching, stated that our 'schools . . . are the main line of defence against pollution in the human environment.'[48] Although the difficulties are acknowledged as formidable, recommendations are made in tones reminiscent of the early progressives' warnings of imminent crises, and their notes of religious fervour. All recent contributors in this field acknowledge the problems—of an individual teacher's conflict with the traditional school; of children's bewilderment on meeting an unfamiliar approach; of the threat embodied in working-class language to a teacher's cultural values—and, in common with supporters of literature and creativity, demand exceptional qualities in the teachers. In order to stimulate discussion in an informal, relaxed atmosphere, they must inspire trust; to create confidence in children about the value of their oral responses, they must be open-minded. They must, moreover, if their interest is to be genuine, get to know the life of the school's neighbourhood. James Britton says of this: 'That it should matter is ultimately a test of our sincerity and of the degree to which we are prepared to throw ourselves into life itself . . . .'[49]

Upon the teaching of 'controversial issues' within the humanities, Lawrence Stenhouse says: 'We are working in a difficult and complex area where relatively high risks are justified by the prospect of substantial rewards.'[50] Echoing the Schools Council Working Paper No. 11 on *Society and the Young School-Leaver* ('there is no doubt that many of the more successful courses have depended upon the particular gifts of the teacher), he states that the role of neutral chairman is not easy, that the teacher's 'personality comes into it'.[51]

The argument of this book is that in response to changes in society and changes in educational theory, English has grown to dominate the secondary school curriculum. It has risen in status, grown bewilderingly diffuse and taken on a powerful sense of moral purpose. The discrediting of formal grammar teaching, part of the complex process which moved the experience of literature, and creativity, to the centre of school English, has meant that English language has been regarded with suspicion by imaginative and forward-looking teachers this century. Within the past ten years, however, as a result of widespread acceptance of research findings in psychology and sociology about language acquisition and its role in educational failure, new approaches have been proposed which, aiming to remedy social injustice, have added another dimension to an already powerful ideology. Today, language teaching as defined by the *Language in Use* team, far from being the despised mechanical routine against which progressive English teachers reacted with literature and creative writing, is proposed as the work of greatest relevance to the majority of our pupils. Whether viewed as an activity to be pursued in addition to these or to replace them, its supporters insist upon the value of its acceptance with a sense of purpose as strong as any other discussed in this book.

Notes

1. *Half Our Future* (London, HMSO, 1963), p. 153.
2. Ibid., p. 15.
3. *The Teaching of English in England* (London, HMSO, 1921), Introduction, p. 10.
4. Ibid., pp. 65 ff.

160/*The Preachers of Culture*

5. *Half Our Future*, op. cit., p. 29.
6. Ibid., p. 153.
7. Sir H. Read, *Education through Art* (London, Faber, 1943), p. 201.
8. *The Teaching of English in England* (1921), op. cit., p. 281.
9. M. A. K. Halliday, A. McIntosh and P. Strevens, *The Linguistic Sciences and Language Teaching* (London, Longman, 1964), p. 103.
10. Ibid., p. 107.
11. M. Andrews, 'The Dynamics of Aesthetic Form', in M. F. Andrews (ed.), *Aesthetic Form and Imagination* (Syracuse University Press, 1958), p. 61.
12. *Half Our Future*, op. cit., p. 103.
13. D. Lawton, *Social Class, Language and Education* (London, Routledge, 1968), p. 152.
14. Peter Doughty, 'Understanding, Exploration and Awareness', in *Exploring Language* (London, Edward Arnold, 1972), p. 31.
15. Ibid., pp. 31 f.
16. Halliday, McIntosh and Strevens, op. cit., p. 105.
17. Carl Rogers, *On Becoming a Person*, (London, Constable, 1961), pp. 34 ff.
18. Quoted by H. Rosen, *Language, the Learner and the School* (Penguin Papers in Education), rev. edn, Part 3, p. 120.
19. Andrew M. Wilkinson, 'The Implications of Oracy', in *Educational Review*, Vol. 2, No. 2 (February 1968), p. 131.
20. *The Year Book of Education* (1933).
21. Halliday, McIntosh and Strevens, op. cit., pp. 227 ff.
22. Ibid., p. 274.
23. Ibid., pp. 243 f.
24. Ibid., p. 229.
25. J. Britton; quoted in J. R. Squire and R. K. Applebee, *Teaching English in the United Kingdom* (Illinois, USA, NCTE, 1969), p. 118.
26. P. Doughty, *Programme in Linguistics and English Teaching* (University College, London, and Longman, 1968), Paper 1, p. 42.
27. Ibid., loc. cit.
28. Ibid., pp. 64 ff.
29. D. Lawton, op. cit., p. 76.
30. Ibid., pp. 140, 158.
31. Halliday, McIntosh and Strevens, op. cit., p. 241.
32. *Language in Use* (Schools Council Publications, 1971), p. 12.
33. James Britton, *Language and Learning* (Harmondsworth, Penguin, 1970), p. 128.
34. Lawton, op. cit., pp. 159 f.
35. P. Doughty and G. Thornton, *Language Study, the Teacher and the Learner*, Explorations in Language Study (London, Edward Arnold, 1973), p. 19.
36. Ibid., p. 40.
37. Lawrence Stenhouse, 'Society and the Young School-Leaver', Schools Council Working Paper No. 11 (1967), p. 39.
38. Ibid.

39. Lawrence Stenhouse, 'The Humanities Curriculum Project', in *Journal of Curriculum Studies*, Vol. 1, No. 1 (November 1968), p. 27.
40. Lawrence Stenhouse, 'Open-Minded Teaching', *New Society* (24 July 1969).
41. Basil Bernstein, 'Social Class, Language and Socialisation', in *Language in Education* (Open University Press and Routledge, 1972), p. 104.
42. *Half Our Future*, op. cit., p. 153.
43. M. A. K. Halliday, 'Linguistics and English Teaching Papers', Vol 3, *Language and Social Man* (London, Longman, 1974).
44. M. A. K. Halliday, 'Linguistics and the Teaching of English', in *Talking and Writing*, (general editor J. Britten, 1967), p. 81.
45. James Britton, 'Their Language and Our Teaching', in *English in Education*, Vol. 4, No. 2 (1970), p. 33.
46. N. Postman and C. Weingartner, *Teaching as a Subversive Activity* (Penguin Education Special, 1969), p. 26.
47. Doughty and Thornton, op. cit., pp. 40 f.
48. Halliday, *Language and Social Man*, op cit. (London, Longman).
49. Britton (ed.), *Talking and Writing* (op. cit.), p. 43.
50. Stenhouse, 'The Humanities Curriculum Project., op. cit., p. 33.
51. Stenhouse, 'Society and the Young School-Leaver', op. cit, p. 1.

Chapter 11

Changing Views of the 'Good' English Teacher

'Perhaps I can clarify my thoughts by saying that
these qualities which in the good teacher of any other
subject seem desirable, in the good teacher of English
seem essential. And the first of these essentials is
affection for the children he teaches. Very little can
be accomplished without this.'

J. Walsh, *Teaching English*

During the past century faith appears to have been transferred from religion and politics to education as the agency most likely to promote greater human happiness. Reorganisation of the schools, changes in the curriculum, improvements in the qualities of teachers are frequently proposed as likely to be effective in the achievement of desired social goals. A sceptical commentator on this optimism writes:

'What is it that can ease racial tensions, revitalise communities, transform our leisure hours, redefine women's role in society and prepare the elderly for a happier retirement? The correct contemporary answer is not God or socialism but education—as anyone will know who reads the appropriate correspondents in the quality press.'[1]

This book has tried to show that specially high optimism has been invested in English as the subject most likely to achieve desirable results. It has, throughout its history, been believed to contribute to pupils' personal and social development. Supporters of English, according to the nature of their dissatisfaction with the education system and wider society, have proposed that teachers involve children in the experiences of literature, creativity, discrimination and classroom talk. They have been deeply convinced about the special power of these activities to promote pupils' development in worthwhile ways.

Having traced the hopes for English to their origins and discussed them in relation to their historical context, this Part will end by considering the different qualities which have been demanded in the various supporters' ideal teachers. From the time when the vernacular literature was recommended as the humane centre of a liberal education until today when English has become bewilderingly diffuse, it has been given the heaviest responsibility in the school curriculum. The responsibilities of English teachers have grown correspondingly heavy and diffuse and, inevitably, men and women with exceptional qualities have been called upon to accept them.

Firstly, it is useful to recall briefly some of the key claims made for English during the past hundred years. In his Report for 1871 Matthew Arnold called literature 'the greatest power available in education'.[2] By 1921, when awareness of the public schools' neglect of pupils' emotions in their education was sharpening anxieties about England's class divisions, statements concerning the subject's power rang with conviction about spiritual salvation. Contributors to the Newbolt Report asserted that 'a realisation of what might be accomplished through English literature . . . would, if it became general among teachers, transform the face of our schools'.[3]

Equally high claims have been made for the various activities which have been gradually added to literature. A collection of essays on the need for increased opportunities for creativity in schools suggests very strongly that it is the cure for a whole range of personal inadequacies —indecisiveness, apathy, aggression, timidity, even hysteria. A contributor directs the reader:

'Just take a good look around you. Those who have lost their individuality really do not know what they want to do, what they themselves feel to be right or wrong, and are not at all interested in what they are doing. Their perceptions are dull. They think in a literal-logical way, possess competitive attitudes, and reject the new and strange. They are confused, bewildered, superficial, submissive and pessimistic. If asked to express their own experiences they may become frightened and frustrated to the point of tears. They may even display more aggressive emotional maladjustments and nonacceptable compulsions.'[4]

The progressives' strong sense of undeserved neglect appears to explain why this kind of exaggeration so often enters their work. Here, characteristically, it is suggested that a changed approach to learning will reform a wide range of attitudes and behaviour. They are, however, not alone in making sweeping claims in tones of confidence and certainty. It has already been noted that scholars of the Cambridge School, largely for similar reasons, frequently expected cultural catastrophe if their recommendations were ignored. Today Peter Abbs, deeply sympathetic with Leavisite English and, like David Holbrook, anxious to adapt it to less-able children, is making very wide-ranging assertions about what English can achieve. His book, appropriately called *English for Diversity*, argues that good teaching, as he defines it, can counteract the mechanism of our society, its synthetic culture. Good English teaching can, he suggests, promote 'awareness of freedom' and 'honest introspection'; it encourages the development of the 'imaginative, inventive and original man', capable most importantly, of 'tenderness and love.'[5]

Recalling, lastly, the two most recent developments in English—the new language teaching and interdisciplinary approaches—we must note that in these areas also the aims are ambitious. In the generally heated climate of discussion about English, their supporters' statements appear coolly expressed and relatively modest. New language teaching is proposed because it can create 'a language environment which makes sense'. The Humanities Project was designed 'to encourage tolerance and the ability to think humbly', 'to assist in the capacity to make value judgements which are based on more than prejudice'. Although passion seems to have disappeared in the transfer of interest from the spiritual to the social areas of pupils' experiences, this impression can be misleading. M. A. K. Halliday asserts, in support of his central argument, that 'it is the teachers who exert the most influence on the social environment . . . by playing a major role in the process whereby a human being becomes a social man'.[6] More suggestively, as far as his perspective on wider society is concerned, he writes: 'the school is the main line of defence against pollution in the human environment'.[7] In reality, supporters of the new language teaching feel as strongly about their proposed social goals as scholars of the Cambridge English School felt about their moral purposes. When James Britton calls upon English teachers to think of themselves as 'missionaries in a new way',[8] he underlines the intensity of Halliday's desire for teachers to fight 'pollution'.

After briefly summarising the key claims for what good English teaching can achieve, we shall look more closely at the actual qualities demanded of its teachers, noting particularly where they differ most sharply. The qualities which Henry Morley, London University's most energetic Professor of Literature, was looking for were both moral and intellectual: 'integrity, opposition to falsehood, quick apprehension, faith in children's goodness, high culture and attainment'.[9] The contributors to the Newbolt Report, stating that literature cannot be 'taught' but is 'communicated', asked for quite exceptional gifts 'and magic of personality'. While retaining the Report's strong missionary element in his recommendations, Leavis, in reaction to the perceived threats to quality of life from the mass media, called for 'warriors', for teachers who would fight. For more than thirty years a sense of impending catastrophe and the insistence upon the need for English teachers' crusading strength against exploitative commercial forces have characterised the Cambridge School's writing about literature and critical discrimination. Fred Inglis, in the 1960s, writes in tones very similar to Leavis and Thompson in the 1930s.

'If, as English teachers, we feel we cannot teach from our convictions, and that moral urgency is unseemly and impossible, then, again, we blink our function and must resign. However Calvinist it sounds, I am asking for a militancy against all that is hateful in contemporaneity, and for a brave access of energy to build on those things we have which are worth the holding.'[10]

The mood here is unmistakably aggressive—'urgency', 'militancy against all that is hateful', 'brave access of energy', all suggest the behaviour of strong teaching personalities, very committed to literature, and prepared to be a positive influence in the classroom. Teachers, as envisaged by Leavis and Thompson, and at times by Inglis must be highly cultivated men of fierce convictions who will inspire their pupils to resist their environment in a similar spirit. Since the early leading figures of the Cambridge School were mainly interested in university English and in improving the experience of English for grammar school pupils, their outstanding concern was with the teacher's relationship with great literature. The early publications were wholly militant in their condemnation of the environment and in their prescriptions about the teacher's role. Although, as we have noted, several important writers adopt crusading tones today in their proposals about the teacher's stance, there are variations, within Leavis's supporters, according to their degree of concern about less-able pupils. Most remarkably, David Holbrook and Peter Abbs have been attempting to adapt the Cambridge School's high valuation of great literature to average and below-average pupils. In *English for Diversity* Abbs recommends non-interference with children's writing, and in *The Exploring Word* David Holbrook suggests a more 'creative' approach to teacher education in the colleges and university departments Unlike the early Leavisites or today's most committed supporters, several influential figures pay sustained attention to the need for warmer relationships between the teacher and his pupils. Leavisite supporters of English—for example David Holbrook, Frank

Whitehead, Fred Inglis and Peter Abbs—who have responded sympathetically to progressive child-centred theories and widespread anxiety about average and below-average pupils, are making intellectual and moral demands upon the teachers which are as heavy as those of Henry Morley. Frank Whitehead, a Cambridge English scholar and editor of *Use of English*, insists upon the teacher's need to be both imaginative and unselfish.

'. . . we have to be prepared to engage ourselves with the real feelings, the real concerns, real problems of our pupils, exploring with them the issues which excite, perplex or distress them. Whatever these issues may be.'[11]

Stimulating awareness in teachers of a child's need for love, sympathy and trust has been part of the special contribution of progressive theorists to current definitions of English. An early example of this can be found in *The New Schoolmaster* (1914). Here Norman MacMunn claims that such altered approaches will 'be a perpetual delight' to imaginative adults and attract more people to the teaching profession. The teacher, he says:

'. . . will be at once the modest, patient, scientific observer and the sympathetic friend of his pupils; he will know how to be silent when there is no need to speak; he will be a natural (never a hypocritical) diplomat, with an instinct for saying with sincerity that which is psychologically apt; he will be profoundly an optimist with regard to individuals and to the mass; from the goodness of his heart he will make each boy feel that no boy is honoured nor more trusted than the boy before him.'[12]

Much more recently, in a collection of essays on what the authors define as a desperate need in the schools for children's creative activity, a contributor insists upon the following extraordinarily wide-ranging catalogue of virtues if a teacher is to achieve success in this area. What is of the greatest interest, though, is the way in which emphasis has moved from the teacher's intellectual distinction to his personal qualities, particularly those which encourage other people's development. The following extract illustrates how progressives can get carried away into making somewhat indiscriminate and unrealistic demands for qualities which are unlikely to be found in the same teachers. Although the writer places 'intelligence' last on his list of requirements, and includes 'intellect' only in so far as it is 'free' and being fostered in the child as a 'faith', nevertheless this is required of the same teacher who must possess all the other abilities and qualities in the six items.

'If the individual is to be led to good health and self-fulfilment the teacher must endeavour to:

'1. Be a person of exceptionally fine character. He must possess the personal stature and human attributes worthy of respect of all others: integrity, sincerity, friendliness, sympathy, optimism, patience, self-assurance, open-mindedness, self-control and intelligence.

'2. Establishes a favourable climate which challenges and allows for creative experience, sets up conditions of inquiry and self-actualisation, and frees the unconscious forces.

'3. Allocate enough time for experimentation, for exploration, for discovery, for incubation of thoughts and feelings, and to guarantee success.

'4. Encourage the learner to find the true, the beautiful, and the good within himself; to solve his problems with more than the literal-rational mind; to exaggerate, distort, emphasise, and abstract, if need be, to relate how he feels and what he believes; to tolerate strangeness; to question bias and prejudice opinions; to hold conventions and customs in reserve; and to develop a wholesome, self-satisfying philosophy of life.

'5. Foster in others a feeling of security, freedom, confidence, belonging, courage, independence; the integrity of thought and action; a faith in the free play of intellect and impulse; an awareness of their own being; an openness to unconscious thinking; a genuine sense of wonder.

'6. Accept and respect individual difference and idiosyncrasies, diversity of behaviour, and artistic manifestations, a variety of values, and the individual's own mistakes and discoveries.'[13]

Thus far, the content and tone of these recommendations reinforce the central theme of our discussion of English teachers. Whether supporters are interested in their encouragement of literature or creativity, they demand outstanding personalities for this work in the classroom. The Leavisite emphasis was upon intellectual distinction and moral courage; the progressive emphasis has been upon personal warmth. Educators who value literature highly and are, at the same time, concerned about less-able children, tend to make heavy demands upon teachers' intellectual and personal qualities alike.

When we examine the descriptions of good English teachers in proposals for the new language teaching and interdisciplinary work, we find that they are, predictably, closer in content to demands made upon those responsible for children's creative work. As mentioned in Chapter 10, James Britton and Patrick Creber advise teachers to accept readily working-class children's playground talk without surprise or disgust. More radically, several figures in this area propose abnegation of the teacher's traditional role. They suggest that, since the child or group of children is the rightful centre of the classroom activity, the teacher should join the class in the role of guide and fellow learner. Anthony Adams, describing his team-teaching experiments, says that the staff's aim was to produce a 'learning team in which pupils and teachers are engaged co-operatively in a series of teaching and learning situations'.[14] His department relinquished gowns and surnames—'we simply were prepared to be ourselves in the classroom as well as out of it'—to further their central purpose which was to secure their pupils' spontaneous, full participation in English lessons. Asking of his teachers 'well-stocked and lively minds and a fund of general knowledge',[15] Adams is, above all, seeking their ability to relax, to be informal, to have sufficient confidence in their adult status to move in and out of the traditional teaching role in order to join the children as fellow pupils. Acknowledging the difficulty of this situation, in which the teacher deliberately refrains from expressing disapproval of working-class children's language, Patrick Creber insists upon the need for confidence. In what he refers to as a 'verbally threatening situation', he says that 'the teacher's inner security must be sufficient for him to retain his capacity to discriminate between the various needs of those in front of him'.[16] Perhaps what we have arrived at is yet another paradox, as suggestive as the others of how very good, as a person, the good English teacher needs to be as defined by the subject's supporters. He must be an attractive personality who refrains from exploiting his power; he must encourage the creative ability in every child while leading him to appreciation of high art; among working-class children he must accept generously everything which is offered to him, mature and sufficiently confident in himself to resist feeling threatened by an alien culture without the support of his traditional teacher's authority.

In Chapter 10 we looked at the way in which the new language teaching relates to developments to integrate subjects into interdisciplinary work. Both arose, to a large extent, out of anxiety about a suitable curriculum for average and below-average children. Both number, among their supporters, educators who wish to promote greater social justice by means of a redistribution of power in the classroom. When, therefore, we come to look at the Humanities Project's supporters' description of the good teacher and good teaching, we arrive at the definitions farthest away from those offered by Fred Inglis. In Lawrence Stenhouse's view, teaching should be 'open-minded'; it should 'permit and protect divergence and maintain individual opinion'. While all this comes very close to the progressives' proposals in Item 6 about 'individual difference and idiosyncrasy', it is very unlike the suggestion that teachers should be 'militant'; and even more unlike Fred Inglis's statement about bravely building upon that which 'is worth holding'. Recommendations made by supporters of the new language teaching and the Humanities Project indicate an area of major conflict inside English teaching. While James Britton and Patrick Creber renounce 'correctness' and 'standards' in expression, Stenhouse renounces authority in content and values. Discussing his position in an article in *New Society*, he says:

'Our strategy must renounce the position of teacher as an "expert", capable of solving by authority all issues about values that arise in discussion . . . . Teaching must be based on discussion and inquiry.'[17]

Though very different from David Holbrook and Fred Inglis, with their insistence upon 'the good society', Stenhouse is, however, equally emphatic about the difficulties facing his teachers and the need for them to have certain personal qualities if they are to be successful. With significantly less intensity than Leavis's supporters, Stenhouse says, nevertheless, that 'the change of role in this kind of teaching is not easy for a teacher to achieve, we have found. His personality comes into it.'[18]

This final sentence marks a useful point at which to end this part. It draws together, by implication, the hopes and anxieties which have been associated with English teaching since it was first recommended as the humane centre of a liberal education. In addition, it anticipates some of the major problems within the subject's current ideology which will be discussed in Part III. What has been noticeable throughout the preceding argument is that supporters have all turned, finally, to the teacher's personality as being the crucial element in English in schools. When literature was the most highly valued experience, the 'personality' needed for success was confidently demanded to be that of a missionary or an ambassador. When interest shifted to the child, and confidence in the old certainties weakened, calls were made for more subtle, gentle and self-effacing figures. Stanley Hall's gold-mining analogy helpfully suggests this shift of perspective. Referring particularly to the teacher's work with adolescents, he writes:

'There is now evolved a penumbral region in the soul, more or less beyond the reach of school methods, a world of glimpses and hints, and the work here is that of the prospector, and not of the careful miner.'[19]

Where the main concern has been the children's experience, in creativity, oral participation or exploration of social issues, educators' imagery has suggested the ideal teacher who can effectively appear to withdraw. The missionary, ambassador and warrior have been replaced by the artist, psycho-analyst and chairman, figures who exercise control without external authority. This, it will be argued in Part III, is an extremely difficult role for the English teacher, who is being asked to achieve complex and ambitious goals while renouncing the traditional supports of 'correctness' in expression and the 'standards' of great literature.

Throughout these first two Parts it has become very clear that educators have been constantly searching for new, more satisfactory models for English. They must be worthy of respect and at the same time be relevant to changes taking place in wider society. Each new definition has produced a matching definition of the subject's ideal teacher. Ever since its development from basic skills into literature, creativity, growth through linguistic competence and engagement with personal and social problems, requirements of the good teacher have turned, finally, upon the individual personality.

Moving away from discussion of the forces in education and wider society most likely to have been responsible for current definitions of English, Part III will be entirely concerned with the subject's teachers. It will explore further the central question raised throughout this book about the special nature of English and its teachers as prescribed by its supporters. Why have we met repeated insistence on the need for people with outstanding personal qualities to teach English in schools? Thus far, this has been discussed in terms of educators' convictions about the power of their chosen activity to compensate for shortcomings in the education system and the outside world. In their view, because English plays such a vital role in pupils' lives, it should be entrusted only to the very best teachers.

While it has been essential to consider these convictions, their content, tone and origins, it is useful now to examine them against a wider context. Firstly, therefore, we shall look at the social background and education of recruits to the teaching profession, in the state sector, from its beginnings until today. It seems highly likely that the persistent demands for English teachers with exceptional gifts are explicable partly in terms of supporters' recognition of the academic and cultural inadequacies of many entrants to the profession. An unintended consequence, however, of their emphasis upon personal rather than academic excellence in English teachers may have been to retard the development of their professional status and confidence. This discussion will be followed by a detailed study of the tensions which can be related to the bewildering variety of prescribed roles for the good English teacher. His role is now not only disturbingly diffuse, but likely, at times, to conflict with the expectations held of it by various groups inside and outside school. It seems very possible that professional confidence is being shaken within English by internal conflict between its supporters, and even more by the misunderstanding and hostility which its teachers can create among staff, headmasters, pupils and parents.

Notes

1. Michael Irwin, 'The Left and Education', in *New Statesman* (4 May 1973), p. 644.
2. Matthew Arnold, General Report for the Year 1871, in *Reports on Elementary Schools, 1852–1882* (London, HMSO, 1908), p. 142.
3. *The Teaching of English in England* (London, HMSO, 1921), p. 106.
4. M. F. Andrews (ed), *Aesthetic Form and Education* (Syracuse University Press, 1958), pp. 61 f.
5. Peter Abbs, *English for Diversity* (London, Heinemann, 1969), publisher's note.
6. M. A. K. Halliday, *Language and Social Man* (1974).
7. Ibid.
8. James Britton, 'Their Language and Our Teaching', in *English in Education*, Vol. 4, No. 2 (1974), p. 33.
9. Henry Morley, quoted in W. A. C. Stewart and W. P. McCann, *The Educational Innovators* (New York, Macmillan, 1967), Vol. 1, pp. 292 f.
10. Fred Inglis, *The Englishness of English Teaching* (London, Longman, 1969), pp. 186 f.
11. Frank Whitehead, 'Why Teach English?' in D. Thompson (ed.), *Directions in the Teaching of English* (Cambridge, Cambridge University Press, 1969), p. 20.
12. Norman MacMunn, *The New Schoolmaster* (London, Smith Elder, 1913).
13. Andrews, op. cit., p. 62.
14. Anthony Adams, *Team-Teaching and the Teaching of English* (Oxford, Pergamon Press, 1970), p. 14.
15. Ibid., p. 88.
16. P. Creber, *Lost for Words* (Harmondsworth, Penguin, 1972), p. 103.

17. Lawrence Stenhouse, 'Open-Minded Teaching', in *New Society* (24 July 1969).
18. Ibid.
19. G. S. Hall, *Adolescence* (New York, Appleton, 1905), Vol. 2, p. 474.

Part III

THE IDEOLOGY
AND THE TEACHERS

Chapter 12

Social and Academic Background of Teachers

'Whilst within the professions in general, academic
ability is expected to be the principal intention of
competence, within the "people-oriented" professions
it is regarded as legitimate to reject the candidates
with outstanding technical ability but the "wrong
personality".'

R. N. Morris, *The Sixth Form and College Entrance*

What we shall be concerned with firstly in this discussion of English
teachers' confidence is the social and academic background of recruits
to the profession. A characteristic statement of George Sampson's
usefully recalls the content and tones of educators' hopes for what,
ideally, should be achieved in English and their sense of the need for
special people for the task. Children, he urged, in *English for the
English*, should be educated against their environment, and one of the
chief ways he proposed was through poetry in the classroom.

'I am thinking of . . . the class of young barbarians whose souls are
to be touched with the magic of poetry and whose souls will certainly
not be touched unless there is first a soul to touch them.'[1]

But souls with the necessary cultural refinement and confidence to
experiment with literature in the interest of the 'young barbarians'
were inevitably rare in the elementary school situation. Creative
teaching, such as Cecil Reddie had introduced at Abbotsholme and
Caldwell Cook at the Perse School, had taken place in small classes
of boys from prosperous homes taught by men educated at public
schools and the ancient universities. In 1943 Beacock acknowledged
this in his tribute to Caldwell Cook.

'One of the biggest problems we have to face is to find men and
women who can learn from Caldwell Cook and teach with his vigour
and enthusiasm.'[2]

Inspectors, however, who lamented the elementary school teachers' reluctance to abandon the old method of rote-learning and collective teaching, referring to them as 'creatures of tradition and routine',[3] appeared to be underestimating the degree of cultural sophistication and professional confidence demanded by the officially accepted, new, 'interest' theories. Contributors to the Newbolt Report regretted that 'teachers seem, at times, to be unaware of or afraid of their liberty and to desire the restrictions that no longer bind them';[4] they seemed puzzled by teachers' inability to be transformed into independent-minded innovators by a changed set of regulations. Their insistence, though, upon the need for higher academic standards in training colleges indicates that some contributors were aware of the indivisibility of cultural confidence and readiness to experiment in English lessons. Comparison between schools like the Perse, upon whose methods the Newbolt Report bases many of its proposals, and those in the state system, exposed the two major difficulties hindering the development of English as a liberal subject: the absence of culture and scholarship in teachers; and the hostile conditions in the schools. However praiseworthy the expressed aims of the inspectors and contributors who proposed widespread adoption of Caldwell Cook's methods, their proposals remained unreal against the context of professional insecurity.

The low standards of teachers' culture and academic attainment, which were regretted by the Newbolt Report, were inseparable from their lowly social origins and the confused, uncertain emergence of their profession. Throughout the nineteenth century, trained and untrained teachers had been recruited from the lower or lower-middle classes, their education deliberately kept to a minimum in order to calm society's fears about their likely social aspirations. From their beginnings, the training colleges were anxious to disclaim responsibility for producing 'empty intellectual pride'. J. Kay-Shuttleworth's *Report on Battersea* (1843), anticipating expressed goals of teacher education this century, asserted that 'the main object of the Normal School is the formation of the character of the schoolmaster'.[5] Character in this sense, however, meant sympathy with the lower classes, readiness to serve their needs without superiority, and reconciliation to 'a life of hard work and comparative penury'.[6] In his view, the teacher's role should be characterised by humility and religious zeal in the task of helping members of his own class. Asher Tropp, discussing the important religious issues which hindered the progress of provision of state education, refers to the Church's role in ensuring the persistently low academic level of elementary school teaching, its fear lest the early religious enthusiasm which inspired popular education gave way to social ambition. The Church's unease reflected middle-class resentment of its stereotype of the overeducted, socially ambitious, working-class teacher aspiring to rise to their level by means of his certificates of education. To allay these fears, the training colleges tried to intensify their students' personal humility and sense of religious mission, at the expense of academic excellence. Kay-Shuttleworth thought thus, about the training of working-class students entering Battersea:

'. . . it [is] essential for teachers of the poor to accept for themselves a way of life little different from that of their charges. It was not the intention of Battersea to encourage students to acquire increased social status or respectability from the training undergone.'[7]

The colleges' failure to reconcile society's and educators' aims, that is to produce low-status teachers capable of academic excellence, gave rise to persistent complaints throughout the century about the low level of attainment of those who had been mechanically drilled in useful knowledge, and inspired only with a sense of religious purpose. In 1852, Matthew Arnold reported thus his reaction to pupil-teachers' performances in examinations:

'I have been very much struck in examining them towards the close of their apprenticeship, when they are generally at least 18 years old, with the great amount of positive information and the low degree of mental culture and intelligence which they exhibit.'[8]

Recruited from the working classes, socially isolated and insecure, poorly educated by their colleges, and denied by the Newcastle Commission such status which entry to the Inspectorate could have conferred, elementary school teachers were made to feel even more frustrated and inferior by the 1861 Revised Code. Although it 'restored efficiency in the drudgery of teaching the 3 Rs . . . it ruthlessly destroyed the culture which was slowly creeping into the schools of the people . . . . For the next twenty years they were sullenly to restrict themselves to mechanical task work, narrow in scope and low in standard.'[9] Matthew Arnold, strongly critical of the introduction of Payment by Results, anticipated the nature of its effects when he referred to future relations between teachers and the Inspectorate as a 'game of mechanical contrivance in which the teachers will and must, more and more, learn how to beat us'.[10] The Code produced an attitude unfavourable to experimentation in the classroom. It diminished such attractiveness as the profession had possessed by reducing the teachers to the status of servants of school managers, permanently fearful of inspectors' visits. It was, therefore, unlikely that teachers who had become dependent upon well-tried 'mechanical' methods, to ensure the continuation of grants, would have the necessary confidence to take advantage of the freedom which, later in the century, the Board and its inspectors were to offer them. Contrasting the innovative schools such as Abbotsholme with traditional state schools, Campbell Stewart refers to the part played by the 1861 Code, saying: 'Its reverberations in the attitudes of teachers in elementary schools lasted until well into the twentieth century and thought of any experimentation in State-supported schools during the period from 1862 was quite killed.'[11]

Nor was this confidence likely to grow from students' training-college experiences later in the century. Students' timetables continued to be filled with fact-cramming about a wide range of subjects, supplemented by manual work and religious services. Lectures were numerous and formal, notes were dictated for memorising, libraries were inadequate, and recreational facilities were poor. The lecturers' salaries, lower than those of secondary school teachers, were insufficient to attract graduate teachers into the colleges; promotion to principalship was unlikely, since most of these went to outsiders, mainly churchmen and graduates from Oxford and Cambridge. William Taylor writes:

'The staff of the colleges in the nineteenth century were not distinguished by their qualifications or accomplishments. Instructing the underprivileged instructors of the underprivileged did not attract many of high academic standing. It was the general practice to recruit staff from the ranks of former students some of whom had no practical experience in schools before taking up their appointments.'[12]

Class hostilities, religious conflict, ambivalent attitudes towards universal education in the nineteenth century, all contributed to the slow and uncertain development of the training colleges. Moseley, commenting on the state of the colleges between 1839 and 1846, thought that 'manual occupations flourished at the expense of outdoor exercise and literary culture', and pointed out that 'of forty students, eighteen spelled incorrectly, twelve read and eight wrote incorrectly, and ten might be characterised as illiterate'.[13] Matthew Arnold, insisting upon the need for teachers to have a higher standard of culture, said in his General Report of 1855:

'It is . . . sufficiently clear, that the teacher to whom you give only a drudge's training, will do only a drudge's work, and will do it in a drudge's spirit; that in order to ensure good instruction from within narrow limits in a school, you must provide it with a master far superior to his scholars.'[14]

The Newbolt Report also complains bitterly about the low standard of English acceptable for entrance to many training colleges. It quotes a witness who gave evidence about students' lack of interest in cultural activities.

'. . . numbers of students arrive at College ill-found in respect of English, and that applies to pupils from secondary schools as well as to rural pupil teachers. Such students are said to be not only without a taste for reading, but defective in capacity for understanding English as well as ill-trained, it may be, in speech and in reading aloud.'[15]

The substance of these and later complaints about the products of training colleges is central to any discussion about teachers' professional confidence. Underlying them is the assumption that, if only their training could be improved or, better still, if they could display exceptional personal gifts, they would be successful teachers of literature to working-class pupils. It is an assumption which ignores the indivisibility of liberal education, with its attendant social and academic confidence, and the leisured origins of university students. These complaints, which persistently draw attention to the students' lack of culture, thus illustrate two main points. They show, of course, the severe discrepancy between the increasingly high expressed ideals for English teaching and the inadequacies of entrants to the colleges. More importantly, they suggest an explanation for educators' tendency to call for personalities with outstanding qualities for the teaching of English. Since teaching in the state sector drew, and continues to draw, mainly from students from working-class backgrounds, with relatively poor academic qualifications, educators deeply committed to English called, and continue to call, for outstanding people to enter the schools. At this early point in the subject's history they tended to reiterate hopes and wishes in the face of students' lack of professional confidence. Later it will be suggested that this optimism has performed a dubious service to the status of the teaching profession.

The students entering teaching were, in general, strangers to that literature which the Board of Education, the Inspectorate and witnesses to the Newbolt Committee were urging them to explore in the classroom. Trained either by the routine drilling of the elementary school or the routine drilling of the secondary school, since both had few cultivated graduates on their staff, they possessed no sustaining cultural traditions of their own. Although many figures in education, philanthropic liberals from public schools and ancient universities, were becoming more receptive to progressive notions about education through art and children's need for play and freedom, they still attempted to impose complex responsibilities upon teachers only very little removed from the backgrounds of their pupils. Romantic liberals' anxieties about social divisions, schools' lack of culture, urbanisation's threats to society's cultural health and, above all, children's personal development, tended to obscure and simplify the problems facing the teachers. During the same period that new freedoms were granted by the Board, and creativity and the love of literature were officially encouraged, the Inspectorate was opposing the entry of elementary school teachers to its ranks on the grounds that they 'are as a rule uncultured and imperfectly educated, and . . . there are special reasons why the bulk of the local inspectors should be unequal to their responsible duties . . . .'[16] In 1910, of ninety-two high-grade inspectors, fifty had degrees in classics and eighty-one came from Oxbridge (it was this Inspectorate which linked the schools with the Board which, as a result of its recommendations, issued regular handbooks of suggestions). The Newbolt Report, drawing attention to the fact that, outside London, only 54 per cent of the teachers in schools and only 38 per cent of the assistant teachers were certificated say, of those who were certificated, that 'they have been neither grounded nor confirmed in the idea of a liberal education.'[17] More seriously, it asserts that 'those who have passed the Preliminary Certificate of the Board of Education will have been tested in reading but only a very serious disability in speaking and reading would have disqualified them'.[18] The Report considered that these teachers were failing their pupils, and held the training colleges responsible for this. 'It is mainly because their education is so defective and their outlook so narrow that they cannot even realise what they ought to be aiming at, much less carry it out.' Its conclusion, which points out the students' humble social origins and impoverished academic experiences, while at the same time indicating the depth of the gulf between hopes and reality, was that only about a third were satisfactorily equipped to teach English.

This chapter also argues that many English teachers in the state sector have, because of their lowly social origins and poor academic qualifications, lacked the professional confidence necessary for imaginative and innovative work in the classroom. The tendencies of educators, particularly in recommendations for English, to emphasise the need for the right personal qualities in teachers, to stress the personal, affective content of the subject, have, it appears, contributed to this lack of confidence. High-status graduates, with 'good' degrees, continue, it will be argued, to view teaching contemptuously. And as far as staffing in English is concerned, the subject's personal, as opposed to cognitive, content appears partly to explain headmasters' readiness to distribute its teaching widely among non-specialists. It is useful, however, at this point, to see the extent to which the situation has changed since the beginning of this century.

Since the creation of the maintained secondary schools in 1902, there has been an improvement in the academic standard of students entering the teaching profession. Gradual but important changes also took place in the recruitment of teachers to the elementary schools. The pupil-teacher system slowly gave way to teacher-training, which students entered from a secondary school, either as free or 'unpledged scholars', or still through the pupil-teacher system. After 1920, the elementary school teacher's status rose as more and more entered college after a grammar school education. Gradually the number of uncertificated, supplementary teachers decreased in the elementary schools and, by 1928, 70 per cent of the training college staff consisted of university graduates. Accompanying the expansion of education after the First World War, the academic quality of staff in the grammar schools also improved. These improvements, however, took place very slowly; before the First World War, secondary education developed very unevenly and secondary school staff tended to be of mixed quality. In 1910–11, out of 5,100 men teaching in secondary schools, over 30 per cent were not graduates, and this was at a time when subjects like physical education, craft and art figured hardly at all in the secondary school curriculum. By 1920–1, the percentage had hardly changed. A sharp increase, however, took place in the 1930s, by which time the proportion of male graduates in secondary grammar schools had increased to as high as 80 per cent. Since 1945, the percentage remained about the same. In the colleges of education, also, the academic standards of the students continued to improve. By 1943, nearly all students entering the colleges had received their preliminary education in a secondary school, had passed the 'School Certificate' examination, and had spent some time in the sixth form. Since 1944, the improvement has been sustained, so that by 1967, 63 per cent of men and women had at least one pass at GCE 'A' level, and only 7 per cent of women and 9 per cent of men were qualified at the minimum of five GCE 'O' level passes.

Nevertheless, in spite of the undeniable improvement in academic standards of staff in the state-maintained schools—during the 1930s grammar school staff tended to be very well qualified as a result of unemployment in the other learned professions—several important factors, all related to professional confidence, seem likely to have hindered the achievement of the high aims of English by teachers in all types of schools. Although graduates in grammar schools and non-graduates in elementary and, later, secondary modern schools have their mainly working-class origins in common, it is useful to consider them separately because of their different experiences in higher education.

As Asher Tropp pointed out, from its beginnings the teaching profession had been 'an important avenue of social mobility for the working-class child'.[20] It seems that this continued, and continues still to be the case. Floud and Scott's research revealed that 'almost half of present-day teachers are descended from working-class grandfathers' and that 'the pull of teaching is still strong for working-class graduates'.[21] Their figures show that while working-class graduates made up one-fifth of the staff in direct grant grammar schools, they constituted one-third of the staff in maintained grammar schools and two-fifths in primary, secondary modern and technical schools. More recently, Kelsall, Poole and Kuhn (1972), noting 'the profound effect of social class on the flow of graduates into particular fields of work',[22] indicate the close relationship between graduates' working-class origins and their decision to enter teaching.

'In all university groupings, graduates from working-class backgrounds were far more likely to think in terms of a career in teaching than were their counterparts from middle-class homes, the proportion overall being 28 per cent and 10 per cent respectively.'[23]

While the majority of middle-class male graduates, from both independent and grammar schools, entered the professions and management, the great majority of working-class graduates from local authority schools favoured teaching. And the authors make the same point in their discussion of women graduates who, more than their male counterparts, entered teaching from both middle- and working-class backgrounds.

'Although more than 40 per cent of the women had a preference for school teaching, this propensity was particularly marked from those from working-class homes, among no less than two-thirds with an occupation in mind planned to become teachers and indeed showed little interest in other kinds of work. Again, the comparative disinclination seen here of the graduate from a high-status home to want to take up school teaching is clearly common to both men and women and is once more almost certainly a reflection of their low evaluation of school teaching compared with other occupations.'[24]

Although their sample was extremely small compared with Floud and Scott's, and Kelsall's national figures, one of the interesting points to emerge from B. Jackson's and D. Marsden's survey of working-class graduates was the very large number who returned to teaching.

'The most striking thing is that forty-six of the sample have become teachers—they themselves are staffing the educational services. There is no other category so large as this . . . only nine girls did *not* become teachers.'[25]

And it appears that, like their predecessors in the 1930s, many of whom perceived their most important work as being in the field of examinations, these graduates support the system of competitive examinations by means of which they achieved their upward social mobility. A comment by a pupil in Jackson and Marsden's sample, who was critical of her education at a grammar school, illustrates something of the realities of English in the classroom.

'The course on Literature was particularly open to sardonic memories. "You had these set books, and then had to answer questions like 'What is it that so-and-so found on the sole of his left foot?'—a fact from page 327!".'[26]

In spite of such memories, however, the working-class graduates who returned to teaching in large numbers 'were well satisfied' with their education. The authors comment somewhat wistfully upon these graduates' conservatism.

'With their own education they were pleased, and most wished to see no changes in the present system, unless it be that grammar schools should be more selective still, and penalties to be imposed to prevent lower working-class children from entering them in any numbers.'[27]

What must be noted is that, since the 1930s, competitive examinations have expanded enormously. The Spens Committee, in fact, supported the conventional notion of the grammar schools' responsibility for their pupils when it reported that professional training was unnecessary for teaching in them. Their time, it was suggested, would be better spent, 'increasing their mastery of their special subjects, than in following a course in the University Training Department'.[28]

Not surprisingly, this view was not shared by the Cambridge School of English. Their opposition to the classics' domination of the ancient universities and public schools, and their support for pupils' personal

engagement with English literature as the humane centre of the curriculum, led them to criticise conventional examinations. They
objected to their measurement of the memorising of literary facts,
knowledge of form and the analysis of literature in the classicists'
mechanical fashion. L. C. Knights's article in *Scrutiny* (1933)
illustrates the bitter opposition by the supporters of Cambridge
English to school examinations in their subject.

'Any English master interested in education who has prepared a
school certificate form knows that bitter feeling of waste . . . . Since
the damage done to education by external, "standardising" examinations is so gross, obvious, persuasive and inescapable, the time has
come to press firmly for their abolition.'[29]

However, in spite of the Cambridge School's and the progressives'
argument about teachers' responsibilities to encourage pupils' critical
discrimination and individual response to great literature, it is very
likely that many teachers subscribed to competitive examinations
partly from a sense of obligation to their pupils. The social origins
of many graduate teachers may not have given them the cultural
confidence of the Cambridge English graduates who were attacking
'standardising' examinations. In addition, they were likely to remain
unconvinced by arguments put forward by school teachers whose
middle-class, academically committed pupils' successes were not
exclusively dependent upon competitive examinations. It is probably
the case that many of the grammar school teachers, whose upward
social mobility had been the result of examinations, felt insufficiently
culturally secure to teach 'creative' English in a school situation where
their 'abolition' might seriously threaten their working-class pupils'
futures. It is significant that, although progressive approaches to
English teaching have gradually been receiving greater official acceptance since the end of the First World War, they have, until very
recently, been most widely implemented in schools for young or less-
able children. Given the social backgrounds of many school teachers
and the expansion of examinations during the past forty years, it
seems unlikely that the expressed high aims of English teaching could
have gained widespread acceptance in secondary education.

At present, however, it seems likely that, once again, secondary
school teachers' confidence is relatively low on account of the poor
academic level of most recruits to the profession. Although there
were many good honours graduates in grammar school staff rooms
in the 1930s, and from those, particularly the middle-class teachers,
came much of the optimistic prescriptive writing about English, this

has been less true since the last war. In recent years, during the expansion of the tertiary stage of education, the situation has changed considerably in the numbers of well-qualified graduates choosing teaching. Recent analysis reveals that during the 1960s (the period of expansion in higher education) the numbers of well-qualified graduates entering school teaching fell noticeably. A writer investigating this comments that 'school teaching has attracted a disproportionate number of those who in terms of first degrees may be regarded as poorly qualified'.[30] Supporting this view, Kelsall, Poole and Kuhn write in *Graduates. The Sociology of an Élite* in a section on career choice:

'Class of degree, too, had an important bearing on career choice . . . the most educationally competent graduates (as measured by degree class) had been especially attracted by the prospect of a university post. Indeed, approximately half of all those with first class honours degrees were thinking along these lines, as were more than a third of those who had gained an upper second. There was a substantial difference between this educational "élite" and the rest of the graduate body, those with undivided or lower seconds were likely to want to take up school teaching, and the remainder were to be spread evenly between teaching, research, design or production, administration and the "other" professions.'[31]

Both pieces of research into graduates' choice of career show that graduates regard the teaching profession as second best. One of the consequences of the expansion of higher education has been, therefore, the failure of teaching to attract able graduates at a time when, as one of the writers points out, 'the schools require more well-qualified staff than ever before, where there are more pupils in school beyond the minimum leaving age than at any previous time'.[32] It seems that a poor image of school teaching has persisted, and that if alternative opportunities offered themselves, well-qualified graduates at college and university level preferred to take these than enter the schools.

Writers in this field suggest a variety of reasons for this poor image and, collectively, they hold some significance for our consideration of the teachers' professional confidence. Making the point that the most exclusive fields of employment were, inevitably, the most prestigious, Kelsall comments on the ease of graduate entry into teaching.

'Thus there seemed to be few barriers against entry to school teaching, for example, and as a result the vast majority of our sample who had thought in terms of such a career were able to achieve their ambitions.'[33]

In his discussion of the large numbers of women graduates intending to teach, Kelsall indicates reasons which, again, are of some significance for the confidence and status of the whole profession. In addition to the shortness of the training, women were attracted to it because they could either leave it at any time and return, or they could obtain part-time employment, both because of the belief that teaching is exceptional in its lack of a 'specialised and rapidly changing knowledge base'. Looking at reorganisation and the movement towards interdisciplinary work in schools, Bernbaum suggests that these may have blurred professional and specialist distinctions and made school teaching less attractive to graduates wishing to continue in close identification with their subject through work with the most able children.

'The growth of the tertiary stage of education has created opportunities for teachers to perform academic roles which never previously existed, to achieve status through undertaking work which is of a high standard and which offers to those that they teach the chance of upward social mobility.'[34]

At every level of the teaching profession the relatively poor academic qualifications of recruits indicate its depressed image in comparison with other careers. Teaching remains unattractive to well-qualified graduates and to those from high-status social backgrounds. Since the great majority who enter the profession appear to have achieved upward mobility through success in competitive examinations, they are unlikely to be wholly resistant to these on their working-class pupils' behalf. Turning now to teaching's largest group of recruits, the non-graduates, we find that it was possible for the majority to become qualified by means of school achievements considerably below those required for a university course.

In 1961–2, 73 per cent of undergraduates had three or more passes at GCE 'A' level, with at least one of those at grade A or B. In contrast, only 9 per cent of trainees in colleges of education, that is non-graduate teachers, came into this category. Whilst only 18 per cent of undergraduates as a whole failed to achieve grades A or B, as many as 71 per cent of non-graduate teachers had no high grades in their 'A' level qualifications. Clearly, in comparison with the whole undergraduate population, the majority of these teachers had low academic qualifications.[35] While first-class graduates appear to hold a poor view of teaching, non-graduates who enter teaching tend to hold noticeably inferior 'A' level qualifications to the total number of sixth formers entering universities.

In contrast with France, where the aristocratic ideal was replaced by the intellectual, the status of the teaching profession in this country is low. In England, it seems likely that the persistence of the character-building model in teacher-training has been largely responsible for a disparaged professional image. A recent study describes the colleges' values in the following terms.

'There can be no doubt that the importance of relationships, of rapport and of "real liking for children" are central to the culture of teacher education in Britain as represented by the colleges of education and central to the socialisation of non-graduate students for the teacher's role. In so far as the colleges of education have a professional concept of the teacher's role, it is one which, unlike many professional concepts, stresses the necessity of sustained and warm relationships with the client.'[36]

It has been widely suggested that the colleges' long-sustained hostility to the basic disciplines of education, their emphasis upon the practical rather than the academic, their desire to invest teaching with social purpose, have all contributed to the depressed status of the teaching profession. William Taylor, in his chapter on the values of teacher education, is explicit about the colleges' attitude to academic excellence.

'Until very recently there has been a tendency for the intellectual performances of both staff and students to be rated lower than the possession of certain other qualities which are believed to be relevant to the task of the teachers . . . [perhaps explained by] the mistaken dichotomy between intellect and character that has affected the whole of educational provision in this country from primary school to university.'[37]

Although not wishing, any more than the progressives, to 'restrict the teacher's task to communication of mere facts and information, nor to deny the importance of his moral function and the need for him to be inducted into this during the course of his professional preparation', Taylor wishes to 'repudiate the techniques of manipulated socialisation that have hitherto characterised some aspects of the training of teachers'.[38] He asserts 'the need for a theory of teaching that no longer makes arbitrary and socially inspired distinctions between intellect and character, that recognises the moral force that inheres in the organisation of academic disciplines, properly taught. . . .'[39] He recommends a revaluation of academic excellence in teacher education as a preliminary to rejection of the currently anti-intellectual, problem-centred approach to students' training. At present, colleges and university departments appear to be more interested in the students' success in changing pupils' values than in their ability to instruct them; their approach to the students' courses, therefore, tend to be equally 'child-centred' and generally unacademic. In a critical discussion of anti-intellectualism in the courses and, given the lofty aims, the ironically low academic standards of the students, an observer of American teacher education has noted the affinity between religious and educational faith.

'The educationist . . . despises the vocabulary of despair, for in the conventional wisdom of education, truth and wish are one. The credo of unlimited hope performs useful functions for education. For the professor or school man who sights the promise of individual salvation the school becomes a church and work a calling. In a profession where frustration and failure are common, the ideology of mass education revives professional energy and protects children against the comfortable cynicism and apathy that might otherwise afflict their teachers.'[40]

The contempt with which well-qualified subject specialists appear to view education is likely to be explained by the ease of entry into colleges and university departments and the very high pass-rates into teaching. In his discussion of graduates' choice of careers, Kelsall pointed out that the great majority wishing to teach found few barriers to their wishes. This lack of exclusiveness, he suggested, lowered the profession's prestige. Interviews for entrance, both to colleges of education and university departments, tend to be of a highly personal nature, selection appearing to take place on the grounds of student commitment to teaching. It seems far more important that the student exhibits the 'right' attitude towards the work than that he exhibits academic excellence. A recent study comments upon this:

'Whilst within the professions in general, academic ability is expected to be the principal intention of competence, within the "people-oriented" professions it is regarded as legitimate to reject candidates with outstanding technical ability but the "wrong personality" . . . training college interviews were more elaborate, placed greater emphasis on personal qualities and less on academic achievement than university interviews . . . there was more interest among training college selectors in dedication to the profession, in leisure interests and in other personality indicators, than in further academic skills.'⁴¹

Assessment, too, tends to be made upon personal criteria. Pass-rates from colleges of education and university departments are, from the perspective of the well-qualified graduate, derisively high. Critics usually arrive at a similar sort of conclusion; as this observer of the American situation states:

'In 1960 some three hundred and thirty five colleges and universities conferred one hundred and twenty thousand earned degrees in education—too few for estimated needs and too many for any hope of excellence. Given the facts of huge numbers, scarce talent and limited rewards, it is unrealistic to suppose that education will be able to recruit sizeable proportions of students from the gifted end of the ability spectrum.'⁴²

It is not difficult to find evidence of dissatisfaction with the academic and cultural quality of teachers. Taylor, aware of the low status of the profession from primary school to university, is clearly critical of the colleges' level of studies. For quite different reasons, mainly because he fears the deterioration of high culture as attempts persist to disseminate it through unresponsive classes of society, G. H. Bantock deplores the unsatisfactory quality of many students; his contention is, like T. S. Eliot's, that, without the consensus and support of wider society, the schools can accomplish little in the way of raising cultural standards. In another context, Professor Jackson, in his classic account of *Life in Classrooms*, comments upon teachers' talk's 'lack of technical terms' and their 'conceptual simplicity'. Teachers have, he observes, an uncomplicated view of causality, an inventive, rather than a rational, approach to classroom events, and an 'opinionated' rather than an open-minded approach when confronted with alternatives. His comments upon what he noticed about teachers' approaches to their work are significantly similar to the actual recommendations made by progressive educators about the good teacher. He reports:

'. . . the intensity of teacher's emotional investment in her work, if we can believe the way she talks about it, often exceeds . . . common concern. In this respect, teachers resemble clergymen, therapists, physicians, and others whose duties link them intimately to the personal well-being of their clientele.'⁴³

In addition to the hopes discussed in Parts I and II, two important features within education itself appear to have contributed to the powerful ideology of English teaching. The first is closely linked with the social origins and academic and cultural attainments of teachers. Since these have been generally unhelpful in promoting sufficient professional confidence to achieve anything resembling the crusade envisaged by the subject's supporters, emphasis has continually been laid upon those inspirational qualities necessary for success. The persistence of emphasis on the personal, in education generally, and in English in particular, may be contributory to the low status of teaching and, consequently, be likely to discourage rather than encourage the most able recruits to enter the profession. Secondly, there are recurrently unfavourable conditions in the schools, and authority's tendency to reflect society's contempt for the 'diffuse' role by treating English in schools as unenthusiastically as it treats religion.

Deploring conditions in the schools—large classes, truancy, interrupted attendance, poor linguistic habits, and a generally hostile attitude towards culture—the contributors to the Newbolt Report called for gifted personalities endowed with enthusiasm, warmth, ability to comunicate, and that elusive magic which could overcome almost insuperable obstacles. It appears, however, that in spite of the movement, at an official level, of English to the centre of the curriculum, in practice the supply of specialist teachers remains insufficient to meet demands. Recent figures indicate that, during the first four years of pupils' experience of English in comprehensive schools, at least 25 per cent of their staff are non-specialists. In secondary modern schools, where the needs as defined by the subject's supporters are most urgent, at least 40 per cent of the English is taught by non-specialists.[44] The gulf is still very wide between aims, 'training the sensibilities of three-quarters of the population', and every-day realities, unless any well-meaning teacher is accepted as qualified for the task. It has been shown that, across all the work going on in maintained schools up to 1968, English had, with 34 per cent, the second highest proportion of non-specialist teaching staff, next to Religious Education, which had 63 per cent.[45] Next to Religious Education, English was, in fact, the subject most frequently mentioned by teachers in comprehensive schools who responded positively to questions about being inadequately prepared for their work.[46]

It seems very likely that, while the expressed aims remain diffuse and vaguely defined, English will be taught in many schools, certainly at the lower age levels, by anyone whose heart is in the right place. It might be more helpful to the subject's status, in spite of supporters' anxieties about examinations, mechanical methods and the need for emotional content, if, instead of being viewed as largely inspirational and, therefore, any willing teacher's undertaking, its goals could be more precisely defined. The heavy price of neglect is being paid in many schools for diffuse and lofty aims which, it is so often insisted, can only be achieved by exceptional people. This view of English in schools seems to arise from the co-existence of a low-status profession with the problems of disseminating liberal culture throughout a largely indifferent society. While it persists, however, focussing almost exclusively upon the inspirational, it is unlikely to strengthen professional confidence or to achieve serious consideration for English in the classroom.

Notes

1. George Sampson, *English for the English* (Cambridge, Cambridge University Press, 1952), p. 90.
2. D. A. Beacock, *Play Way for English Today* (London, Nelson, 1943), p. 105.
3. S. Hoare, Speech to House of Commons (March 1921), in *Hansard* cols 277–8.
4. *Teaching of English in England* (London, HMSO, 1921), p. 57.
5. J. Kay-Shuttleworth, Second Report on Battersea; quoted by R. W. Rich, *The Training of Teachers in England and Wales during the Nineteenth Century* (Cambridge, Cambridge University Press, 1933), p. 65.
6. Rich, op. cit., p. 87.
7. W. Taylor, *Society and the Education of Teachers* (London, Faber, 1969), pp. 93 f.
8. Matthew Arnold, General Report for the Year 1852, in *Reports on Elementary Schools, 1852–1882* (London, HMSO, 1908), p. 16.
9. Rich, op. cit., p. 179.
10. Matthew Arnold, General Report for the Year 1867, in *Reports on Elementary Schools*, op. cit., p. 115.
11. W. A. C. Stewart, *The Educational Innovators* (London, Macmillan, 1968), Vol. 2, p. 4.
12. Taylor, op. cit., p. 204.
13. Moseley, Report of Committee of Council on Education, *Minutes* (1847–8), Vol. 21, p. 477.
14. Matthew Arnold, General Report for the Year 1855, in *Reports on Elementary Schools*, op. cit., p. 48.
15. *The Teaching of English in England* (1921), op. cit., p. 171.
16. Hoare, op. cit., cols. 277–8.
17. *The Teaching of English in England* (1921), op. cit., p. 25.
18. Ibid., p. 168.

19. Ibid., p. 169.
20. A. Tropp, *The School Teachers* (London, Heinemann, 1957), p. 186.
21. J. Floud and W. Scott, 'Recruitment to Teaching in England and Wales,' in A. H. Halsey, J. Floud and C. Arnold Anderson (eds), *Education, Economy and Society*, (Glencoe, Free Press, 1961), p. 533.
22. R. K. Kelsall, A. Poole and A. Kuhn, *Graduates. The Sociology of an Élite* (London, Methuen, 1972), p. 110.
23. Ibid., p. 73.
24. Ibid., p. 142.
25. B. Jackson and D. Marsden, *Education and the Working Class* (London, Routledge, 1962), pp. 156 ff.
26. Ibid., p. 123.
27. Ibid., p. 192.
28. *Report of the Consultative Committee on Secondary Education with Special Reference to Grammar Schools and Technical High Schools* (Spens Report), (HMSO, 1938), p. 300.
29. L. C. Knights, 'Scrutiny of Examinations', in *Scrutiny*, Vol. 12, No. 2 (September 1933).
30. G. Bernbaum, 'Educational Expansion and the Teacher's Role', in *Universities Quarterly* (March 1967), p. 159.
31. Kelsall, Poole and Kuhn, op. cit., p. 84.
32. Bernbaum, op. cit., p. 161.
33. Kelsall, Poole and Kuhn, op. cit., p. 93.
34. Bernbaum, op. cit., p. 163.
35. William Taylor, calculated from annual reports of the Central Registry and Clearing House for the years concerned, *Society and the and the Education of Teachers*, op. cit., pp. 176 f.
36. Gerald Grace, *Role Conflict and the Teacher* (London and Boston, Routledge, 1972), p. 23.
37. Taylor, op. cit., p. 294.
38. Ibid., p. 295.
39. Ibid., pp. 295 f.
40. M. Bressler, 'Conventional Wisdom of Education and Sociology', in *Sociology and Contemporary Education* (New York, Random House, 1963), p. 83.
41. R. N. Morris, *The Sixth Form and College Entrance* (London, Routledge, 1969), pp. 142 f.
42. Bressler, op. cit., p. 86.
43. P. W. Jackson, *Life in Classrooms* (New York, Holt Rinehart & Winston, 1968), p. 144.
44. *Statistics of Education, Special Series One*, Survey of the Curriculum and Deployment of Teachers (Secondary Schools) 1965–6, Part 1: 'Teachers', p. 85, Table 16.
45. *Statistics of Education*, op. cit., pp. 49, 97, Table 16 .
46. T. G. Monks, *Comprehensive Education in England and Wales* (Slough, Bucks, NFER, 1968), p. 75.

Chapter 13

The English Teacher's Role: ·
Strain and Conflict

'Some of us need to know that we are successful in
what we do. This is your own need to believe that
you are succeeding. There is no way of knowing your
success in English as there is in Maths. I aim to
get them to perceive relationships—to become
aware—this can't be measured by exams. It depends
on your own faith in yourself—some are certain that
they are doing well—I'm not yet certain. Perhaps we
need to be accepted as successful by other people'
(man certificated: age 46: s. modern).

Quoted by G. Grace in *Role Conflict and the Teacher*

The content and tone of discussion about the aims of English teaching during the past 150 years testify to its supporters' view that the
subject is of special importance in pupils' lives. Prescriptive writing
insists upon the need for exceptionally gifted people to take on this
responsibility, and, on occasions, it goes as far as to claim that neglect
of drama, or creativity, or literature, will stultify pupils' personal
development or precipitate cultural catastrophe. Teaching, however,
in spite of its generally high aims, is a low-status profession, apparently
unattractive to many students from privileged social backgrounds
or with good academic qualifications. It may be that the widely
acknowledged anti-intellectualism in teacher education is an important discouragement to precisely those recruits who might work
with the greatest confidence, particularly in English. It also seems very
likely that the emphasis in the prescriptive writing upon the affective
and personal in English may create difficulties for many recruits to
the profession whose own upward mobility has been through competitive examinations. Certainly, it seems possible that the shift of
emphasis this century from the cognitive to the affective in English
has made it more vulnerable to casual treatment in the schools as
far as specialist staffing is concerned.

Bearing in mind the specially high aims of English as described in

Parts I and II, these last chapters are primarily concerned with the question of its teachers' professional confidence. The subject's supporters, as we have noted in many instances, state or imply that this is essential to English teachers' success. They are called upon to teach 'from their convictions', or to be ready to resign, or to be sufficiently secure within themselves to resist feeling threatened by the language of working-class pupils. All the dominant imagery of the prescriptive writing underlines this assumption; preachers, missionaries, ambassadors, warriors, psycho-analysts, artists and even 'crap-detectors' are, ideally, figures who have confidence in themselves.

Among the professions, though, the teacher's role is the least precisely defined, widely acknowledged as being the most diffuse, and thus most open to conflict. Gerald Grace begins his discussion of this in *Role Conflict and the Teacher* in the following way:

'It is claimed (Reisman *et al.* 1950, Floud 1962, Wilson 1962) that roles having a moral and ethical orientation and which are concerned with the transmission of values, are exposed to considerable conflict in the cultures of advanced industrial societies. This conflict arises because of the breakdown of value consensus, because of changed attitudes to authority and because of the growth of hedonistic and other-directed philosophies of life. Certain roles are seen to be in a 'confrontation position' with the developing tendencies of a culture and the teacher's role is characteristically regarded as one of these .... Potentiality for conflict has been suggested from a variety of sources—the diffuse nature of the role (Wilson 1962), teachers' concern with status (Tropp 1957), their exposure to conflicting expectations (Merton 1957), the affectivity and moral orientation of the role (Floud 1962; Wilson 1962) and characteristics of the organisational setting (Corwin, 1965; Hoyle 1965).'[1]

This chapter suggests that progressive English teachers are likely to experience strains and tensions that are more severe than those felt by other members of staff. Grace's research showed that the greatest professional confidence, that is the least role conflict, existed in those teachers whose aims were the most narrowly defined, whose role was clearly prescribed, and whose certainty of consensus of purpose with fellow staff, parents and pupils was the strongest. The least role conflict was thus experienced by graduate specialists working mainly with sixth-formers and receiving feedback about their effectiveness through pupils' success in examinations. Conversely, teachers in the 'value' subjects experienced the greatest role conflict, particularly when they were working with low-ability pupils or in situations where they 'felt uncertainty about actual learning achievements'. This response about satisfaction within teaching illustrates something of the difference between the cognitive and the affective subjects as represented by mathematics and English.

'Some of us need to know that we are successful in what we do. This is your own need to believe that you are succeeding. There is no way of knowing your success in English as there is in Maths. I aim to get them to perceive relationships—to become aware—this cannot be measured by exams. It depends on your own faith in yourself—some are certain that they are doing well—I am not yet certain. Perhaps we need to be accepted as successful by other people.'[2]

As it has been seen to touch upon every aspect of pupils' lives, most particularly the emotional, English has become increasingly diffuse. Moreover, there are within it, more than most other subjects, marked political differences between the leading figures in the field. As they relate to decision-making about priorities and responsibilities in the classroom, these differences must affect many English teachers' sense of purpose and professional confidence. We shall, therefore, look at the outstanding disputes within prescriptive writing about English. In addition, we shall discuss the areas of likely conflict between English teachers supporting the dominant ideologies and the expectations held of them by some parents, headmasters and fellow staff.

Before examining conflicting views about priorities within the four main activities within English—literature, creativity, discrimination, and classroom talk—it is useful to consider the term 'political' in reference to definitions currently being made by leading figures concerned with English in schools. Within the last ten years, during which time interest had shifted to the curriculum of the average and below-average child, widespread dissatisfaction has been expressed with the traditional grammar school education. Its specialist, academic, authoritarian elements have been persistently criticised, partly because they ignored progressives' demands for children's activity, participation and development through discovery, and partly because of the perceived irrelevance of this education to the lives of working-class children, the majority of whom have failed to benefit from it. Progressives, and radicals supporting reorganisation of the schools and the introduction of non-streaming, are carrying their attack upon the grammar schools' élitism into the curriculum, dismantling the traditional subjects by rearranging them through interdisciplinary work, projects and themes. As this relates to English, the central concern of which has been the dissemination of liberal culture

throughout society, it has undergone considerable revision. Literature, usually the major part of English in the grammar schools, has
received the most severe overhauling, but because of the current un-
acceptability to many educators of a 'middle-class' curriculum for all
our pupils, every activity in English has been given a different set of
emphases. It will be recalled that for Arnold, and his successors who
contributed to the Newbolt Report, education's primary responsibility was the dissemination of culture, particularly literary culture.
Their most bitter regret was that, while utilitarianism persisted in
education, the lives of the masses were untouched by the refinements
of high art, and as a consequence, they argued, the social classes remained divided and mutually hostile. Better teaching, it has until quite
recently been believed, will in time affect the working classes with a
sense of excitement and satisfaction which great art can inspire. *The
Report of the Harvard Committee* (1946) took up this theme:

'. . . today, we are concerned with a general education—a liberal
education—not for the relatively few, but for the multitude—the task
of modern democracy is to preserve the ancient ideal of a liberal
education and to extend it as far as possible to all members of the
community . . . . To believe in the equality of human being is to believe that the good life, and the education which trains the citizen for
the good life, are equally the privilege of all.'[3]

Referring to what it calls 'the problem of . . . less gifted young people',
the Report says that 'the aim is to educate them by exactly the same
ideals of schooling as everyone else, yet by means which shall be as
meaningful to them as are more abstract means to the more abstract
minded'.[4] Thus, the central aim is still to bring everyone as close to
appreciation of high art as they and the gifts of their teachers make
possible. And it is an aim which appears to be shared by many
grammar school teachers.

'Apart from the social purpose of the school, and in spite of the
demand for scientists and the resultant earlier specialisation, I consider the purpose of a grammar school . . . goes back to the Renais-
sance . . . to give an introduction to the humanities and a training in
the intellectual processes, and thus to provide a healthy counter-
balance to the cinema, ITA and Radio Luxembourg . . . .'[5]

Recent anxiety, however, about the grammar schools' perceived
responsibility for reinforcing divisions between the middle and work-

ing classes, and about the wastage of talent which their continued existence perpetuated, has brought their traditional curriculum under severe attack. In addition, as far as English has been concerned, others besides progressives and radicals have questioned the value of academic approaches for working-class pupils. G. H. Bantock and David Holbrook, who are very concerned about exploitation by commercial culture of working-class pupils, have argued that the watered-down grammar school curriculum has failed to affect the lives of the great majority. Although not wishing to disturb the present social system in any fundamental way, they, like the radical educators, have proposed the revival of popular culture. Instead of set books, periods of literature and preparation for examinations, they propose more mime, dance, poetry reading and writing, an affective education for pupils unreceptive to the academic, and susceptible to the commercial. Thus, both radicals and élitists have severely shaken the early certainty about the worthwhileness of attempts to disseminate liberal culture as widely as teachers' skills and school conditions permitted. And within recent years, the question of which culture is for whom is being raised in connection with every one of their activities. If literature and its related activities are tainted with 'middle-class' exclusiveness and, it appears, that teachers engaging pupils in these are 'imposing' alien values upon working-class pupils, it follows that they must move into the lives of working-class pupils to encourage that culture which, up till now, the largely irrelevant curriculum has 'stifled'. Teachers frequently express anxiety and bewilderment about the changes which their early aims have undergone. Referring to the 'varied but quite clearly defined curriculum area which is the English teacher's province', a teacher writes in *Use of English*, that 'it hardly seemed likely that teachers could lose confidence in their [the aims'] importance or ignore their relevance to each other'.[6] The article regrets the English teachers' apparent need to demonstrate the social relevance of their work, ascribing to the social sciences, current distrust of élitism and patriotism, and fragmentation of English into psychotherapy, linguistics and socio-scientific examination of the media, responsibility for current confusion and uncertainty.

It appears from articles like this that many conscientious English teachers see themselves faced with strongly expressed views about their role which are based upon different interpretations of social justice. Are they perpetuating social divisions by exclusively concentrating upon the child's own culture, or encouraging sensitive response to environment and pride in individual identity? Commenting upon this recent dilemma within the humanities, and English in particular, John and Pat White write:

'What is most remarkable here is that both right-wing and left-wing educationists seem to agree about the need to insulate class cultures from each other. On the right we see a Black Paperman like Bantock arguing that popular education should develop the folk-culture of the working classes; and on the left, dozens of sociologists, or sociologically orientated specialists in other fields, English especially, propagating via a doctrine of cultural relativism deriving from social anthropology and the sociology of knowledge a new monolithic working-class system.'[7]

After surveying the general scene, it is useful to look at existing differences between educators about each of the four main activities.

The teaching of literature has been the activity most profoundly affected by these conflicting views. Pupils of Leavis continue to support his concept of the centrality of the literary experience, denying its identification with middle-class culture and the charge of imposing alien values upon working-class children. As recently as 1966, Americans at the Dartmouth Conference were left with the impression of English teachers' solidarity of purpose, their loyalty to Leavis and 'the great tradition' of English literature. Their aim was to promote children's growth, and they hoped to achieve this by introducing them to literature, and stimulating creativity. Although very concerned about the curriculum for less-able children, they did not propose to abandon literature, still defining it as vital to an affective education. Although G. H. Bantock and David Holbrook attack the 'watered-down' curriculum for secondary modern children, they insist upon the value of literature in the school experience of all pupils. They suggest approaching the average and below-average children through mime, dance and personal composition. Nevertheless, the proposed stimuli are myth and folk song and, hopefully, these are meant to lead on to the poetry of Blake and Shakespeare. Like Arnold and Leavis these writers, concerned above all with what Holbrook calls the children's 'humanity', believe that this can be touched and sensitised by engagement with great works of art. Today, Holbrook and his supporters, opposing the shift of emphasis to 'relevant' social or environmental studies, simply disclaim the accusation of endorsing middle-class values; they insist upon the universality of the literary experience which, if neglected, will mean severe imaginative deprivation for children continually exposed to what, they argue, are the banalities of the mass media.

Their opponents appear to be divided about where they wish to place their emphasis, although united in the desire to diminish the importance of literature by delaying or rearranging it. The *Language in*

Use team argue that the stress, within English for the majority of pupils, should be upon the means of improving their social competence, and that literature, if it is to be enjoyed, must be introduced after the children have achieved linguistic confidence. Halliday and Doughty, while not wishing to remove literature from English courses, wish to give it a smaller place because there is so much more to be done. While the team express guarded enthusiasm for continued inclusion of literature in English lessons, the supporters of humanities teaching tend to regard classroom study of the complete play, novel or poem as suspiciously supportive of the traditional teacher-directed curriculum. As concerned as the *Language in Use* team with the less able, but generally more inclined to rearrangement of the specialist curriculum for political reasons, humanities teachers give priority to 'controversial issues' over literature, turning to it mainly for material usefully illustrative of their chosen topics. Several significant trends in education are discernible here. There is the wish to give children greater opportunity to talk, thus removing importance from the text and the teacher to the pupils; 'discussion diffuses power, or at least suggests that it might be diffused'.[8] There is the desire to blur distinctions between subjects in order to show children how knowledge is related rather than separated, strengthened by the radical conviction that dismantling the traditional curriculum is part of a movement to promote greater social justice. Reflecting bitterly upon what he perceives to be a serious deterioration of purpose within English studies, a teacher ascribes the shift of importance from literature to 'relevant' social topics to the influence of *Culture and Environment*.

'These tendencies in English studies, towards uncertainty of aim, triviality of content, neglect of the imagination, and concentration upon ephemeral social issues, evolve directly or indirectly from the first attempts to use the English lesson as a time for training the critical intelligence and equipping it to engage successfully with the worst aspects of modern society. That is, they derive to some extent from *Culture and Environment*. I can think of few ironies more bitter than that.'[9]

The unwillingness of some English teachers to teach literature stems from their convictions about the neglected richness of working-class culture. While the *Language in Use* team wish to order priorities differently and the Humanities Project's teachers wish to rearrange literature to illustrate relevant social issues, there is an extreme form of resistance to literature on the grounds that it is part of the 'syllabus of established middle-class culture'.[10] In *This New Season*, a book about English teaching in Stepney, Chris Searle expresses his belief in the validity of working-class culture and the English teacher's responsibility to encourage children's pride in their own identity. Literature, apart from a reference to the Liverpool poets, is excluded from his working-class pupils' experience of English in school. Instead, Searle proposes stimulation of pupil's personal writing about their feelings and environment. Having identified the academic curriculum with competitive examinations and the status-seeking of the middle classes, Searle excludes all works of art from the classroom except the pupils' own creations and those which reflect their lives.

Although their reasons differ and their perspectives on literature conflict, the élitists like Bantock and Holbrook and a radical like Searle face English teachers with proposals based on similar assumptions. Arguing that the curriculum of the working-class pupils should be specially chosen to suit their environment, experiences and abilities, they indicate their lack of interest in the question of academic achievement with its possibility of pupils' upward social mobility. Bantock and Holbrook seek no reorgansation of the social structure, investing their hopes for greater happiness in the power of creativity and great art to bring self-awareness and fulfilment. Searle, and teachers with his views, reject the present social system, recommending that ways be found to give working-class pupils confidence and pride in their cultural identity. They do not propose to enter into work in school which makes achievement in competitive examinations possible, having judged this to be highly undesirable.

Turning to the field of children's creativity we find that the area of agreement is far larger than that about literature. So strong have been the influences here—of progressivism with its romantic view of childhood's vision, of anti-industrialism, of egalitarianism which has democratised art in every form, of therapy—that the great majority of educators wish to encourage pupils' growth through creativity. Disagreement is mainly about whether great literature or the children's own environment and experiences should provide the stimuli for this work. It is a debate which reflects the overall political dispute about the role of high art in the classroom. While Bantock, Holbrook, Inglis and those English teachers who support the 'élitists', recommend the employment of stimuli drawn exclusively from the music, painting and literature of high art, and make it clear that they view creativity partly as a way back into appreciation, a radical teacher like Searle rejects this culture completely. Unlike the élitists, many of whom wish to compensate for working-class children's loss of traditional agricultural satisfactions through a mainly affective curriculum, Searle recommends creativity to strengthen working-class children's confidence and pride in their own identity.

The severest critics of exclusively personal, creative writing are the *Language in Use* team, who argue that such work does not help pupils achieve social competence. Peter Doughty expresses his suspicion of the limited nature of the 'creative' approach.

'The only kind of written work acceptable to many teachers at present is written work that is recognisable as one variety of the language of literature, that is, intensely autobiographic, densely metaphoric, syntactically highly informal, and devoted to the accurate reporting of personal response to experience. . . . From the point of view of the pupils' needs as a whole . . . the limitations of this assumption are immediately apparent . . . it ignores the nature and function of technical varieties of English, that is, the workaday language of a complex industrial society.'[11]

The charge is that exclusive concentration upon the personal can, in its effects, be socially divisive. Unless working-class children are given linguistic means of control over the disciplines of the curriculum, and situations in the outside world, they are unlikely to stand much chance of being upwardly mobile. What this criticism draws attention to is the bitter truth about teachers' exclusive concentration upon creativity with working-class pupils. Whether this is stimulated by the myths and ballads proposed by David Holbrook, or is a reflection upon the living conditions of society's victims suggested by Searle, teachers' limitation of the pupils' work in English to 'personal' writing can be interpreted as giving their support to the *status quo* of the social system. Since this decision relates, in English, to what has come to be accepted as a key element in children's potential to achieve at school, that is their linguistic competence, the English teacher has a heavier responsibility when he attempts to resolve it than staff concerned with other parts of the curriculum. He has to decide whether it is more in his pupils' interests for him to accept the existence of the present social structure and to give them help to advance within it, or for him to have rejected it, on their behalf, as stifling, competitive and exploitative and to encourage them to find fulfilment within themselves and their environment. It will be appreciated that these decisions within English teaching, as they are seen as likely to affect pupils' future working and leisure conditions, might be poignantly uncomfortable to resolve for working-class teachers. Having achieved professional status by means of success in competitive examinations, they are likely to feel a sense of obligation to working-class pupils to equip them in a similar way. It is unlikely to be easy for them to decide, on their working-class pupils' behalf, that personal fulfilment derives solely from their inner selves and their environment, unrelated to questions of higher social status and improved working and leisure conditions. What is certain, however, is that currently English teachers are being urged by the majority of voices in their midst to concentrate upon encouragement of their pupils' creativity.

And as discussion moves on to include the other major activities within English—critical discrimination and classroom talk—it becomes clear that the central difficulties remain. Firstly, there is very general agreement that these are worthwhile; indeed, as was noted in earlier chapters, their supporters tend to make very strong claims for the benefits which they confer. Within each, however, as with literature and creativity, there are firmly held opposite views on where the main emphases should be placed. The crucial question of 'standards', of teachers' commitment to what have traditionally been accepted as cultivated or educated taste and speech, recurs in connection with both these activities with disturbing persistence. In the area of critical discrimination there is, as there was about children's creativity, a general consensus that it is a highly desirable activity for all pupils. Where differences exist they are about how far into the mass media the teacher will go in order to create dissatisfaction with its worst products. In *The Living Tradition*, Frances Stevens notes that when a master states that 'it is the function of the grammar school to fortify the pupil against the debilitating effect of mass influences', this represents 'a fairly widespread opinion'.[12] In a Schools Council Project on the *Mass Media and the Secondary School*, the authors report that the English teachers in their sample unanimously condemned the mass media, were very unfamiliar with it, viewing it as their responsibility to provide resistance against it. They report on the teachers' tendency to regard children either as 'lambs to the slaughter' or 'Zombies', and themselves as providers of some sort of antidote. Commenting upon the teachers' attitude to the media as a threat, the Report states:

'. . . it is in English lessons that the assumptions of curriculum culture come into head-on collision with the pupils' experience of the pop media. English and pop offer pupils two contrasting modes of understanding and expressing emotional experience, the one based on linear communication and literary skills, the other on multiplicity and movement.'[13]

The Report strongly regrets the English teachers' entrenched stand, their unfamiliarity with the pop world, arguing that English teachers are very unlikely to be effective in protecting children from the worst products of the media, if they condemn and ignore all of them. The Report criticises those English teachers who are inflexible about the superiority of high culture, not because its authors reject a hierarchy of standards but because they fear lest this superior attitude hinder teachers in guidance of pupils towards appreciation of the mass media's better products. Its authors believe that 'Teachers can ignore this important part of adolescent experience only by risking the alienation of a large section of the school community',[14] arguing, in addition, that 'pop is not a unitary phenomenon, and a number of diverse styles co-exist under this general umbrella heading'.[15] Suggesting that media-based teaching should be an integral part of all secondary school courses, the Report proposes that it should have three aims: to encourage pupils to be discriminating; to give them understanding about how the media have developed and currently operate; and to provide opportunities to create their own material in this area. Although deeply critical of English teachers who are superior about the products of the media, the Report's descriptions of, for example, mainstream pop ('predominantly concerned with romantic love themes and are usually performed in a mechanical way') convey very clearly that it wants media-based lessons to stimulate enthusiasm for other available varieties. It is not recommending this work simply as entertainment, but to provide opportunities for children to become aware of the wide range of experience the media offer. What this Report confirms, therefore, is that support for discrimination is widespread. Apart from the extreme radicals who wish the schools to accept, uncritically, the validity of pupils' outside school experiences, there are two major kinds of support for this activity: exclusive concentration upon great art and the children's work to provide an 'antidote' to mass culture; or work *within* the media as suggested by the Schools Council Report.

In contrast with educationists' enthusiasm for discrimination by whatever means, deep divisions exist within educators' perceptions of children's oral work. As discussed in Part II, this activity has come into prominence within the past ten years as linguistic competence has been identified as the factor differentiating middle-class and working-class children's achievements in school.

At first, when popularisation of Basil Bernstein's work on the elaborated and restricted code gained widespread acceptance among English teachers, there was much enthusiasm for suggestions for work in the classroom which appeared to offer compensatory experiences for what was too readily accepted as his diagnosis of working-class pupils' verbal 'deprivation'. Recently, however, indignant rejections have been made of what several radical educators have erroneously perceived to be Bernstein's indictments of working-class speech. The same radicalism in education which has been discussed in relation to creativity is currently very vociferous in its objections to what is taken to be Bernstein's high valuation of the elaborated code, that is middle-class speech. *This New Season*, the most recent and persuasive expression of this, insists upon the strengths, even superiorities, of working-class speech. The disagreement has become very bitter. In spite of Bernstein's disavowals and modifications, and his acknowledgement of the richness and vigour of working-class language, his critics insist upon his responsibility for reinforcing the schools' prejudices against their working-class pupils. Labov, his main critic in America, claims that working-class mothers are not non-verbal, 'they differ from the middle-class mothers in the contexts which evoke universalistic meanings', and that Negro and working-class children *will* talk, if the standard formal interview situation is adapted to them.[16] Labov, and in this country Harold Rosen, argue that it is less a matter of the middle classes' ability to employ a specially complex speech code than of social convention's acceptance of a form of speech employed by people of whom society approves. These critics carry further the views described in Part II, about 'linguistic table manners'; they claim that, in some respects, working-class speech is superior. Labov says that:

'. . . [Bernstein's] views are filtered through a strong bias against all forms of working-class behaviour, so that middle-class language is seen as superior in every respect—as "more abstract, and necessarily more flexible, detailed and subtle".'[17]

Claiming that, if an adult enters into the 'right social relation with a a child if he want to find out what a child can do', he suggests that 'in many ways working-class speakers are more effective narrators, reasoners and debators than many middle-class speakers who temporise, qualify and lose their argument in a mass of irrelevant detail'.[18] This strong reaction against Bernstein confronts English teachers with an important decision about their approach to this part of their work. On the one hand, they can decide to accept the difficult conditions, acknowledged by Lawton and Creber, of disguising their sense of superiority of their own language while leading working-class children into a greater range of linguistic skills. On the other hand, like Labov, Rosen and Searle, all of whom resent the 'myth of verbal deprivation . . . because it diverts attention from the real defects of the educational system, to the imaginary defects of the child',[19] they can encourage greater informality to give working-class children confidence in their own identity and culture. The New Left in English take further than the *Language in Use* team the notions of informality in school and more ready acceptance of children's enthusiasms from the outside world. Like Nell Keddie in *Tinker, Tailor . . .* they are bitterly critical of much that goes on in most schools on the grounds that it assumes the goal of making 'children more like teachers'. Supporting strongly the notion of cultural relativism, she argues that 'It would be more sensible to consider how to make teachers more bicultural, more like the children they teach. . . .'[20] Demonstrating the close affinity between the contemporary radicals in education and the early progressives who reacted against utilitarianism, she writes angrily:

'. . . many children come to school to find their experience disvalued and discounted: they are treated as empty, to be filled with knowledge, rather than as experienced participants in a way of life that has its own validity.'[21]

Searle, like Nell Keddie, shares Labov's views, attacking middle-class speech by saying that 'to elaborate is not necessarily to clarify, it is sometimes more likely to complicate and often to confuse'.[22] Rejecting the notion of giving working-class pupils greater linguistic competence to achieve in school and wider society, he wishes to bring about fundamental changes in the social structure productive of a new set of values. Although society remains competitive, he and teachers with his views place faith in the value of working-class culture to provide greater satisfaction than the attempt to achieve upward mobility.

'The teacher of English must stand up and affirm the working-class loyalties of the language that his students speak. He must not accept those judgements pronounced by an alien culture upon his own culture and the culture of the children he teaches, but move towards establishing criteria developed through the culture of their own social class and belongingness. A language of clear insight, empathy and solidarity is not a restrictive code of language, but an unbounded code of language.'[23]

While these differences may present some teachers of English with an exciting and stimulating challenge, it must be allowed that they could confuse a great many, particularly those who are working with less-able children and feel inadequately prepared for this.

We noted earlier that the greatest professional confidence seemed to be experienced by teachers whose role was most precisely defined and who received feedback through their pupils' examination achievements. Since such achievements are generally highly valued by pupils' parents and fellow members of staff, it is possible that English teachers who define their role very differently may encounter conflict which could undermine their professional confidence. As far as pupils' parents are concerned, the possibility of conflict exists, of course, for all teachers introducing innovation into the curriculum and general organisation of the school. Hostile reaction to schools like Countesthorpe College and Wreake Valley, in Leicestershire, testifies to the vulnerability of teachers to criticism and misinterpretation when there is lack of consensus between their goals and those held by many of the parents. Interdisciplinary projects, mixed-ability teaching, informal methods and freedom of choice, in so far as they create parental anxieties about academic achievement, can provoke bitterly expressed dissatisfaction about what are commonly perceived as failures of discipline. However, conflict between staff and parents may, even in these schools, be at its sharpest for English teachers. To a far greater degree than teachers of other subjects with a measurable and recognisable cognitive content, conscientious English staff influenced by progressive notions deliberately set out to seek expression of children's personal experiences and opinions. Informality, personal confidences, criticism of established middle-class institutions, and acceptance of playground language are likely to be viewed by parents as particularly characteristic of the English teaching in innovative schools The goals implicit in the following extract are unlikely to be approved by many parents, least of all by working-class parents who, it appears, tend to hold an instrumental view of the schools. A teacher writes:

'The conditions that foster language growth are by their very nature anti-authoritarian. Liberal English teaching is more than a pedagogic idea: it is a political one . . . . It is wrong to speak of "a change in teaching method" when a moment's reflection persuades us that what we are involved in is nothing less than a revolution in social relations in the English classroom and to a lesser extent within the total institutions we work in. It is no accident that the shift from prescriptive English teaching to an expressionistic approach has been accompanied by a shift from a regulative teaching style to a much more permissive and egalitarian one.'[24]

Although English staff working in this way will probably be strongly supported by the prevailing ethos of a progressive school, they may be far more isolated in traditionally organised institutions. Headmasters, as well as many of the older staff in these, tend to see themselves as custodians of society's values and, as such, they are generally unsympathetic towards the new radicalism, as expressed above, in English teaching. Those, therefore, who set out to change relationships between staff and pupils, to encourage working-class speech in the classroom, to stimulate discussion of personal and social issues, can appear to be seriously disruptive and, in pursuit of their aims, find themselves in stressful situations. English teachers who are interested in oral and written expression of individual experiences are, inevitably, at the centre of the school's expressive relationships with its pupils. As a result of assignments inviting confidences about family and other outside school relationships, they are likely to get to know pupils more intimately than other members of staff. Adolescents defined as troublemakers by the school can place English teachers in difficult situations; the 'good' English teacher is likely to know about their experiences of sex, drugs and violence and must decide whether their knowledge belongs to other members of staff. Frequently, the pupil who is unco-operative in other lessons becomes an 'interesting' pupil in English, someone about whom the teacher can become defensive and consequently come into conflict with authority. When the school supports authoritarian relationships, and insists upon enforcement of traditional discipline, the English teacher who encourages greater pupil participation can experience considerable strain. In working-class areas, having been urged by linguists to be more flexible in his attitude towards children's accents, pronunciation and conventions, he will be unwilling to criticise and correct their language. The conscientious English teacher who wishes to increase his pupils' confidence will be more ready than other staff members to ignore language normally unacceptable in school. This 'permissiveness', along with his encouragement of accounts and discussions of normally unacceptable subjects, can, therefore, bring the English teacher into conflict with his headmaster, fellow staff and, in a special sense, even with the pupils themselves.

As a result of Chris Searle's dismissal after the publication of *Stepney Words* and the Croydon pupil's suspension for his 'obscene' essay, it was proposed at the 1973 NATE conference at York to give the organisation's support to English teachers in similarly unsympathetic schools. Referring to these cases as 'just the tip of the iceberg', Rosen said:

'We are concerned with fostering teaching of English in which children are encouraged to use their own language about things which concern them, as opposed to English as simply literature or a means of communication. This has led to controversy recently and will continue to do so in the future. I think the back lash against this kind of teaching is now beginning at grass roots level in particular areas and schools.'[25]

NATE's response to these admittedly extreme cases usefully suggests the organisation's acceptance of the inevitability of some sort of conflict between its members trying to practice current theory and the schools' authorities. The somewhat disturbing implication for English teachers seems to be that hostile reactions to their work indicate the extent to which they are being successful; it leads once more back to the insistence in the prescriptive writing upon the need for exceptional men and women to do the work effctively.

Whereas Searle clashed with his headmaster and the Inspectorate, Anthony Adams, an English teacher who introduced new approaches into Churchfields School, records the uneasy relationships between his team and the rest of the staff. From his account, the reader gets the impression that Adams's fellow staff were not only suspicious of his deliberate informality but may have been irritated by the self-righteousness into which his defensiveness had led him.

'Very often the English Department, if it is working along the lines that I have been described in this book, may appear to be opposed to the social and cultural values of the school in general; in such cases there is usually little difficulty in getting co-operation from the pupils. This fact can, of course, lead to some resentment as far as other departments in the school are concerned . . . we still have our colleagues to contend with. One must expect a great deal of criticism.'[26]

Although the other staff say that they resent the English staff's failure to teach conventional English language, and that the children do no 'work' in English, Adams claims that, in reality, they resent the children's enjoyment of these lessons. In his view, the team is essential to support and protect the forward-looking English teacher against the misunderstanding and hostility of the rest of the staff room.

'It is certainly true that working as part of a team enables one to withstand the pressures that would otherwise break one down; far too many progressive and liberal teachers in the past have foundered understandably enough because they were struggling alone.'[27]

Searle's dismissal, the school boy's suspension, Adams's reference to 'struggling alone' all illustrate the kinds of staff-room tensions which can be created by conflict between the progressive English teacher's definitions of character' and that of his fellow staff and the school authorities.

This book's study of the origins of English teaching in schools has shown that as a subject it has come to be invested with very high hopes. Literature, creativity, discrimination and classroom talk are all claimed by their supporters to have important roles to play in children's development and in the promotion of greater social justice. At every stage of the discussion attention was drawn to the repeated demands within the prescriptive writing for teachers with exceptional personal qualities. What this final part is suggesting, however, is that, particularly as it is currently defined by progressive and radical educators, English is likely to place its teachers in uniquely stressful and vulnerable situations. It raises, therefore, the question of English teachers' professional confidence, asking whether this is not being undermined rather than strengthened by the subject's current diffuseness and, at times, conflicting ideologies.

It must, of course, be acknowledged that ever since the Cambridge School insisted upon its special role in affecting the quality of pupils' lives, 'good' English teachers have risked conflict with authority, particularly with headmasters representing traditional values. Indeed, the militant imagery of the Leavisite prescriptive writing underlined the view the Cambridge English teachers held of themselves as doing battle with the current literary orthodoxy. Resisting the classical treatment of English, with its emphasis upon grammar and elegantly written essays, many Leavisite teachers deliberately conflicted with the academic establishment. Encouraging the personal response to literature, valuing experience above knowledge, critical of anthologies' noble sentiments and refined sensibilities, teachers from the Cambridge English School appeared to threaten prevailing definitions of literary studies. Nevertheless, in spite of the School's hostility to *belles lettrism*, its own élitism has fused gradually with the conservatism of public and grammar schools. As developments in wider society have diminished the status of the classics, schools have accommodated the Leavisite English teacher as supportive of traditional values. It seems likely that today only his literary élitism and sense of messianic purpose might antagonise his colleagues, many of whom may share their pupils' enjoyment of popular culture. The radical English teacher, though, is much more likely to be perceived as embodying a threat within most traditionally organised schools and must, unless working in a team, be prepared to be discouraged when he is misunderstood by other members of staff. The conscientious English teacher who supports any of the current orthodoxies, most particularly those recommending pupil-directed learning, sometimes deliberately setting out to redistribute power through changed approaches in the classroom, is likely to antagonise or mystify some groups with whom he comes into contact inside and outside school. Except in the few highly innovative schools, he must be prepared to be either a stranger in the staff room or hope to belong to a closely knit team, defensively united against the rest of the staff. What appears to happen (from descriptions in books and articles, accounts from rueful English teachers at conferences and students on teaching practice) is that a committed group of English staff are in running battle with a confused headmaster until the central inspirational figure of the team loses heart and leaves for another post. The highly personal nature of the subject means that any successful group of staff is bound by inward loyalties rather than supported by the school as an institution. Thus, when these weaken, little remains to support the other members of the group. Team leaders like Anthony Adams have expressed their dissatisfaction, and personal observation has confirmed that English teachers who are influenced by any one of the previously described ideologies are likely, except in the most exceptional circumstances, to experience considerable professional unease and alienation.

This being so, the situation can be particularly distressing for new recruits to the profession. An important result of the high expressed aims of English, however interpreted, is that most students enter the schools with equivalently high expectations, and, given the problematical nature of their relationships with working-class pupils, fellow staff, parents and school authorities, these are likely to be severely tested in classroom experience. What frequently happens is that young teachers entering the profession believe that if they have the necessary 'personality', adolescents will readily value the arts, be creative, participate in discussion and adopt liberal attitudes towards other groups in society. The discovery that their audiences 'are not ready for the message and that they do not have the skills to make them ready',[28] can lead to disappointment and cynicism. Moreover, the 'cultural shock' to students in training and young teachers' can be exacerbated by their discovery that headmasters, parents and fellow staff members hold different perceptions of the school and of 'character-building' from their own. In this area, knowledge about social structure, the school as an institution, and the history of their profession might be more helpful during the period of training than prescriptive, activist approaches characteristic of colleges and departments of education. The persistent calls to battle in the field of English studies are probably contributory to that assumption of martyred rectitude which sharpens potential staff-room antagonisms.

In 1969, writing about *Teaching English in the United Kingdom*, American observers reported upon the strong missionary element in the subject.

'They [the teachers] were all working to make their society a more democratic one, and they were all convinced that English was an important basis for the changes to be made . . . they feel they are part of a highly significant national, social and cultural movement in which the school is playing a central role. As one of them put it, "Teaching English is teaching a way of life".'[29]

They comment upon English teachers' emphasis upon the personal, the felt response, the expression of individual experience, noticing that many graduates valued these above pupils' *knowledge* of literature. This observation leads one back again into the confusion of good will and arrogance at the centre of the cultural debate. Graduates, 'often the products of a selective grammar school education, were pacing the new developments . . . they knew literature . . . they sometimes refused to teach it to their classes'.[30] In this Report, and in retrospective articles on the Dartmouth Conference, American observers comment, in some amazement, upon English teachers' apparent lack of concern about the potential social divisiveness of this stance. Since 1969, however, as reaction has taken place and strengthened against widespread acceptance of Basil Bernstein's theories, support for working-class culture has produced unwillingness to 'impose' middle-class speech patterns, thus increasing the likelihood of this divisiveness. While society remains unchanged in rewarding academic achievement, English teachers, in particular, carry significant responsibility in their refusal to teach literature or to employ opportunities for working-class children to extend control over their language. The American observers commented upon what new recruits to the profession discover, sometimes with shock and disappointment, that for anything positive to be achieved by the teacher who values the affective above the cognitive in English, exceptional personal qualities are essential. On this the Report comments:

'At its best the spirit is crusading and alive; at its worst, it is intolerant and neglectful of many literary values . . . too many lessons lack closure, direction, or planning . . . and time passed in the classroom is not easily distinguishable from time out of school.'[31]

Notes

1. G. R. Grace, *Role Conflict and the Teacher* (London and Boston, Routledge, 1972), pp. 4, 13.
2. Ibid., p. 49.
3. Report of the Harvard Committee, *General Education in a Free Society* (London, Oxford University Press, 1946), pp. ix, 53.
4. Ibid., p. 96.
5. F. Stevens, *The Living Tradition* (London, Hutchinson, 1960), p. 109.
6. 'Why Have Things Gone Wrong?', in *Use of English*, Vol. 23, No. 4 (Summer 1972), p. 335.
7. John and Pat White, 'Slogan for Crypto-Élitists', in *The Times Educational Supplement*, No. 3,006 (5 Jan, 1973), p. 2.
8. E. P. Clark, 'Language and Politics in Education', in *English in Education*, Vol. 5, No. 2 (Summer 1971), p. 102.
9. 'Why Have Things Gone Wrong?', op. cit., p. 336.
10. C. Searle, *This New Season* (London, Calder & Boyars, 1973), p. 15.
11. P. Doughty, 'The Relevance of Linguistics for the Teacher of English', Paper 1, *Programme in Linguistics and English Teaching* (London, Longman, 1968), pp. 65 f.
12. Stevens, op. cit., p. 108.
13. G. Murdock and G. Phelps, *Mass Media and the Secondary School* (London, Macmillan, 1973), p. 19.
14. Ibid., Foreword.
15. Ibid., p. 89.
16. W. Labov, 'The Logic of Nonstandard English', in P. P. Gigliogli (ed.), *Language and Social Context* (Harmondsworth, Penguin Modern Sociology Readings, 1972), p. 191.
17. Ibid., p. 183.
18. Ibid., p. 193.
19. Ibid., p. 180.
20. Nell Keddie, *Tinker, Tailor . . .* (Harmondsworth, Penguin Education, 1973), p. 10.
21. Ibid., p. 15.
22. Searle, op. cit., p. 136.
23. Ibid., loc. cit.
24. Clark, op. cit., p. 102.
25. Harold Rosen, reported in *The Guardian* (3 August 1973), p. 7.
26. Anthony Adams, *Team-Teaching and the Teaching of English* (Oxford, Pergamon Press, 1970), p. 173.
27. Ibid., p. 182.
28. Kevin Ryan, 'The Teaching Intern: A Sociological Stranger', in *The Journal of Teacher Education*, Vol. 17, No. 2 (Summer 1966), p. 189.
29. J. R. Squire and R. K. Applebee, *Teaching English in the United Kingdom* (Illinois, USA, NCTE, 1969) pp. 42, 234, 235.
30. Ibid., p. 47.
31. Ibid., pp. 99, 177.

Chapter 14

Interest and Enjoyment: Teachers and Pupils

The Aims

> The Humanities Course aims to give you an opportunity
> to discover more about yourself and the world of
> people in which you live. It is intended to increase your
> awareness of other people's experiences and of your
> own—of beliefs, thoughts, attitudes and relationships.
> It is to give you a chance to explore your feelings, to
> to express your ideas and to create your own versions
> of the world which you find.
>
> >   The Humanities Course
> >   Student's Guide
> >   The Bosworth College
> >   Desford, Leicester

> Every class . . . was a kind of happening . . .
> Everything was geared to feeling not knowing.

> J.R. Squire and R. K. Applebee, *Teaching English in
> the United Kingdom*

At the end of his enthusiastic review of *English for Diversity*, in which
Peter Abbs asks 'why do we fail to teach the mother tongue freely,
honestly, joyously?', and answers that 'there must be something in
our society which flinches from the liberation of the whole, unpredict-
able, perhaps unmanageable human being', Edward Blishen expresses
agreement with the author's explanation. Regretting teachers' failure
to encourage creativity in the classroom, he, too, refers this to society's
shortcomings.

'There must surely be some such explanation. The flow of books crying for a new approach to English teaching never ceases: yet the dark
fortress of common classroom practice looks as though it could sit
out the siege for ever.'[1]

Blishen choses his imagery without irony, apparently sharing the widespread conviction and hope that if the 'flow' and the 'crying' mount, the stubbornness of classroom practice will eventually be defeated. This book has suggested, however, that this is unlikely, arguing that many teachers' resistance to new approaches should be considered in the light of the profession's history and status, and the inevitable strain and uneasiness associated with their role. Conditions in many schools, moreover, in terms of large classes, insufficient time and shortage of specialists, remain unhelpful to teachers in their efforts to disseminate culture, stimulate creativity or promote greater social justice by means of pupil participation. Above all, English teachers may be discouraged from adopting the recommended new approaches by the possibility of conflict with pupils' parents, their fellow staff and headmasters, some of whom may misunderstand the contemporary shift of emphasis from knowledge and formality to feeling and freedom.

Despairing references to some sort of generalised social timidity in the face of liberated individualism are not useful substitutes for inquiry into the realities of professional anxieties and insecurities. They avoid raising questions about the quality of lessons produced by new approaches, ignoring the structural difficulties these create for teachers, as well as the complications which they can introduce into relationships with pupils. The increasingly heavy stress placed on the prescriptive writing, particularly as it relates to creativity and oral participation, upon the felt instead of the known has made the organisation of lessons more complicated. In addition, it is likely to have produced uncertainties in teachers and pupils about how much learning has been achieved. As we have seen, romantic progressivism, with its valuation of the individual child and suspicion of teacher-directed instruction, has played a major role in reducing the academic content of English and in increasing encouragement of pupils' own creations. In recent years this tendency has been accelerated by the radical influence in education with its insistence upon the cultural validity of groups in society previously rejected or ignored by the schools. A representative viewpoint is expressed by Nell Keddie in her introduction to Tinker, Tailor . . . when she suggests that 'school education is historically and technologically stagnant . . . the insistence upon literacy is peculiar to education and not to the life worlds of the learners . . . in most other contexts of their lives'.[2] The subversion of absolutism by the sociology of knowledge, that is 'its conception of societies as products of competing definitions and claims to cognitive and moral legitimacy rather than integrated around a core set of absolute values',[3] has led, certainly in America, to strong support for the perspective of cultural relativism. There the discussion centres mainly around the Black American culture, whereas here it centres upon the school's acceptance or rejection of working-class culture. The romantic progressive view of children has conspired powerfully with the romantic radical view of working-class culture to move the personal (what Nell Keddie calls the 'everyday') to the centre of the classroom experience, particularly in English and the humanities. If this is what is meant by 'new approaches', 'teaching the mother tongue joyously', and liberation of the 'perhaps unmanageable human being', it might be more helpful to indicate how very difficult this appears to be to do well than to make generalised criticism of wider society. This book ends by suggesting that progressive and radical educationists may have increased teachers' vulnerability by recommending pupil-directed learning and replacement of the cognitive by the affective in the classroom. By placing teachers in situations where certainties about what has been achieved have been diminished and successful lessons turn upon enjoyment and interest, they are likely to have seriously undermined professional confidence. High valuation of experience and feeling and suspicion of intellect and organisation can, it will be argued, be held responsible for those unstructured lessons, most generally about the mass media or 'controversial' issues, in which any discussion is rated as having been a good discussion. New approaches, therefore, will be considered now as highly problematic. Designed to diminish the teachers' control, they may be offering pupils, particularly from the working classes, classroom experiences of dubious quality.

As far as literature is concerned, high valuation of feeling and experience has meant that English teachers have had to try to come to terms with Leavisite, progressive and radical hostility to examinations. From their differing viewpoints educators supporting any one of these ideologies have insisted upon the greater value of experience than mere knowledge of literature. Thus, until such time as examinations are designed to measure reliably qualities like appreciation, sensitivity and sincerity of personal response, the literature teacher remains in a dilemma as far as his approach to the texts is concerned. Examinations continue to confer respectability upon school subjects, something which English teachers would not wish to lose. Nevertheless, it is often regretted that, in general, they test pupils' knowledge rather than their capacity to *experience* literature. The English teacher omits preparation for examinations at his peril; pupils will either not 'know' the work sufficiently well to achieve success, or, against the context of an examined curriculum, will fail to take literature seriously. As with most unexamined parts of the curriculum, only the exceptional teacher can stimulate sustained interest in the work. Because of the perceived close relationship of English with pupils' total growth, its dependence upon enjoyment, and teachers' failure leaving a gap likely to be filled by the mass media, many teachers suffer anxieties about the role of examinations. In practice, many conscientious English teachers lead double lives. Ideally, their work lies far from coarse testing processes, and yet pupils and parents appear to persist in holding an instrumental view of the school. Although the teacher can, with a clear conscience, ignore preparation of pupils for English language now that examination practice in this area reflects current movements away from formal grammar, he remains in difficulties with English literature.

Unless exceptionally confident and gifted, English teachers face difficulties without examinations. Quite apart from the problem of their subject's status, if they reject the security of set books they have the responsibility of choosing literature relevant to their pupils' lives and giving it meaning beyond that yielded by one superficial reading. If they reject teaching knowledge about literature, which is generally agreed to be mechanical, 'academic' and dull, they have to work out ways of making each text personally meaningful to all their pupils. Success here appears to be elusive. American observers, visiting several of the best English schools, reported upon their impressions of literature lessons. Noting the extent to which feeling was valued above intellect, they wrote:

'Every class . . . was a kind of happening . . . At no time are the students given a conscious method of analysis or the language to talk about literature, or language as a study of form. Everything was geared to feeling not knowing.'[4]

These observers agreed that lessons in the best schools were designed to generate pupils' personal response, to engage their inner selves. But while agreeing that, at its best, this could produce periods of excitement in the classroom, they expressed doubts about the achievements of less-inspired teachers. Since there appeared to be little observable coherence or continuity in literature lessons with energetic gifted teachers, anxiety was expressed about the likely effects of widespread commitment to the exclusively personal in English. Analysis of a number of English teachers' usual approaches appears to justify this anxiety; clearly, many teachers find it very difficult to be both personally exploratory and effective. Douglas Barnes comments upon English teachers' heavy dependence upon factual questions. The ability to probe, to draw children out, to 'reach down into them' appears to be rare in teachers.[5] Opponents of examinations in literature sometimes fail to recognise their supportive nature to average teachers who find it difficult to generate classroom excitement. Teachers facing large classes in areas unsympathetic to the culture of the school are not helped in their recent liberation from traditional grammar and crowded syllabuses by vague exhortations such as those found in the Introduction to the Penguin English Project. Providing, it says, 'a chance for relaxed involvement', it asserts that 'too many of us struggle still to test our powers of instruction by devising exercises for the children. . . . But it is not possible to mark the Inner Light, and "becoming oneself" is not a competitive process'.[6] The Project is anxious to avoid prescribing approaches for teachers, illustrating the contemporary official desire for teachers to grasp their freedom: 'There is no special way to read or look at any of the books . . . we should all be able to suit ourselves.'

Somewhat censoriously, its authors quote the following extract from a review to illustrate their view of the good teacher.

'Unhappy the teacher who cannot structure the teaching situation so that oral and written expression springs spontaneously from the challenge to the mind; the kindling of the senses and the heightening of the emotions that these books provide.'[7]

The central problem arising from creative work in the classroom has already been discussed in Chapter 13. Teachers must define their views about the kind of stimuli they employ, about the role of high culture in this work with working-class children, as well as gauging its value in their pupils' lives, and their degree of responsibility for finding time for 'technical' writing. On a day-to-day level, they face problems of evaluation and planning. Each teacher, if he is to move beyond grateful acceptance of anything which his pupils produce, has to work out what he means by 'imaginative growth', and how to encourage what he perceives as progress or improvement. With each class or, ideally in the view of some eductors, with each pupil, he has to follow a course somewhere between lesson-by-lesson stimuli and the 'mechanical' superimposition of a syllabus. While clearly favourably impressed by the high level of creativity achieved by pupils in British schools, American observers again had reservations about its 'occasional' nature, and the difficulties this work presented in terms of guidance or promotion of development. About one teacher's stimulation of poetry writing they commented: 'Never, however, did she give any advice or concrete suggestion for improving the poems.'[8] Noting the high value teachers invested in imagination and individuality, they expressed doubts about the value for the children of an exclusively romantic approach to their creative work.

'The general absence of correction and revision is directly related to the prevailing conception of writing as the expression of personal experience. . . . Knowledge is considered almost detrimental to the aims of the school; "Presenting kids with knowledge can stifle their creativity".'[9]

Fred Inglis and David Holbrook urge English teachers to stand firm against the forces of commercial entertainment. The majority of writers in the field, however, recommend the inclusion of media-based lessons; either they hope that teachers will succeed in encouraging appreciation of the media's superior products, or they believe that the school should include the children's outside interests within its activities. The Schools' Council Report on English teachers and the media, which criticises the traditional view of the English teacher as representative of high culture, suggests that, to be effective as a guide to discrimination within the media, he must be much more familiar with his pupils' entertainment. This point of view, widely shared and certainly given forceful expression by Newsom, raises several problems. It is extremely difficult, given the time he needs for preparation and marking, for the teacher to become as familiar as his pupils with current pop records and favourite television programmes. If he considers this desirable and possible, however, he is likely to find it difficult to overcome being an 'outsider', because he is not an adolescent whose emotional world is in process of creation by the enthusiasms and changing fashions of pop. And, in contrast with the mass media, the teacher will always be out of date. Supporters of discrimination through his familiarity with the media are putting the teacher under an obligation to understand the teenage complex of current idioms and their implications, clothes, personalities and magazines supporting the popularity of a star or group; the words of the lyrics alone are not what constitute the potency of pop songs' appeal. Any teacher, however 'good' his relationship with his pupils, must to some extent be viewed with distrust by them in this area of his work—because he is an adult, and a teacher. However tactful his approach, unless his aim is merely to bring the children's world into the school, his efforts are designed to create dissatisfaction with a world of pleasure skilfully constructed as the adolescents' own special experience; indeed, its promoters exploit its difference from adult experience to strengthen the passion of the loyalties.

Thus, in addition to their lack of familiarity with the majority's taste in pop, and lack of training in handling film and records in the classroom, there are problems arising out of the children's reception of such lessons. Young teachers are likely to be dismayed to discover, having decided to take lessons involving pop music, that if their choice of records fails to coincide with current enthusiasm, they encounter greater boredom and scorn than if they had brought the totally unfamiliar into the classroom. Unless the school becomes a part of the mass media, it is difficult to see how these lessons will appear to the children as anything more than pathetic imitations. It is possible to argue that, since the world of pop, hero worship, adolescent fashions, is deliberately contrived to be uniquely theirs, so attractively non-school, a teacher runs the risk of resentment, particularly from girls, if their preserve is intruded upon by the school. The whole approach demands plentiful time, reliable and easily available equipment, carefully planned links between lessons and, above all, delicacy in the treatment of emotionally cherished material. After deciding what his aims are in this area, the teacher needs to be far less of an amateur than he generally is, to do anything in detail about the complex organisation of press, advertisements, television programmes and promotion of pop records. As they are at present conducted, it appears that many pupils do not consider these lessons as 'real work'. Although the Schools Council Report says that English teachers can ignore this [mass media] only by 'running the risk of alienating a sizeable section of the adolescent school population,[10] they point out that working-class pupils tend to view 'media-based lessons' as 'timewasting'. They say that of the pupils they interviewed, 50 per cent of these from working-class backgrounds did not want them. This Report points to an aspect of the progressive teacher's and, in particular, the English teacher's problems in this summary of its authors' impressions:

'. . . the so-called "Newsom" children . . . appear to show the least enthusiasm for this proposal [media-based lessons] while those in grammar schools and in the top half of comprehensives where innovation is much less likely, would apparently very much welcome the idea of more media-based teaching.'[11]

Progressive and radical high valuation of interest, enjoyment and activity largely explains the current popularity of classroom discussion, particularly of controversial issues. It is prescribed on the grounds that these lessons can become pupil- rather than teacher-directed and, since the teachers cannot possibly be experts or authorities on these issues, their altered status will encourage previously rejected or neglected groups of pupils to express their opinions. The Newsom Report is very enthusiastic about discussion, or what it calls 'mutual exploration'. The teacher's role in this is 'to be an open-minded person with whom one can trustfully roam'. The language here hopefully evokes the pleasing picture of confidence-giving, intimate classroom conversation, 'open-minded', 'exploration', and 'roam' suggestive of profitable freedom. Evidence from observers, from prescriptive writing and, indirectly, from the material of the current anthologies designed to stimulate this work, however, all suggest that discussion of any quality might be very difficult for teachers to achieve.

One major problem which they must face is the confusion which their invitations to discuss sometimes create in pupils, particularly from working-class backgrounds. Musgrove and Taylor's research into children's perception of the teacher's role shows that they 'expect to be taught, to have mysteries explained',[12] and that they give 'most weight to the good teacher's teaching, least weight to his personal qualities'.[13] Teachers offering pupils opportunities for classroom participation are likely, therefore, as Denis Lawton suggests, to bewilder and alienate their working-class pupils. They do not, it appears, perceive discussion as 'real work', any more than media-based lessons.

Many teachers do not find these lessons easy, as Douglas Barnes discovered when he noticed the infrequency of open-ended questions in English lessons. Or, if they are successful in choosing provocative material and stimulating initial interest, they either choose not to or are unable to extend the discussion in a meaningful way. The American observers (recording, it must be noted, work in the 'best' British schools) commented that many oral lessons were 'little more than directed play'. They complimented the teachers upon their ability to stimulate talk, but had reservations about the lessons' lack of structure and discrimination.

'Brilliant in creating a situation for informal talk and affective response, the teachers are willing to accept comments as they come, one as good as another.'[14]

Patrick Creber who, in *Lost for Words*, strongly supports teachers' efforts to encourage pupil-directed discussion, admits that '. . . the teacher's new, less formal role is not an easy one. What he has to do is often a good deal less clear than what he is not to do'.[15]

The prescriptive writing makes it very clear that these lessons are meant to be undirected and that teachers are discouraged from being or behaving like experts on the issues under discussion. Success, which appears to depend very heavily upon the teachers' personalities and intuitive grasp of the classroom situation, is not precisely defined. By implication, it has been achieved when children, normally difficult, unresponsive or passive at school, have contributed to these discussions, have had their comments accepted and developed by the teachers' sympathy, receptivity and ability to grasp possibilities for further inquiry. Although several writers, like Creber, acknowledge the difficulties involved in this and, like Stenhouse, suggest that the teachers' personalities figure very largely, there is a widespread tendency to neglect consideration of how well informed they might need to be. Nell Keddie, in an article reporting upon inquiry-based learning in a comprehensive school, indicates that C pupils were getting little benefit from this. She explains the failure of these lessons in terms of the teachers' preconceived, inflexible notions about what constitutes 'ability'. Their stereotypical expectations of working-class pupils, she suggests, explain their speedy closure of 'everyday' contributions to the discussions, adding, only in passing, that the teachers' unfamiliarity with the material 'complicated the matter'.[16] Looking, however, at these teachers' failure from a different perspective, an unintended consequence of progressive and radical educationists' low valuation of teachers' expertise might be their inability to see the possibilities which exist within some pupils' contributions. Discussion of controversial issues may be an activity in which the teachers' expertise is outstandingly necessary for the benefit of all pupils involved in it.

Many English and humanities teachers are, in general, insufficiently well-informed to chair classroom discussions profitably about complex social and international issues. The contemporary tendency to stress the value of the children's opinions, when some are drawn only from their experience of the media, can diminish and trivialise the subject under discussion and leave pupils merely exchanging prejudices. Without strong support from the relevant specialisms, the English teachers alone are unlikely to lead their pupils very far into greater understanding. From Nell Keddie's article it seems that it can be precisely those pupils for whom these lessons were designed who lose most heavily when teachers are too insecure or too ignorant to seize and build upon the potential of their inquiries. Instead of criticising the teachers for their unreadiness to rate these children more highly than A pupils ('It would seem', she argues, 'to be the failure of high-ability pupils to question what they are taught in schools that contributes in large measure to their educational achievement'),[17] she might be of greater help to them by recommending that they should become more familiar with the material. It is surely of dubious value to these and to all other pupils to have their opinions left unchallenged or leadership of their discussions taken over by the most aggressive or confident members of their class.

The conclusion seems difficult to avoid that if English teachers are to achieve the ambitious goals described in progressive and radical educational writing, they must reconsider the functions of knowledge and the traditional skills of literacy. If pupils of all abilities are to become seriously engaged with the examination of controversial issues, to arrive at critical perspectives on established institutions, they must possess the relevant information and appropriate tools of inquiry. Exclusive attention to enjoyment and interest can trivialise issues, confine children to their own experience, with all the inequalities within this which they bring to school, and put the teachers' confidence and effectiveness at risk. Neil Postman wants teaching to be a 'subversive activity' and teachers to be 'crap-detectors'. Neither subversion nor detection, however, is likely to be searching or long-sustained by those teachers whom he is discouraging from teaching literacy. Both he and Nell Keddie express reservations about teaching reading, she because it does not belong to the 'life-worlds' of most learners, and he because he believes that its most important function has been 'to make students accessible to political and historical myth'.[18] Without literacy, however, it is supremely optimistic to believe that pupils' critical faculties can be developed by teachers' personalities and whatever visual stimuli are available. Interest, enjoyment and feelings alone are unlikely to promote achievement of this complex goal.

Much of the recently published material for work in this area reflects radical and progressive ideas about English teaching. Its contents derive largely from twentieth-century concerns, make a very strong visual impact, and are chosen and arranged to be stimulating and provocative. Photographs, and personal accounts of experience in poetry and prose, are grouped around selected themes; in *The Receiving End* (Penguin Project Stage Two) the emphasis is upon minority groups traditionally unjustly treated by established authority—peasants in underdeveloped countries, Negroes on the 1963 Washington March, school children, housebound wives and mothers. The same political radicalism, it appears, inspires the publication of these anthologies as well as the contemporary criticism of literacy. Their dependence upon the visual, the personal and, frequently, the highly sensational, reflects Neil Postman's ideal school of the future as described in 'The Politics of Reading'.

'As he is now provided with textbooks, each student would be provided with his own still camera, 8 mm camera and tape cassette. The
school library would contain books of course, but at least as many
films, records, video tapes, audio tapes and computer programs . . . .
Entirely new methods of instruction would evolve. In fact, schools
might abandon the notion of teacher-instruction altogether. Whatever discipines lent themselves to be packaged, linear and segmented
presentation would be offered through a computerised and individ-
ualised programme.'[19]

Anthologies like *The Receiving End* are, clearly, meant to be exciting
and stimulating. They bring the outside world into the school, are
judged 'relevant' to children's interests, and are visually dramatic
in their appeal. What is disturbing, though, if they are intended to
serve the new ideal of radical educationists critical of literacy, is
that they are likely to replace one political and historical myth merely
by another. As they stand, it is difficult to see how they can take
pupils more reliably to the truths of complex issues than finding out
and knowing more about them. When D. H. Lawrence attacked
literacy for the great majority he was expressing part of his wish for
them to be relieved of mental consciousness, to be rid of the myth,
as he saw it, of equality. Radicals such as Nell Keddie and Neil
Postman are also attacking literacy while prescribing ambitious and
complex goals, like crap-detection, for the teachers. There seems to
be some vague hope that teachers will be able to keep the excitement
going of exploding political myths, while at the same time. implant-
ing the appropriate information.

What seems most likely is that many teachers will feel unable to
compete, particularly when getting the pupils down to continuous
discussion and search for information, with the exciting stimuli of the
anthologies. There will almost certainly be some depressing days
when pupils are not interested in Hiroshima, race riots or sexual
deviancy, days on which teachers will ask themselves some disturbing
and unprofitable questions. Perhaps these are, in fact, boring subjects? Perhaps, if they were 'better' teachers, the pupils would be
interested? Or, as Nell Keddie observed, interest and inquiry-based
lessons might face teachers with the discovery that the A type, mainly
middle-class children are ready to be stimulated to do their individual
research and that the C type children are unresponsive. It appears
that 'interest' theories lay many traps.

Since English developed from the rudimentary skills of literacy
into the humane centre of the curriculum it has had high hopes invested in its activities and its teachers. Gradually, as progressive
theories have fused with the powerful tradition of anti-industrialism

to place the child and his creation alongside great works of art, the teaching of literature as the content of English has been eroded. This was a process which began with dissatisfaction with the classical curriculum, with the 'undeveloped heart' of upper-class English society. It has been accelerated by romantic progressivism, and is on the way to being completed by romantic radicalism. In their early days of responsibility for forming the characters of all their pupils, English teachers were asked to be inspiring—to negotiate as ambassadors of culture, to fight like warriors against commercial forces. Since then they have been told constantly that their sensitive and sympathetic guidance is indispensable in promoting their pupils' growth—but that they must withdraw, be inconspicuous. Today, advised to renounce their knowledge and control, they are asked by the radicals—as are all teachers—to stop being teachers altogether, to be, simply, people who help other people. In Postman's ideal future:

'. . . teachers would have to stop acting like teachers and find something useful to do, like for instance helping young people to resolve some of their more wrenching emotional problems.'[20]

While the exceptional men and women will always achieve success on their own terms, the great majority will find this task very difficult to achieve. Like Arnold's preachers, they are 'likely long to have a hard time of it'.

Notes

1. Edward Blishen, 'Stepmother Tongue', in *New Statesman* (10 April 1970), p. 523.
2. Nell Keddie, *Tinker, Tailor* . . . (Harmondsworth, Penguin Education, 1973), p. 16.
3. M. F. D. Young, *Knowledge and Control* (London, Collier-Macmillan, 1971), p. 6.
4. J. R. Squire and R. K. Applebee, *Teaching English in the United Kingdom* (Illinois, USA, NCTE, 1969), p. 870.
5. D. Barnes, *Language, the Learner and the School* (Harmondsworth, Penguin Papers in Education, 1971), rev. edn, p. 22.
6. P. Radley, Introduction to *Teachers' Handbook to Penguin Education Project*, p. 7.
7. H. M. Saxby, review from *Reading Time* of Penguin English Project (Stage Two).
8. Squire and Applebee, op. cit., p. 138.

9. Ibid., pp. 154 f.
10. G. Murdock and G. Phelps, *Mass Media and the Secondary School* (London, Macmillan, 1973), Foreword.
11. Ibid., p. 146.
12. F. Musgrove and P. H. Taylor, *Society and the Teacher's Role* (London, Routledge, 1969), p. 14.
13. Ibid., pp. 23 f.
14. Squire and Applebee, op. cit., p. 101.
15. P. Creber, *Lost for Words* (Harmondsworth, Penguin, 1972), p. 65.
16. Nell Keddie, 'Classroom Knowledge', in Young, op. cit., p. 154.
17. Ibid., p. 156.
18. Neil Postman, 'The Politics of Reading', (Harmondsworth, Penguin Education, 1973), p. 89.
19. Ibid., p. 93.
20. Ibid., p. 94.

Index